C000229319

Humble Pie

Humble Pie

A Roe Stalker's Bedside Book

Richard Prior

SWAN·HILL PRESS

All illustrations by Jeppe Ebdrup

First published in the UK in 2006
by Swan Hill Press, an imprint of Quiller Publishing Ltd

British Library Cataloguing-in-Publication Data
A catalogue record for this book
is available from the British Library

ISBN 1 904057 89 6
   978 1 904057 89 5

Printed in England by Cromwell Press Ltd., Trowbridge.

Swan Hill Press
An imprint of Quiller Publishing Ltd
Wykey House, Wykey, Shrewsbury, SY4 1JA
Tel: 01939 261616 Fax: 01939 261606
E-mail: info@quillerbooks.com
Website: www.countrybooksdirect.com

Contents

For Sally

Who deserves so much more than just this.
But she has my heart already.

Introduction

Roe deer have been a love affair of mine since I caught up with my first buck fifty-three years ago. Then they were detested as an unmitigated pest, now they are established as a valued and valuable quarry species. Roe are charming, graceful, and above all highly successful in our overcrowded island.

This book is intended for any deer enthusiast to dip into – bits and pieces of roe lore which have tickled my curiosity or puzzled me over the years. There are also a few stories, without which no gathering of stalkers is complete. Inevitably in the Sporting Answers feature of the *Shooting Times* the same queries crop up time after time, and a few of the most recurrent have been included, with the Editor's kind permission. There is also some material from the defunct and lamented *Stalking Magazine*, again with permission which is acknowledged with gratitude. Christopher Borthen has also meticulously corrected the outflow from my quavering and corroded pen. Jeppe Ebdrup has produced some of his inimitable drawings to enliven my pages. I am grateful to him.

Special thanks are due to the many landowners, their agents, foresters and gamekeepers for enormous tolerance while, as one put it, I was running a private zoo at his expense. And also to many fellow-stalkers who have so generously shared their knowledge. Most of all to my long-suffering and amazingly supportive wife who, having made the calamitous decision to marry a stalker, stuck to it through thick and a great deal of thin.

Research on roe has proliferated in recent years so that we know things about them now which used to be pure speculation. Even so, they are such variable animals that we will never be able to reduce them to any sort of text-book creature. At least I hope not!

Eating Humble Pie

According to Brewer's *Dictionary of Phrase and Fable,* to eat humble pie is: 'To come down from a position you have assumed, to be obliged to take a "lower room".' Anyone who stalks deer or tries to predict their behaviour is more likely than most to finish up eating humble pie in quantity.

On a hot, thundery day in early August with no wind, one might expect the roe rut to be in full swing. Not so; it was going on madly in yesterday's cloudburst, and to make it really sting, the action was all over the boundary on your neighbour's land, or so he delights in telling you just to rub salt in the wound. Today the roe all have hangovers and won't be about until late. Or go out for one or two does on a crystal clear January dawn and as the sun gets up they should all be out fluffing their feathers and getting warm with a few press-ups in the lee of that hedge. Not so – they knew you would be out early on such a lovely morning, so the order of the day is *Keep down until he's gone to breakfast.*

In magazine articles one tries to do a bit of crystal-ball work on what the deer will be doing in two months' time. Of course everyone knows better, disproving everything from long, personal experience – and they are usually right. Join me round the humble pie again!

With roe especially, we are dealing with an incredibly adaptable animal whose mode of life allows it to study human behaviour round the clock and whose brain is quite up to analysing the difference between threatening and harmless behaviour on our part, and of adapting meal times, love life and everything else to swing the balance of survival heavily in its favour. That is probably what makes woodland stalking the maddening challenge most of us so much enjoy. I don't like to think of the number of times I've proved a false prophet when the deer once again have thumbed their noses at me, my theories and my efforts to outwit them.

Even if you think that you have sorted out the habits of the deer on your own ground reasonably well, you have only got to go to the next county, the next wood even, to see the infuriating creatures doing just the opposite. It is humbling, but that makes the occasional victory all the sweeter.

So it is appropriate that the term humble pie does originate firmly with deer. Why *humble?* Referring to Kenneth Whitehead's monumental tome *The Encyclopedia of Deer* we read:

> <u>Numbles</u> *Originally the liver, kidney and entrails of a deer (the word later became* umbles, *then* humbles – *hence* Humble pie*). At a hunt feast in former times a pie made from numbles was served to the hunt servants, while the nobility ate haunch and saddle.*

I wish he had written more about it, for I can't help feeling that humble pie in its material form continued to be enjoyed into much more recent times. In fact, has it ever died out? Deer keepers have never been in the upper income bracket and maybe the tradition and recipe has been handed down in one or other of the great estates, so many of which had deer parks. When I was selling venison on behalf of my employers (and was earning under ten pounds a week, plus dog allowance) by some zoological anomaly the local deer certainly existed without heart, liver or kidneys. They also seemed to have very short necks! We learned, no doubt like many a deer keeper before, that much could be done to keep a growing family from semi-starvation with such a source of rich, if homely, protein. Humble pie? Not at that stage, but certainly liver strips fried or baked; kidneys grilled or reinforcing a stew constructed out of neck meat. Above all, heart muscle minced – the perfect basic material for anything from spaghetti Bolognese to something near cottage pie. Nothing was wasted.

Returning to the metaphorical, how can one ever dodge those endless series of outings with nothing but humble pie to show for thought, effort and alarm clock wear? Maybe one thing might be consciously to relax more, enjoy the outing for itself and not measure success by the number of shots. Long ago a fellow deer keeper was telling me about his employer, a very good stalker and shot, but whose stalking was limited to short weekends away from the highly competitive business of which he was Managing Director. 'We'd go out on Friday night when he arrived and he'd practically run through the woods – I had a job to keep up with him. Then on Saturday he would slow down a bit and begin to see deer. By Sunday morning he was relaxed and we'd stalk properly and probably shoot a buck. But then it was back to business, and he'd be just as bad again by the following Friday!'

Too many of us are the victims of the same stresses, or at least are affected by the universal drive not to 'waste time'. So what about stepping out of the car in the dawn, and taking a deliberate interval to attune yourself to the woods before setting off. Where is the wind? Was it dark and cold last night, so that the deer will show up in sheltered places, or was the moon near full with a clear sky allowing night-long feeding? Are the leaves crisped with frost, or could you take *this* path, rather than *that* one? Is all quiet, or can you hear the distant bleating of sheep in the valley field? In that case the plans you made last night must be scrapped. The deer won't be there like they were last time. In five minutes or so you will have a better chance of avoiding a liberal helping of that humble pie at breakfast!

1 WHAT MAKES THEM TICK?

What Are They Thinking?

 You may go out stalking at ungodly hours of the morning because you tell people you love to watch deer and listen to the birds, or just because your wife snores, but sooner or later you have to bring home the bacon. Consistent lack of success is bad for self-esteem and makes the neighbours begin to talk.

As a desperately keen beginner I prowled the woods, mentally red in tooth and claw, at first carrying a fearsome 12-bore Paradox shotgun/rifle which would have rolled over a couple of tigers, let alone a fifty pound roe buck. It took me four years of frantic endeavour to get my first buck because I hadn't the least idea what they did, or when. Misdirected enthusiasm gets you nowhere, and that is just where I got until I sat down and thought. Not about the glory of shooting one of those enormous but elusive roe bucks, but the real reason why they never happened to be where I was. I had never tried to put myself in their shoes, as it were, or tried to guess what they were thinking that particular morning or evening.

An old keeper/poacher told me: *'You've got to be in the right place – at the right time!'*

His idea of the right place was flat against a beech tree where he could pour a load of BB from his 12-bore into a fallow buck's ear as it passed within a yard or two, but he was uncanny at choosing just the right tree.

Times change, but to have any consistent success you have to know your quarry as well as he did; not just what it looks like, or what it is supposed to do according to the books, but really understand it as you do your friends. Within their limitations, deer are just as individual as humans, and above all, they are not fools. Do not underestimate the capacity of a roe or fallow buck, especially one living close to civilisation, to observe us, separating the menacing from the innocent, the walking stick from the rifle, and modify his behaviour accordingly.

Similarly, if your stalking takes you to the remoter, heather- or

Sitka-covered hills, don't assume that because the deer may not see a man from one month to another that they live in a state of confiding innocence. Just for the reason that human contact is an event, they are likely to be really wild and unapproachable. Their suburban cousins which are so accustomed to the close proximity of man become, if you like, discriminating: connoisseurs of humankind. Another element in their behaviour is that if you run blindly for a quarter of a mile on the hill you will probably be out of trouble. Try the same thing in suburbia because somebody happens to come past and you have probably risked your life crossing a main road and finish up in a playground.

Obviously, before you can begin to appreciate these finer points of deer behaviour, you need to have a solid data base: What makes your suburban roe buck tick? What he would do normally if his territory wasn't invaded at first light by joggers, at last light by courting couples and during the day by chaps cutting logs with a chain saw. What makes a hill roe move at certain hours of the day, or why does he tend to appear on the burn sides, and not in that convenient open space where you could so easily shoot him?

Like other ruminants, the roe has a neat regime for feeding in reasonable safety. He quickly picks off enough leaves to fill his first stomach with roughly-chewed mush, and then retires into thick cover to do a better job of mincing it up in peace. Lying down in a sunny place, chewing the cud may take a leisurely quarter of an hour. Successive balls of food are brought up, thoroughly chewed and returned to a different section of the rumen where indigestible cellulose is broken down by a collection of primitive plants and bacteria, allowing the cell contents to be absorbed. After a siesta (roe rarely sleep as we do) and a stretch, he will wander out and repeat the process. In really natural conditions they like to go through the day, and most of the night if there is a moon, feeding at three hourly intervals.

Forget this dusk-and-dawn business: that only developed when deer discovered that humans are slow to get going first thing, and inclined to retire and chew the cud (or whatever) towards evening. As soon as they find that there are suspicious goings-on in the early mornings, they will adapt accordingly.

The weather has a fundamental effect on deer movement. Like ourselves, they feel the cold, don't like going out in the wet, and will only leave a warm bed in the rain if the trees start showering them with cold drips. Wind makes them nervous, because their scenting powers on which they rely to a great extent, are less reliable, particularly when the air is dry. Watch a doe who is suspicious of you, but can't catch the scent. She will probably lick her nose repeatedly, which is to moisten the air as it enters the nasal passages. Moist air carries scent better. She will jerk her head up and down, which is not only to get a better view of a suspicious object, but to test the air currents at different heights.

Cold winds, or driving rain are no more pleasant to roe than to ourselves, and we have mackintoshes. So do not expect to find them out in the open, but sheltering in the lee of trees or thick hedges. When the sun comes out, ten to one a buck will get up, stretch, shake himself and then go in search of the deer equivalent of a Mars Bar.

Thinking about shelter, never forget that a roe is much nearer ground level than we are. Heather-living roe sometimes seem to endure dreadful weather, lying out on the open hill while the rain or snow drives over them. Mark carefully where one of these hardy beasts has been lying, put him up and find the place. You will probably discover that there is a warm pocket of air just there, but only up to the height of a sitting roe's head.

Food, and the search for it, dominates their lives. Roe are very discriminating feeders, and they need a much higher level of nutrition than a red stag, for example, or a dairy cow. While they will take some grass or young cereals, their principal resources are the leaves, twigs and buds of trees and shrubs which are more nutritious. Anything young and luscious attracts them, while the nutritive quality is at its best. Brambles and coppice shoots (the regrowth after a tree has been felled) are picked out. Ivy and willow leaves are also very high on the preference list, so if your stalking is in good roe habitat, where there is a plentiful supply of these, you can expect deer to be numerous and with good body weights.

Do your homework during the day (when deer expect humans to be about) and do it openly, with cracking twigs and heavy footfalls, to show them that you are harmless. Look for browsed twigs and brambles, a sharp cut-off line on ivy-covered tree trunks where the deer have shaved off every leaf as high as they can reach (about four feet, or 1.2 metres, in the case of roe) and cut stumps which have had the new shoots removed. If deer are responsible, the twig ends will be chomped off roughly. Hares and rabbits leave a clean cut because unlike deer, they have cutting teeth in the upper as well as in the lower jaw.

These investigations during the day can also reveal evidence of deer presence and movement. There will be footmarks *(slots)* in any muddy patches, but often across rather than along human paths. Their own regular tracks *(racks)* across ditches and banks are often a give-away, but for Goodness' sake don't try to follow deer paths through the undergrowth. First of all, they never seem to lead anywhere, and more important, you will frighten the local deer out of their wits. They are quite used to noisy humans coming and going in the woods during the day, but on the whole we keep to the rides and tracks, or advance boldly into the thickets in order to cut trees down or even drive pheasants. These are things which are well understood by the deer. On the other hand, if they become aware that someone is crawling menacingly along their own private ways – that is terrifying.

The best way of getting into the recesses of the woods is to volunteer as a beater in the winter shoots. The deer are going to be disturbed anyway, and the discipline of beating means that you have to go into bits which might look pretty uninteresting or uninviting. It is a very good idea in any case to get along with the shoot, and the gamekeeper if there is one.

Woodland roe do not move far anyway, which is another important fact to hoist in. One will always get fed with stories about where they come from or go to, but the fact is that a mature buck or doe is much more static than the average middle-aged householder. Once a buck or a doe has established a territory (and the two sexes live somewhat separate lives) they will stick to it through thick and thin. Only total loss of cover and lack of food during the winter, or constant disturbance will induce them to shift. Nor do they have to go regularly to the nearest water hole to drink, so it's no good lying up for them as if you were in Africa. Another widely-held idea smashed.

In one way roe are quite different from humans in their mode of life: the young of the previous year are forcibly ejected before the arrival of the next batch. These sad and shattered youngsters, suddenly turned out by their

previously doting and protective parents, have to make their own way in the world. It is nature's way of regulating the population. Each May or early June these outcasts have to go off to find a home for themselves. A wood which has sufficient mature deer exports most of the yearling crop as surplus to requirements, and in a deer-crowded countryside they may have to travel for days and miles before finding either a vacant territory or some sort of cover which is not attractive enough to hold an older buck.

Your piece of stalking may be good enough habitat to export deer, or it may be firmly on the receiving end of the influx of yearlings. Observe the deer methodically enough to realise this vital piece of information, and you are at least halfway to success because you are beginning to know your deer, not as targets, but as the fascinating and highly individual 'people' they are.

Antlers – Why all the Fuss?

No subject among stalkers – except possibly ballistics – releases more cubic yards of hot air than antlers.

Most of it is about the question of whether a particular set is 'good' or 'bad'; whether or not the late owner ought to have been shot.

The joke is that all this, quite unconsciously, demonstrates one of the principal functions of antlers: to divert the predator's attention away from the unassuming, but infinitely more biologically valuable female!

In fact, antlers are fascinating structures, quite apart from their qualities as trophies or walking stick handles. It is worth giving a moment's thought to why deer go through such an apparently wasteful process in which they spend quite disproportionate amounts of minerals and energy in growing large skeletal structures, only to discard them after a few short months.

From the time of *Triceratops* and the other horned dinosaurs, it has been quite clear that there must be advantages in having spikes on your head, but deer antlers are totally different from such bony protuberances, although one must assume that the basic purpose must have something in common.

The last of the dinosaurs vanished from the earth nearly a hundred million years ago, while the first true deer probably evolved about sixty-five million years later, so far as we know. Maybe the remains of something older will eventually emerge from the primeval slime, but if it does, the probability is that bumps of some sort will be found on its skull.

The earliest deer ancestors are likely to have had furry pedicles, rather like the modern giraffe. Some authorities have suggested that later forms had antler-like structures of bare bone. Fossil skulls of *Merycodonts* which lived in North America in the Miocene Epoch (thirty-five to fifteen million years ago) would pass for modern roe, but even their six-point spikes are not supposed to have been proper antlers, because they were never shed.

To some extent this seems a much more economical strategy than annual shedding and regrowth, but because bare bone is essentially dead, there is no way of growing a bigger set to match progressive increases in body size and weight between youth and maturity.

As weapons of offence and defence, tusks would seem to have some advantages, but as antlers developed in length and complexity, so did the tusks become progressively reduced. Chinese water deer, probably the most primitive true deer, have long tushes in the upper jaw developed from the canine teeth. Muntjac, which existed fifteen or more million years ago, have short antlers and long teeth. Red deer, which only evolved in the last million years or so, have the great antlers with which we are familiar, but only vestigial tusks.

Male deer are constantly faced with the need to impress rivals. No doubt big antlers help with the deception, let alone if you hang tufts of grass on the points as the Père David stags do. There were some interesting experiments on an unfortunate caribou stag which was fitted with several sets of clip-on antlers. His attitude to the rest of the herd, and theirs to him, varied according to whether he had normal antlers, overgrown ones, or just juvenile spikes. The long-term effect of this experiment on his personality was not recorded.

The actual process of growing antlers is fascinating and extraordinary to watch, while the physiological changes which make annual casting and regrowth possible are quite unique, yet we take it all very much for granted.

Casting involves physical changes in the structure of the antler, just below the coronet, leading to a layer of cells becoming weakened by decalcification or bone resorption. A buck shot just before casting shows a fracture line on his pedicles, but the antlers retain their strength nearly to the day when they fall off from their own weight. Sometimes, the process is accelerated by chance, if the beast jumps down a bank, or pushes through a thick hedge, jarring them off. I also suspect that there is some irritation or discomfort which would explain why fallow deer, in particular, can do quite a bit of fraying damage just at casting time in the spring. This threshing might accelerate antler cast.

The action is triggered by progressive lowering of male hormone level, which is in turn controlled by the pituitary gland under the influence of sunlight. The same change in hormone balance starts regrowth of the new antlers. Goss, in his formidable book *Deer Antlers,* suggests that casting in itself does not trigger regrowth. In some deer species there is considerable delay between the two events. In roe, there is normally a thickening of flesh round the pedicles before casting, and the scar which results is very soon covered over by new velvet.

Sometimes the old antler fails to shed, and new growth laps round it to make a ball-shaped mass of antler. It is not uncommon in young fallow bucks, and some of the older St Hubert Club stalkers will remember that the red deer in Thetford Forest occasionally grew knobs the size of tennis balls instead of antlers. I was fortunate to shoot one of these 'Knob Stags' in 1965. It was four years old, and to all appearances normal except that his testicles were unusually small.

We tend to take velvet for granted, without sparing a thought for such a curious substance. To take an example, nerve tissue once damaged is not capable of regeneration, yet growing antlers in velvet are sensitive and well supplied with nerves, as well as a plentiful blood supply which makes them warm to the touch.

As well as being hairy, giving rise to the name, velvet is also shiny. Hair follicles are produced as the antler elongates. Each is supplied with a gland which secretes an oily substance. One could speculate whether this oil is a fly-repellent. Certainly, stags and fallow bucks in late summer are increasingly worried by insects as the velvet decays. Is this the attraction of rotting tissue, or the progressive failure of the repellent supply?

Despite all the theoretical stuff about heredity, or 'blood lines', within the capacity of each species an ample food supply is the over-riding influence on the size of antlers which deer are capable of growing. Producing such large bony structures is a severe drain on any animal. The majority of our deer pick up a meagre living compared to farm animals, or similar species in countries where the climate is kinder. One has only to look at the enormous bodily development of second-generation farmed deer whose parents were wild-caught from the Highlands and stunted by malnutrition. The stags' antlers are unrecognisable except by the general shape.

Of course heredity has a profound influence, especially in the type or form of the antlers, but a stag cannot be expected to produce vast, spreading antlers if he was at starvation level when he was trying to grow them. Lack of sufficient food, as in the case of Highland red deer, can also be aggravated by disturbance to the point of actual starvation. Constant incursions by humans on their feeding range can inhibit deer from foraging sufficiently to lay down the reserves of fat which are essential for survival through the winter. Those that survive have not recovered in time for the late spring flush of grass and heather on the hill to benefit antler growth.

Roe grow their antlers when food is at a minimum because of their habit of casting in late autumn. The influence of variations in nutrition, from year to year, is so marked that a buck may be completely unrecognisable by his antlers from one year to another.

Injuries to antlers while they are in velvet can produce the most bizarre malformations, but provided the pedicle is not affected, the malformed antler will be cast at the end of the season, and according to theory, a normal one will grow in due course. Even with this fairly straightforward rule, there are some disturbing exceptions which appear either to prove it, or cast doubt on its validity. Victor Manton, who was Curator of Whipsnade Zoo for years, told me of a wapiti there which had one tine bent in velvet when it was being handled. The bend in this tine persisted, though in diminishing degree, for several years after the original trauma although of course his antlers were regularly shed. Explain that one!

We cheerfully say that antlers grow in the relative absence of male hormone, hardening and losing velvet in time for the breeding season. If so, how does the muntjac manage, now that his antler cycle is linked to the seasons since they were imported to our temperate climate, but the female persists in breeding non-seasonally? Does he send for a friend if he happens to be in velvet at the critical moment? Somehow I doubt it!

Thank Goodness, there are still large areas in the deer scene where we know a great deal less than we think. That is what makes it all worth while.

Two Sets of Antlers

It is on record that the Père David deer at Woburn earlier this century sometimes shed their antlers twice in a single year, possibly due to the high quality feeding which was available in those sumptuous times. Anyway a queer beast like that might do anything! To hear of our familiar roe bucks doing the same thing is almost unthinkable and yet two cases are on record, one of which came to my notice many years ago quite by chance.

June is Heartbreak Month, when roe does with a fawn at foot get killed in farm crops or on the road. In addition, otherwise kindly and thinking people pick up roe fawns, thinking that they have been abandoned. The fawn is loved for its looks and confiding nature, and almost invariably dies within a few weeks with heartbreak for all involved. Rearing young deer requires expert help, including immediate therapy for shock, plus long-term devotion and stock-manship which is usually beyond the average household. It can be done, as the following account reveals, given sufficient whisky and porridge, but sadly 99 per cent of rescue attempts end in failure. It is better to put them back quietly where they came from unless the mother is definitely dead.

Back in 1966, I had a message from a Mrs Lucy Henderson in far-off Achnacarry, Inverness-shire saying that her six-year-old, tame roe buck 'Bonky' seemed to be ill, as he had shed his antlers in May, and was now in velvet. Was he turning into a perruque?

Obviously this was a very unusual situation indeed, not only the odd date for antler-cast, but the very fact that the buck was six years old and still tame! Long before that age a hand-reared buck can be expected to be too quick with his antlers to be safe except behind bars.

> . . . regarding my pet deer Bonky, which I got as a poor little thing half dead and starved on May 7th, 1959. His mother must have left him among some brushwood and branches quite close to our house when it was born, as it wasn't properly cleaned and its eyes were gummed up. We took it home but it couldn't move; we rolled it up in a warm towel and put it in a heated oven to revive.
>
> We warmed some milk and added a teaspoonful of whisky to it and fed him with a small teaspoon. He was very weak for a while and we did not expect him to live. We kept him in the warm house and soon he was getting quite lively and to run about. Everywhere I went he followed me and would squeak whenever he missed me. I used to get up in the night and give him some milk. I had to wash his mouth after each feed and then give him a sponge down as he didn't like to be dirty.
>
> I fed him with Jersey cow milk from Achnacarry dairy: if the dairymaid happened to be away for the weekend and someone strange in her place he would not take the milk: he must have got the different scent. I would have to put my hands in it before he would touch it. When he started to eat I started to give him some porridge and milk with sugar in it, which I must say he is still taking. I kept him in a large tea-box in the house until he got too big and his little horns began to grow. His first lot were very short and tiny but he had a habit of rubbing them against the furniture in the house, so my husband built a shed for him to stay in. He had electric light and a good straw bed to lie on. It must be kept clean and all his dishes for food washed every day, or else he won't take it. His food consists of a dish of washed sliced potatoes and carrots, bowl of porridge and fresh milk, one of flaked maize, mixed grain and cattle cubes. Bowl of clean water. He also likes rowan leaves, oak leaves, beech leaves (when they are young and tender) alder and heather which has to be tied in bundles and hung up in his shed.

In November he casts his horns, just a matter of days between, and by the end of February the velvet is rubbed off. He rubs them against branches and the fence posts. They bleed quite a lot and they look very tender and sore for a few days. Strange enough this year [1966] he cast them again in May, one on the 20th and the other on the 22nd. We have had six pairs of perfect horns with three points on each and very, very rough and jaggy at the base of the skull. The ones he has on just now after casting them in May are small bush ones, very rough and tiny, just like his first horns only much rougher. Up to date [28.10.66] he has still got them on, but I notice that they are beginning to swell at the skull and the wee horns are beginning to sound quite boss if you touch them.

He has plenty of space to romp about in, and loves to play about when the children are playing in the school playground quite close to him. When they are playing football he runs and jumps and kicks his hind legs up in the air. We gave him a red ball and he has some great fun with it himself. He never tries to jump the fence, not even a very low one that divides his grounds; he walks right round it and goes through the gate.

He has got past the rutting season, he is just a bit unsettled and off his food slightly. He goes round his territory and rubs all the places with his head and leaves a brown sticky substance and a peculiar smell like apples. He is like that from the middle of August until about the beginning of October, but I can't say that he has ever been wild with anyone that lives in the house. He certainly does not like strangers to come too close to him. If he gets too annoyed he barks like a dog. I can do anything with him.

The one thing he can't stand is the Tick Fly [Deer Ked?] He comes running to me to comb him and take them off. We have tried him to take salt lick, but he won't touch it. He often eats some fresh salt, ground, or ashes.

Since I got him he has never been out at night and loves to go to his shed for a lie-down during the day. He goes to his bed about five o'clock and I let him out about nine in the morning. He makes a great fuss of me and licks my face and arms. If I am going anywhere and want to get him in early to his house I just have to call him and he comes running for a piece of cake or some sweet biscuits. He is also very fond of tea leaves and cigarettes and would eat any amount of them. How we found out he likes cigarettes: whenever I went to the grocer, if I bought them and put them in my basket, wee Bonky would smell them and go quite frantic until he got one. He would nose about in my basket until he got the packet, take it out and chew to get the packet open.

Tourists passing would stop and see Bonky and offer him a cigarette, but he would not take anything from a stranger. He always smells anything before he ventures to eat it, but immediately I would take the cigarette in my hand and offer it to him he would eat it at once.

What a wonderful person Mrs Henderson must have been. I feel so sad never to have been able to meet her. From her account one can see the sort of dedication needed for success with a fawn.

In November that year, I had another letter from Achnacarry with a few more details of this very unusual buck.

> You were making enquiries about Bonky and when he first grew his horns. The first year we got Bonky he grew those buttons between November and December (the dates I can't tell you) they were very small, just like a little acorn . . . About his antlers, at the present time as I told you they are small very short ones. The velvet is off them for some time. They are by no means soft and he is likely to cast them again at any time as I notice there are new ones beginning to push them off, as they are very itchy and he likes to get them scratched. You were also asking if he marks his territory at any other time. Between May and June he has this peculiar scent and if you stroke or pat him there is also a brown dye comes off him. At that time he walks up and down the fence which he could easily jump: it's only an ordinary garden fence between three and four feet high.
>
> Bonky is very content. If it's wet and cold he won't come out of his shed; he lies and chews his cud. As long as his tummy is full he doesn't want to move about.
>
> . . . I hope some of these items I have told you about will be of some interest to you. We are very proud of Bonky as everyone told me I wouldn't be able to keep him more than a few days.
>
> yours very sincerely
>
> Lucy Henderson and Bonky

Years later, when I happened to be near Achnacarry, I called in, hoping that Mrs Henderson might still be there, but sadly I was too late. If any of her family read this, I would like to record my gratitude for the trouble she took in replying to my questions. The charming letters which I had from her surfaced recently, and deserve a wider public among others who love the small deer and their strange and captivating ways.

Watching Them Watching Us

We tend to think of roe as animals of dusk and dawn and there are certainly peaks of activity round those times, depending on wind and weather, but where roe are undisturbed they are busy at intervals during the day. What happens during the night is anybody's guess! When scientists started radio-tracking roe in heavily-disturbed woods they noticed that the whole pattern changed as soon as night fell, some bucks even occupying different nocturnal territories from those they defended during the day. Of course that is all part of the admirable way that these deer observe our comings and goings, adapting their way of life to take advantage of ground which would be dangerous when people are about. How often have farm men told me that in places where a keen stalker is invariably out every morning before dawn, they see more roe about after breakfast than first thing!

If you spent a frosty night sitting under a hedge what would you do in the morning, lacking a Kelly kettle? Run about, play tag with your girl friend and generally warm up? Of course you would, and the deer do just the same. One has a fellow-feeling for them as the rising winter sun sends long shadows across the hoar-silvered stubble. Fawns play recognisable children's games among themselves; mothers and young dash here and there along the warming slopes; even staid mature bucks rouse themselves and have a playful dig at the nearest underling. That is, if the sun does rise. Otherwise they stand hunched up under the nearest hedge looking just as miserable as one would feel under the same circumstances until some member of the group decides to make the effort and search for breakfast.

A group of roe are often to be seen in the long field opposite my study window, giving a wonderful chance to observe their routine. They appear as soon as the crop is harvested, giving one the impression that the field had been their home most of the summer. There seems to be plenty of new weed growth to eat among the unploughed stubble, with occasional forays up and down the hedges. I notice sudden long absences for reasons unknown. Maybe they get a fright or worse from the local poachers, dislike some agricultural spray which has been applied or just become bored by the browning weeds and take off for better feeding in the woods.

The big field is a bit of curving downland where a safe shot would be difficult because of a road on the top side and our village in the valley bottom. They seem to be mostly undisturbed, able to live a fairly normal life. Across the main road is a wood which probably provides shelter at other times. The make-up of the group varies in number and in membership. There may be anything from three to seven, sometimes, two does with their fawns and two mature bucks, sometimes three does and one fawn. How many individuals are involved?

From studies on roe abroad we know that the behaviour of deer living in the fields varies materially from roe living exclusively in thick woodland but even so they conform pretty closely to the typical behaviour pattern of woodland roe: short periods in turn of feeding, cudding and loafing. Three or four hours later the whole process is likely to be repeated through the daylight hours, given a reasonable lack of disturbance. After feeding the group would lie down, mostly just above a slight ridge across the hill where there was once a hedge, presumably taking advantage of the run of the wind and good visibility all round. On cold mornings and to shelter from cold wind or rain they might be found under a hedge but grazing, even in heavy rain usually means an expedition well away from cover.

Downland deer are quite a challenge to the stalker, not only because of the difficulty of getting into reasonable range over open and all-too-often flinty ground, but from the unpredictable way they seem to move about. Like hill roe they make better use of their eyes, rather than relying on hearing and scent like woodland deer and when a suspicious movement has been spotted the whole group is likely to decamp into the next field before settling down, or over the next hill or two in the case of moorland roe. The deer on one farm of about a thousand acres where I stalked for years gave the impression that their range was more or less the same as the farm boundaries, though the fencing was no different round the perimeter. If they were moved one could be fairly sure of finding them again at the other end of the farm, a weary trudge. Moved again, they would be back where they started and only if a group was really pushed would they jump the wire fence and depart for the neighbour's coverts. This gave opportunities of catching up with them – provided that the stalker's legs lasted long enough to traipse about most of the day. After a few end-to-end migrations they could usually be found in a large group sitting in the exact middle of the biggest field. Downland fields are Texas-sized if you are trying to crawl across to a group of highly suspicious deer about 400 yards from the nearest cover!

Even in woodland there may be wider movements than might be expected. The annual forced migration of yearlings trying to find any un-occupied ground is well known and their travels can take them many miles. Towards fawning time some does will move, presumably to an environ-ment which they think is better for the young fawns, sometimes a considerable distance. This is most noticeable where roe are living on steep hillsides where the chosen fawning ground is likely to be in the lush level meadows near water.

Alan Newman, a professional stalker in Surrey, tells me that even large bucks may desert their usual territories in the middle of the rut, only to re-occupy them a few days later, driving out any interlopers. Certainly I have had doubts about the morals of some of the bucks which I watched regularly who had unexpected absences, either late at night, or for a few days.

Hill roe and those inhabiting some of the more exposed young conifer plantations are capable of making significant movements to lower ground in winter, pushing up again in the spring. I have seen them existing happily in the high alpine pastures with the chamois in Austria at 2000 metres (6,500 feet) from where they certainly would have had to retire at the onset of cold weather. Of course the most extreme can be seen among the Siberian and Chinese roe, some of which migrate *en masse* from the mountains, travelling great distances to places where the snow cover is thin enough to allow them to evade the wolves. Once the snow reaches a depth of half a metre even these big roe flounder in the snow and make easy prey.

Next time the local guru tells you flatly that roe are territorial, or have a very limited 'home range', say 'Well . . . I'm sure they are – sometimes'.

Malformed Antlers and Fly-Strike

According to Shakespeare, human flesh is heir to a thousand natural shocks. Roe seem no better served by life – at least Hamlet could not expect to be devoured piecemeal, even though he was thinking of ending his life at the time. Among the 'natural shocks' which torment the daily life of deer is the liability to be attacked and sometimes gradually eaten alive by egg-laying flies.

The deer warble is well known because of its cousin which used to attack cattle before the eradication scheme got going. Nostril flies, one species for roe, mercifully uncommon in this country and another for red deer and fallow, squirt their already hatched larvae into a deer's nose where they wax fat and horrid. Deer keds emerge as winged flies in September but on alighting on an animal's coat (or a tweed jacket for that matter) they shed their wings and spend a furtive life running sideways among the hair, doubtless to the discomfort of the host.

One of the most revolting states which a stalker can discover in a deer he has shot, and one which must be tormenting to the animal concerned, is the maggot infestation resulting from fly-strike by greenbottle flies. Shepherds are familiar with this problem, but the unfortunate roe have no dips or agrochemicals to protect themselves from the pest. Greenbottles are attracted to any decaying matter, or an open wound. If this happens to be in an accessible place and the beast is in reasonable health, constant licking soon clears the eggs away and no harm comes. However, a wounded animal may be too stiff or too hurt to get at the wound, the maggots hatch and start eating away first skin, then muscle and even into the bone itself.

Bucks suffer more than does; partly no doubt because of their aggressive habits but also because their antlers and the surrounding area of the skull are inaccessible. Bashing one's head against fences and vegetation may be the only way open to combat unbearable irritation and of course this only aggravates the problem.

Bucks with very large coronets often have trouble because the skin between gets progressively squeezed up as antler growth progresses in the spring. By May this skin can actually mortify; along comes the greenbottle as it does to a sheep with a dirty tail or some deep-seated wound under its wool.

I remember shooting one buck in Wiltshire which had two tight white rings below its coronets – the tails of maggots eating away at the pedicles. I was so disgusted that I left the head to rot out, retrieving it later when the worst was over.

Another, a full perruque, found by Dorset Head Keeper Ron Thorpe, was similarly heaving with the pests beneath the skin. This one had died, but whether from the maggots or as a consequence of growing a perruque head could not be established. A passing car could also have brought its misery to an end.

The whole question of fly-strike was brought up again when Ron brought in another, this time a massive, multi-point head found dead by the beaters in a pheasant drive. Some time later, it was brought to me again by a different messenger with the usual request for a pronouncement on how it died.

It is one of those trophies with an immense tanglement of points in every direction – ten of them, above good coronets. A buck of late middle age according to his teeth. Looking at the frontal bone the activities of maggots were all too evident; the surface eaten away between the eye sockets and the central suture penetrated down to the brain. There were also some holes in the skull behind the left pedicle. Whether the maggots had killed him was anybody's guess.

The ability of wild creatures to survive wounds and infections which would be fatal to fragile Man always amazes me. Perhaps they have no realisation of the grave injury done, pain apart, so the shock is purely physical rather than mental as it would be with ourselves.

One real curiosity of these fly-struck heads is how often they are either malformed or multi-pointed. One assumes that the maggots, having feasted themselves to maturity in a comparatively short time would pupate as rapidly as their cousin the bluebottle does, especially when kept for fishing. However, if their presence is the cause of the malformation, they must have been present the previous summer, before the malformed antlers were grown. Are the maggots one sees, therefore, over-wintered larvae from the original strike, or a second generation, attracted by the unhealthy state of the unfortunate buck's skull? Who would be a roe buck!

The alternative is, of course, that the malformed antlers have nothing to do with the fly-strike. In that case, either the eggs were specially difficult to dislodge because of the shape of the antlers, or the root cause, presumably internal, of the malformation makes the animal more susceptible to attack. All I can say is that I have a number of heads with no visible reason for sometimes gross malformation, while all but one of my fly-struck heads are non-typical. The one exception was a buck which harboured a couple of maggots, no more, in the detritus between the coronets. Maybe this one was in the first stages of a continuing process which would have resulted in a malformed set of antlers the following year. Presumably the activities of just two maggots would attract other flies in due course. Alas! Poor Yorick!

All this talk of infestation reminds me of an early BDS Symposium at the London Zoo on the subject of parasites. The first lecturer was hardly into his detailed description of various creepy-crawlies before nearly every member of the audience was covertly scratching, just at the thought.

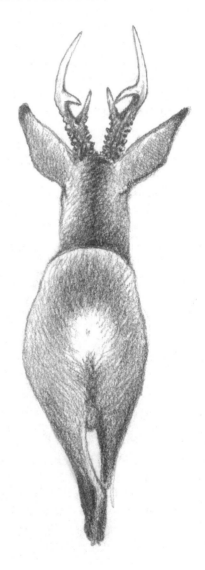

When Roe Bucks Fight

Fights between roe bucks are rarely witnessed but this does not mean that they are rare. The rutting battles of red stags on the open hill can be watched from a distance and during the middle of the day; often all that is seen of an engagement between roe may be momentary glimpses of russet bodies in the undergrowth, and possibly the click of antlers. One must get up early or stay out late to get even that far. But fighting is not uncommon even well before the period of the rut.

Unlike most other deer, roe are territorial in habit and fierce competition for desirable territories develops as soon as the bucks' antlers become clean in the spring. In common with the majority of free-living animals, physical conflict is avoided whenever possible and usually arguments are settled by threat display. This takes the form of challenge barking, scraping with the forefoot (a signal indicating ownership) and the habit of fraying small trees, a so-called displacement activity, which can result in serious damage to forest plantations. Fights develop only when these threats fail. Even in the middle of a desperate bout the combatants often break off and revert to threat. However, once committed to fighting roe bucks display astonishing strength and agility.

On 17 June one year I was able to watch a fight that took place, for once, in an open field and which was unusual for the lack of preliminaries. I had gone at daybreak to a deep fold in the downs called Chickengrove Bottom where roe often feed in the long field threading a valley between scrub-covered hillsides. Conditions were not ideal: overcast and humid with occasional sprinkles of warm rain.

A two-year-old buck was already out feeding, and a doe which I had half disturbed wandered away to join him. Some time after five, the buck crossed the field and jumped a sheep fence into some thick blackthorns. Almost immediately he was bundled out by a heavier buck with a short, massive head. Presumably the old gentleman was annoyed by the sudden arrival of a competitor in the middle of his territory or otherwise they may have had angry words earlier. They ran into the centre of the field, and then turned to face one another.

Then followed a typical roe fight. The bucks advanced with heads nearly at ground level until they were perhaps a yard apart, then giving a simultaneous spring they met antler-to-antler, each shoving in an attempt to get the other off balance. In spite of the disparity in size they appeared to be fairly well matched, and first one then the other would be forced back but always managing to retain a footing. Once or twice the youngster slipped as he was run backwards at full tilt, but he regained his balance and never disengaged his head to allow a sideways stab into neck or flank by his adversary.

After the first long spell, during which their movements were sometimes too fast to follow, they stopped as if by mutual consent and stood eyeing one another, moving slowly about fifteen yards apart and pretending to feed. Then their heads went down once more and the battle started again as fiercely as ever. If they drifted near the fence between bouts, this seemed to trigger renewed action, although the old buck made no attempt to pin his adversary against it, as he could have done at one moment. On the other hand, they both tried to take advantage of a slight bank which crossed the battleground. At the end of half an hour both had lost their original fire without either being obviously beaten. However, a points decision was apparently accepted: the young buck broke away and was escorted back down the field at a walking pace. The doe, who had been a passive witness of all this remained quietly feeding.

Some fights finish only with the death of one buck, but it is difficult to assess how frequent this may be. In the thick cover of summer only chance leads to the discovery of a dead roe and unless it is very soon after the event, little evidence but bones is left for a post-mortem. Cases have been known of death by stabbing when the beaten buck has been pinned down, and of the four bucks which I found dead after one rut, more than one may have been killed in this way. Decomposition made it impossible to be sure. Other injuries are most likely to be inflicted during the initial impact, when the antlers are driven together with all the power of both bucks' haunches.

If they have normal headgear, the brows and back points provide an effective guard. But if one contestant has exceptionally long tops or lacks all points, a 'murder buck', the impact can be sufficient to drive an antler tip through the other's skull. I have seen five heads with similar wounds, though only one buck had died as a result. The brain was exposed in each case. Possibly the relief of pressure by this violent trepanning operation provides its own cure.

In *British Deer and their Horns*, Millais illustrated a buck which had been killed in this way. The top of his adversary's antler had broken off and was embedded in the skull to a depth of one inch (2.5cm). The antler was driven in slightly to the right of the central suture, behind the pedicle. All the skulls which I have seen had been pierced at this point, which rather reinforces the evidence of 'handedness' in roe. Roe usually run their rutting rings anti-clockwise in the same way that horses prefer to lead with one leg rather than the other. There is some evidence that dogs share the right-handed bias shown so clearly by most human beings, and this may apply equally to deer or other beasts whose actions are much less easy to observe.

Interlocked Heads

The chances of entanglement between such short, simple antlers, must be remote. However, cases do crop up from time to time. Of course this is much more rare with roe than among deer species with more complicated antlers, like fallow or caribou. Only one case has been reported comparatively recently – a pair of typical mature bucks firmly locked head-to-head which were found dead near Cullompton in Devon in 1999, but several cases were reported in the early 1970s. One pair was found in Northumberland by Mr A Lyell. In this case one of the combatants had a very unusual thirteen-point head which no doubt contributed to the tragedy. His age was estimated at seven years. His opponent was a four-year beast with a fine head of 25.4cm.

In the South, a pair of interlocked skulls, both standard six-pointers was picked up by Major-General Lipscombe, who offered his young daughter sixpence (old money) if she could separate them. Luckily she failed! They probably became fixed at the moment when, as happens in all roe buck fights, the two bucks lower their heads and jump together in the same way that rams fight. Presumably the combined force of their impact and an unlucky angle was enough to make the antlers spring slightly and then lock together so that one buck broke his neck and the other miserably starved to death.

Shortly afterwards three other sets were reported. One pair came from the New Forest, where they were discovered in a recently-decomposed state by the New Forest Buckhounds. They hung for many years in the Court Room of Queen's House in Lyndhurst. Another pair of large, heavily antlered animals was found in Sussex, and a fourth example came from Wiltshire. The latter was more unusual. Not only were the two adversaries badly matched, but one was alive when found. The survivor was not the heavier of the two, but a three-year buck with thin, poorly developed antlers. The larger was an exceptionally massive nine-point buck whose antlers were exhibited in the British Pavilion at the World Hunting Exhibition in Budapest in 1972. Efforts were made to separate the two bucks in the cause of humanity. The antlers of the younger buck were sawn off, but he did not survive.

Soon after that another tragedy came to light at Chicksgrove, near Tisbury in Wiltshire. When these animals were found they had been dead some weeks, but during the past rut they had obviously been fencing with one another in a thickly bushed hedgerow, with a maple stem acting as a barrier between. Not only had they locked antlers, but the maple also became involved and they had no chance of freeing themselves. They had clearly been there many days before they died. This again was a well-matched pair of bucks, both with well-developed antlers, one with six points, the other with five.

23

In Konrad Lorenz' animal studies, his dog Bully would gallop backwards and forwards one side of the garden fence, barking furiously at a canine enemy who did the same thing on the other, both knowing well that any risky extension of hostilities was impossible. The bucks at Chicksgrove had apparently been using the maple tree, and probably the wire fence too, as a barrier from behind which to threaten and posture.

Roe bucks are certainly inclined to overindulge in threatening behaviour when there is a barrier between them. Sometimes large, serious patches of fraying damage are due to neighbouring bucks (and red stags too) having a satisfying and unhazardous morning hate at either side of a ditch or rabbit fence. The two Wiltshire bucks were probably indulging in this sort of 'brinkmanship' but, like human hotheads before them, took matters too far.

Colour Variations in Roe

I am grateful when anyone rings me up bursting with news of an unusual roe which he has seen or shot. Most often it is a malformed head, sometimes a perruque or even a hermaphrodite. What is startling to the stalker concerned may not be all that uncommon but none the less it is all part of the generous way deer enthusiasts exchange news. Once in a while not only is that understandable degree of exaggeration lacking, but the event is truly rare. Such was the case when I had a phone call from Mark Howell, a stalker from North Dorset, to say that he had shot a black roe. If confirmation was needed, a second call from Brian Booth provided eye witness to the doe's essential blackness.

Black roe are, of course, well known in certain parts of Europe, notably North-West Germany and parts of Holland. When Joop Poutsma took me round the reclaimed Polders of North Holland we saw a number of them, standing out among groups of normal colour. He told me that up to ten per cent of the population there are black. Admittedly it was raining enough to flood the fields again, which always makes deer appear darker, but they did look coal black rather than dark brown.

So far as Britain is concerned, melanism in roe is a real rarity. Only in one area, in Dumfries-shire, is there a long-recognised tendency for a proportion of roe to be very dark indeed. Records of them go back as far as 1968. It was probably about ten years after this that I saw one myself, standing out in a Molinia-grown ride between two massive blocks of spruce.

Scotland apart, I only know of two unconfirmed reports of black roe.

J G Millais in his mammoth three-volume work *The Mammals of Great Britain & Ireland* (1906) wrote that a black roe had been seen at Whatcombe, near Milton Abbas in Dorset 'a few years ago'. Presumably that meant in the closing years of the nineteenth century. No doubt such a good natural-ist would have been careful to check any unusual sighting, but it has something of the ring of hearsay and one is bound to treat this report with some caution. Everyone knows how deceptively dark a roe of normal colour can appear in certain lights, especially if its coat is damp.

In *Deer News* for January 1966 Arthur Cadman wrote that a black roe buck had been seen on three occasions in the New Forest. It had a black caudal patch and a six-point head which seems fairly definite. However, it was never photographed or reported as having been shot, so Mr Howell's doe must rank as the first confirmed example from England.

Photographs show that its coat colour on the back was as dark or darker brown than a 'black' fallow, shading to fawn on the insides of the legs, belly and cheeks. The target or caudal patch was white, in contrast to the New Forest sighting. Brian Booth estimated that it was a middle-aged animal and in good condition. By coincidence or otherwise, it was shot not many miles from Whatcombe, the location of Millais' report.

Mark Howell tells me he mostly operates on farmland where the deer need to be controlled. On 17 December he had been called out by a North Dorset farmer and took up a strategic place to overlook some set-aside fields. Nothing came out until it was pretty dark, when one doe did emerge and paid the penalty. It was only when he came up to deal with it that Mark realised that it was black, and of course then regretted his decision to fire on such a curiosity. However, we all know the pressures on a stalker under similar circumstances to show willing. Apparently it had not been seen before.

Maybe it would never have been seen again, and then I have to admit I might have been a bit sceptical about a 'black' roe, seen only in the winter dusk. Certainly one swallow doesn't make a summer, or one black roe a trend. As they used to say '*What's hit's history – What's missed's mystery!*'

That was in the days before photography. None the less, it will be inter-esting to wait and see if any others are reported in the same area over the next few years. She must, of course, have had fawns somewhere, but they would not necessarily be black.

If one accepts the two previous sightings, it does appear that very occasional melanistic roe may crop up without any likelihood of perpetu-ating the strain. Whether the anomaly is caused by some accident of birth or a recessive gene occasionally displaying its existence is more than I can guess.

In contrast to melanism, a degree of albinism is not uncommon in roe, and there are reports most years of odd ones turning up. By no means all of them have pink eyes. A young deer may be parti-coloured, possibly with only one patch of white about it which expands with age if the animal survives. There was a doe in West Dorset who had a round spot just where you would aim for a heart shot. Surprisingly she survived for several years, the area of white growing bigger all the time. Eventually she disappeared without trace. I have shot a buck which was dashed with white all over, and had another in Cranborne Chase which was pure white from the start. This beast was seen three times in its entire life. I saw it once at the age of two or three; one of my guests spotted it again in late middle age, and it was found dying of senility by a walker eight years after the first sighting. All these appearances were within two hundred yards of one another, so one is led to conclude that it was there all the time. If a Persil-white buck can escape notice to that degree, and in a wood that was not only regularly stalked but driven for pheasants every winter, is it surprising that we should find bucks which are strangers, lose others on which we were relying, or under-estimate our roe populations?

Many stalkers (and drinkers!) on Speyside will remember the skewbald buck which frequented a field just outside the Glanfarclas distillery a few years ago. It was eventually killed by a lorry and was fully mounted. I remember seeing it in this state at the Moy Game Fair. The photo I took at the time was reproduced in my book *The Roe Deer* (Swan Hill Press). Other Scottish records have come from Fife, Argyll and Perthshire.

One commentator in Germany has stated that where odd-coloured roe are to be found there is a degree of interchange between white and black, so that one individual may change between the two extremes, black, for example in summer coat and white in the winter. I would be glad if any

reader had information on this rather surprising theory.

The marked difference between the roe of southern England and Scotland in the colour of their perianal patch (the unfortunately named *target),* is curious. Those of the north keep the clear white through the summer which is a characteristic of nearly all roe in winter coat. Their south-county cousins prefer a modest lemon-yellow or even light brown for their summer coat. Has this a bearing on the vexed question of their country of origin? Who knows? There is more about this in a later chapter.

Typical Questions on Roe and Deer Generally

How is it that deer can eat prickles, like brambles and roses?

Watching a deer feeding on brambles makes one wince, but both they and roses are a favourite food, as so many gardeners know to their cost. There is one pointer – the roof of the mouth is very hard, also a prickly twig is often chewed off with the broad molars rather than nibbled. Even so, deer do prefer the less thorny and younger shoots if there are any. In a garden they will go for modern varieties of roses which tend to be less well-armed, rather than the old-fashioned types with real hard spikes. Similarly, they prefer younger, tender bramble leaves, but if there is nothing else, they still chew away!

Last September I think I saw a roe doe eating mushrooms. At least there were some in the field which I found had been nibbled when I went to look. Is this a normal part of roe diet?

There are plenty of references in the literature of roe eating mushrooms of various sorts. You will find an illustration of roe deer digging out fungi in J G Millais' classic *British Deer and their Horns*, published at the end of the nineteenth century. Curiously enough, in a lifetime of watching deer I have never actually caught one in the act, though I have been shown the small pits dug by roe in Denmark in search of some sort of fungus, exactly as drawn by Millais. Sadly, we do not have too many places where field mushrooms grow these days, but there are plenty of other sorts for the deer to find, so I don't think the habit is too common in my part of the world.

Arthur Cadman found that the New Forest sika deer had a preference for a false truffle called the *Lycoperdon* nut which they detect and dig for. Red deer are also known to eat fungi on occasion.

A lot of the roe deer feeding on my fields have very dirty backsides. Are they diseased, and should I try to shoot them in case they infect my stock?

Deer go out on the fields in late winter and spring because their preferred browse is short, and to take advantage of the nutrient-rich shoots. As the spring growth gets going they do tend to scour on this diet, but it's very unlikely that they are diseased. If you are concerned, take some dung samples to your veterinary surgeon and ask his opinion.

How did red deer and roe arrive on the Hebrides? Were they imported originally, or could they have swum?

Although there may have been human intervention in some cases, red deer and roe are quite powerful and bold swimmers, which is surprising considering their slim legs and feet. Fishermen quite often report seeing both species quite far from land. In spite of fierce tides between the islands, attempts to swim two or three miles would possibly succeed, though with inevitable cases of drowning.

I am a beginner in the stalking business, and am trying to learn the jargon. Some of it is confusing: what, for example, is 'pronking'? It doesn't seem to be in any dictionary. Nor are 'fewmets'. Can you help?

Deer stalkers do seem to wrap up their talk with some esoteric terms, some of them coming from the Middle Ages. 'Fewmets' used to be the term in medieval hunting circles for a deer's droppings. Detailed study of them was supposed to show if that deer was *warrantable* (a suitable beast to be hunted). 'Pronking' does not date back, but it is a very descriptive term for the gait of a fallow deer bouncing away, all four legs in the air.

The different deer species move in quite individual ways. Red deer walk, trot, canter and gallop rather like a horse. Fallow, when they are not pronking, walk and trot and may gallop after the first alarm. Sika deer, too, may bounce a few times, often looking back to see what has alarmed them, but then move more like red deer.

Roe at leisure have a very cow-hocked look but when alarmed break into a graceful bounding run, interrupted at intervals by a space-consuming leap.

Muntjac skulk, head-down when pottering about but they also scuttle with considerable speed, when they can resemble a small pig.

All species cat-jump over surprisingly high obstacles, and they can also creep under fences. When you have some more experience of watching deer you will find it easier to distinguish the species by the way they move.

Are all young deer spotted? If they are, is this because they all trace back to a common ancestor?

All the deer we have in Britain have spotted young, and I suspect this is a characteristic which is shared with most if not all deer species. The reason is likely to be a practical question of survival of the fittest. That is, all newborn deer have to rely on immobility and concealment to avoid predators. A brown coat splashed with white tones blends in perfectly with the sun and shadows in a woodland or moorland environment.

Last May I shot a roe buck which weighed 44lb cleaned-out and with the head and lower legs cut off. Is this weight very unusual?

Forty-four pounds (20kg) is a very big weight for a roe. It indicates a 'quite clean' weight (head and legs on) of about 52lb (23.5kg) and a live weight of around 70lb (31kg). Recorded weights tend to be unofficial and open to question, but weights of up to 88lb (40kg) live, or 64lb (29kg) quite clean have been reported. Some does also achieve a great size: the largest I have noted was 29kg clean, or 64lb. A formidable matron!

I've been brought a young roe fawn which a passer-by thought had been abandoned. As they have handled it, I will have to try to rear it – what is the best thing to feed it on?

Far the best thing is to put it back! If the fawn has been licked, the mother bond will probably be strong enough to overcome any man taint. They are terribly difficult animals to rear, and even if you are successful – what are you going to do with it? Male roe get really dangerous because they have no fear of man, and even the does are a problem in the garden, to put it mildly! You can't return a hand-reared fawn to the wild; it won't know how to look after itself, and no wildlife park or rescue sanctuary is a suitable place for an adult roe. Look at the section earlier called 'Two Sets of Antlers' to see just how much may be involved.

There has been quite a bit of excitement round here because there have been several reports of a white deer (we aren't sure of the species). People want to know if they are very rare, and whether it is an albino. Can you tell me please?

In your part of Hampshire there are several species of deer, so it's not possible to be specific. However, one does find genuine white deer in all species and these are not necessarily albino (with pink eyes). White red deer in the Highlands are encountered from time to time and used to be regarded with superstitious awe. There are herds of completely white reds in some Continental parks. White fallow deer, in contrast are relatively common as it is one of their normal colour phases (the others being black, common, and menil). With roe, white or parti-coloured animals do turn up, but fairly rarely. If they are allowed to live, the white tends to spread through life. Try to have a look at your white deer and find out a bit more about their species.

*I shot a roe buck last night and when I gralloched it, the lungs were
attached to the ribs on one side. Otherwise it was in good condition. Have
you ever seen a similar case? What do you think was the cause?*

With the rough life that roe live, it's not uncommon. I have asked vets about
this sort of anomaly, and the answer is that there has either been some disease
in the lungs in the past, or an injury in this region which causes the lungs
to adhere. If the lungs are apparently healthy, then I would suspect the buck
had been hit by a car – look for evidence of cracked ribs. Otherwise it could
be injury caused by the illegal use of small shot. I hope this is not a problem
in your area.

*I shot a poorish roe buck the other day which when I skinned it was
infested with maggots along its back. What are they, and should I ditch the
carcass?*

These are warble fly larvae (*Hypoderma diana*), which are much more
common on red deer. In this country they are only found north of the
Scottish border. Eggs are laid on the legs, which hatch into larvae which
migrate to the back, where they grow into the large, disgusting maggots
which you found. Although very disfiguring, they do not affect the meat,
as they lie directly under the skin. When due to hatch they tunnel through
the skin, leaving holes which spoil it for tanning, and emerge as flies resembling a common house-fly.

*Though roe deer literature often catalogues the disappearance and
reintroduction of roe deer in England, I can find little reference to their
fortunes in lowland Scotland, particularly the Forth/Clyde valley.*

    *The late keeper on the estate in East Lothian where I stalk could
remember the recolonisation of the estate by roe as recently as the 1940s.
Was this entirely a result of southern spread from the Highlands, or was
there northward spread from the Borders, or even reintroductions to
the Lothian estates? Are there any reliable sources of records regarding the
return of roe to this area?*

This is a subject which has fascinated me, and I have done some research
which is set out in my book *The Roe Deer* (Swan Hill Press) and G K
Whitehead's monumental tome *The Deer of Great Britain and Ireland* (1964).
The situation can only be summarised here. It seems likely that roe were
never eliminated completely from Southern Scotland and the Borders
region. They were present near Hexham in the reign of George I (1714 to
1727) and a pack of roe hounds was operating in Co. Durham in 1847.
Some were released at Drumlanrig, Dumfries-shire in 1860, but J G Millais
wrote in *British Deer and their Horns* (1897) there were 'no roe, at least until
recently, in either Berwickshire or Roxburghshire and though some

appeared in Selkirkshire, on the Duke of Buccleuch's estate, they were killed off as they interfered with the foxhounds'. In 1892 Evans wrote 'It may also be seen from time to time in parts of East Lothian (the woods at Humbie and Salton, for example).' They had reappeared in the neighbourhood of Berwick on Tweed by 1900. I personally think that traces may well remain of the local, south-Scottish race, which is probably identical to the likely source of immigration from the English side of the border. Analysis of roe DNA has so far failed to produce proof of the genetic origins of our roe, but it is possible that more may come from this quite soon as the technique becomes more sophisticated.

Why do roe sometimes give a tremendous jump when they are running away?

My idea is that a high jump gives the deer more of a panoramic view of where to go and what is chasing it. There could also be an advantage in breaking the scent line of a pursuing predator. Sometimes these jumps cover many yards, and could puzzle an animal following the track nose to ground.

There are a lot of horse chestnut trees round here and the fallow seem to be eating the conkers. I thought they were poisonous. Are they being eaten by some other animal? I have also seen fallow and roe picking up green acorns, which I know are very bad for horses and ponies. How do they cope?

No, fallow do seem to love conkers and don't suffer any apparent after-effects, in fact I have shot a buck whose gullet and rumen were full of the newly-fallen nuts – and swallowed whole too! You are right that too many green acorns can be toxic, to deer as well as other stock due to the high tannin content. They lost at least one fallow in Attingham Park one year from eating too many when the British Deer Society made a visit and other cases are on record. However, later on when they are brown acorns do form a

31

Humble Pie

very valuable resource, especially to roe bucks because they are a source of protein through the winter months when they are growing their antlers. In places where other winter fodder is scarce, the relative abundance of the year's acorn crop makes a big difference to the size of next season's antlers. Deer can take a variety of leaves and fruit which are poisonous to other stock, such as yew. Under normal conditions their habit of wandering as they browse probably prevents them getting an overdose, but in very snowy weather when choice is restricted, or in park conditions, death can occur. The danger is greater if the foliage is wilted, for example with fallen or lopped branches.

When I boiled out a roe buck's head last summer I found that there were two supplementary teeth in the upper jaw. Is this very rare?

These are rudimentary canine teeth, which although not normally present in roe do occur from time to time. Normally less than a centimetre long outside the gum, unless you look for them you don't know they are there! They are usually rather loose in the sockets, and there is a suspicion that quite often they are lost by the time the buck is two or three years old. It sounds as if yours are rather larger and better-seated than many examples.

The phenomenon is not rare. The tendency is more marked in areas of very good feeding and in the south of England it has been suggested that about ten per cent of the roe may grow vestigial canines. The teeth are normally loose in their sockets and can easily be missed. Mostly they are not noticed and are either discarded with a standard-cut trophy, or with a long-nose cut come away with the tissues of the palate when the head is boiled out.

Anyone with a collection of long-nose or full skull trophies can easily check for the presence of sockets and so assess whether his roe do display this anomaly. Otherwise it is a matter of feeling that area of the upper jaw when performing the gralloch.

My son and I had just finished potting a few clays, and no sooner had we got in the car (parked literally in the field where we had been firing away) than a nice muntjac buck appeared from a nearby hedgerow and started feeding. The fallout from the shot had probably been all round him a few minutes earlier.

Was he just deaf, as he certainly wasn't blind? Suburban deer do have to put up with living cheek-by-jowl with mankind and seem content to do so, but to expose oneself quite so readily to would-be hunters did seem rather rash and out of character, especially when you remember how many times you can go out, sit quietly for two hours and not see one.

I think you have the answer when you suggest that as other people use the place for shooting practice the buck was used to the noise and had learned that it did not threaten him. They do get very clever at interpreting our behaviour so that they can live successfully in close proximity to man. Of course if you lived with lions, you would be pretty interested in their feeding habits! They aren't fools. You ask if this is a common experience. Yes, one of the biggest roe bucks on Salisbury Plain lived in the bushes behind the stop-butt on the pistol range at The School of Infantry, and more lived in the impact area, with large-calibre shells landing all round. I expect muntjac are the same. The roar of motorway traffic must be pretty terrifying, but they make use of the embankments. Adaptability is a big part of their success.

What on earth happens to my roe after the rut? Here, the rut usually tails off about 10 August and suddenly I can't see anything but a few does wandering about. One of the old books spoke about a period of semi-migration or restlessness among roe at that time – is there anything in that? If there is, why don't I see other people's bucks suddenly appearing to replace mine?

I have read the book you refer to, and it may be true in some districts that some roe tend to change their ground, especially where something in the habitat changes, for example the harvest, a plague of flies, increased keepering activity where grouse are concerned, or with the approach of partridge shooting.

On the whole, I would suggest that your bucks are still more or less where they were. The territorial males will have been exerting themselves with little time to feed during the rut. Once the excitement is over they do stay very quiescent until the beginning of September, presumably recruiting their strength. One of the curiosities of roe digestion is that the absorptive surface of the rumen (stomach) through which much digested nutrient passes, is capable of increasing or decreasing. Thus at very active times of the deer year their metabolism increases in activity while at others, especially in winter weather, it decreases. This allows the beast to remain relatively inactive without losing significant body weight. I suspect that this post-rut period may be a time when this mechanism clicks in, explaining why one sees so little activity. On the other hand, it may just be that the bracken just about hides everything! If you have access to harvest fields on your stalking ground before they all disappear under the plough, there is a good chance to see what the breeding success has been by calculating the doe/fawn ratio in preparation for the cull, and to collect the balance of your yearling buck cull which were not shot early on.

Typical Questions on Antlers

I have a queer roe skull with the two antlers apparently joined at the coronets and for about a third of their length, like a unicorn. Is this very rare, and what is the cause?

So-called coalesced heads are not at all common, so your trophy is quite a curiosity. Bucks with this malformation are usually pretty old, and were probably born with the pedicles rather close together. With each year the pedicles shorten and thicken so that they virtually fuse. With the new growth of antler having no space for velvet in between, the bone can literally join although you can often see a line marking one beam from the other.

One of my roe bucks cast his antlers in the middle of September this year. I think it is a natural cast, rather than an accident, as he seems otherwise perfectly fit. Is this very unusual? He looks fully mature, but not specially old.

If this was entirely natural, it's certainly exceptionally early. Antler cast normally does not start until October. As a rule the older bucks are the first to cast, yearlings being the last towards the end of the year. However, there are exceptions, and this could just be one of these. Other possibilities are accident, disease or injury. Bucks hit by cars often have their antlers broken off, especially if they were near to casting and therefore weakened above the pedicle. The other cause of premature casting is the loss of male hormone either through internal disease or physical castration, which can happen through getting hung up on a wire fence.

All through this season I have seen a roe buck with multi-point antlers on my stalking. Although it would be a very interesting trophy, I think he is quite young and have left him until next year. Is his head likely to be the same, but bigger next time?

Roe are very prone to grow malformed antlers, and these may be derived from different causes. If the growing antlers, but not the pedicles, were damaged while the buck was in velvet, perhaps by impact with a fence or a vehicle, they may finish up like a bird's nest because the growing tissue was damaged. However, when these antlers are discarded in the autumn, the new set are likely to be completely normal. Permanent malformations which continue from year to year result from injury to the pedicles, to the body (such as a broken leg) or to the beast's hormonal system.

Some bucks in captivity, where the cast antlers were kept each year have grown really ugly heads at some stage, only to produce splendid typical ones afterwards. I went to see a buck who was the survivor of two orphaned twins. At five and six years old he grew truly magnificent six-point heads nearly 30cm (12in) long, but his four-year-old cast antlers were a mess and would have put him on the cull list on any well-run estate. In the wild, of course, a buck growing dissimilar antlers in successive years would not be recognised as the same individual.

If you have a big cull of young bucks, then it's probably best to weed out ugly heads especially if the owners look in poor condition. Otherwise, a healthy buck with a large but imperfect head might well get the benefit of the doubt.

I picked up a roe antler in the woods recently. What makes them fall off?

The annual antler cycle is controlled by glands under the influence of day length. Curiously enough, antlers are cast and re-grow when the level of male hormone in the body declines. The bony pedicle weakens just under the coronet and eventually gravity or accident jars off the old hard antler. In most deer species re-growth starts immediately, under a covering of velvet which has a plentiful supply of blood vessels. When the antlers are full-size again, the male hormone level rises, the velvet decays and exposes new, white bone (sometimes bloodstained) which colours progressively through fraying on bushes and so on. Most deer shed in spring; roe are different and lose their antlers between October and December.

I found a cast antler the other day, which is the first I have ever found. What happens to them?

Considering how many deer there are about, and the fact that all males cast their antlers every year, it is surprising how few do get found. Of course, roe and muntjac antlers are fairly small, and lying in the sun and rain they soon get bleached. It needs a pretty sharp eye to spot them in the undergrowth among the twigs and leaves. They often get jarred off when the buck pushes or jumps through a hedge, leaving them in exceptionally difficult places to search. Most often it is just luck finding one. A friend in Cumbria dropped his stalking stick and picked up a twig with it. This turned out to be a tiny cast antler with six true points but only about five centimetres long. Probably a remarkably large example of a fawn button, grown in the fawn's first winter and shed in February. That's real luck! It is true, as you suggest, that the deer themselves eat them, presumably for the minerals, but so do a variety of other animals, rodents in particular, so that a cast antler left undiscovered for a year or so is usually nibbled away considerably.

On 31 March, in a piece of mixed woodland we surprised a roe amongst the thicket. Both of us had it in sight a minute or so. It barked at us very gruffly before disappearing, still barking. We could not see any antlers, but neither of us noticed a tush on the still very creamy caudal patch. Is there such a thing as a roe hummel?

True roe hummels are very rare. In my life I have only ever seen two undoubted examples. This contrasts with red deer. Hummels are not uncommon among Highland red stags and they are often successful in holding hinds against normally-antlered opponents. It was always supposed that the condition was hereditary and that in consequence hummels should be shot as soon as possible, but experiments some years ago proved that this was not so.

In *Shooting Times* of 16 September 1976 the celebrated roe enthusiast Henry Tegner reported that a true roe hummel had been shot in Northumberland. In 1992 Mr A Cohen shot a buck with very slight knobs on the skull not visible externally. It was very old and had only one testicle. This must have been another true example regardless of the anomaly in his anatomy. Shortage of testosterone would not produce a hummel, but the exaggerated antler growth of a peruke.

I think it is quite possible that the buck you saw was indeed another hummel, though without at least a long and clear look through binoculars one cannot be sure that it was not an unusually aggressive doe whose anal tush was not plain to see.

I have been given a roe skull which has fantastic pearling right up to the tops but is very light in weight and the bone seems very brittle, even porous. One stalking friend has said it is a 'mossed head' and the other a 'peruke'. What does this all mean, and what is the cause?

Roe, more than other deer species, are liable to grow malformed antlers. One cause of this is temporary or permanent malfunction of the hormone supply, primarily testosterone. Rather surprisingly in a way, antler growth takes place normally when the hormone supply is at a low ebb. When the reproductive cycle kicks in, rising levels of hormone stop growth and cause the antler to harden and the velvet covering to decay and fall off. Any malfunction of the hormone supply, when the antlers are in velvet or otherwise, can create abnormal growth. Castration has the most immediate effect. The antlers of a buck in velvet at the time of castration continue to grow in an uncontrolled way, producing a wig-like mass, which gives rise to the name peruke (or perruque). Castration of a buck in hard antler leads to premature casting, after which a peruke will start to develop. In either case this mass remains soft, sometimes growing down across the eyes and blinding the beast. Eventually the peruke becomes infected, leading to death. Besides injury to the genitals, birth defects or disease can have the same effect. If the velvet on a peruke is stripped away, the antler mass will be found to be soft and porous, as you describe.

If the interruption to the hormone is only temporary, the antler mass will harden with a resumption of supply, resulting in unnaturally heavy pearling which has hardened. Even then, it is liable to be lighter in density and may be fragile. This is normally called a 'Mossed Head'.

So, as you have found, the dividing lines between normal antler, mossed head and peruke are matters of opinion, even between experts!

I have just shot a queer roe. It has massive antlers in velvet which look diseased. When I gralloched it, I couldn't see much in the way of testicles, and though it appeared to be male, it had teats. I suppose this is what is called a peruke, but could it be half-male and half-female? Someone said it is an 'antlered doe' but it has no female externals except for the teats. Was it right to shoot it?

I have had a careful look at your photos, and the animal is definitely a buck, though the testes are rudimentary.

Antlered does are found regularly. They are usually very old females which (like some other species) have started to show male characteristics. Normally the antlers are short and always in velvet, but cases have been known where an antlered doe has finally formed a peruke. Kenneth Macarthur, widely admired for his deep knowledge of roe, had a tame doe which actually did that in extreme age. The half-way stage – a hermaphrodite – commonly has the externals of a female but grows antlers which are clean and hard due to the presence of some quantity of male hormone. Such animals are really rare, but the condition for some reason is more often found in roe than in other deer species.

Do roe bucks in velvet feel the cold? During the recent bitter weather I saw plenty of young bucks and does, but the seniors who are more forward with their antler growth don't appear. Can they get frostbite?

The antlers of any male deer while they are growing feel warm to the touch due to the abundant blood supply in the velvet. I think they might well add to a buck's discomfort in strong cold winds and make him seek shelter more than the well-insulated does. Younger bucks are showing less antler growth in January and February and might be less affected.

Yes, growing antlers can get frostbitten so that when they eventually harden the tips will be missing. This is a well-known phenomenon in Central Europe, but is less common in Britain because of our milder climate.

There may be another reason for your seeing more does in late winter –

the foetus which has been semi-dormant since the rut last August attaches itself by a placenta and commences rapid growth. The doe is likely to react by feeding more intensively.

In the spring, older deer start to shed their coats earlier than the youngsters. They can look extremely bedraggled and wretched. The winter hair loses its insulating quality even before it falls out, and if this coincides with a period of cold wet weather, they certainly do suffer miserably. A heavy infestation of lice, often associated with poor condition, exaggerates the problem and one can see the unfortunate animals literally shivering in the cold wet weather we often seem to have in April.

Questions on Inter-Species Relations

Where I stalk in Somerset we have had muntjac off and on for several years in addition to a good roe population, but they don't seem to build up in numbers. Do the two species compete, or are the roe aggressive to the smaller deer?

While there are places where roe and muntjac co-exist, the penetration by muntjac into areas which are already well populated by roe has been slow and spasmodic, as you describe. Like lots of animal questions, the reasons are likely to be complex, but there are some possibilities which may apply to your ground: muntjac are shorter in the leg than roe, and so the browse line in woods heavily populated by roe or fallow may be too high for them.

While their habitat requirements are roughly similar, muntjac are very much at home in very thick undergrowth. If your woods are more open, they may make a better habitat for roe.

Muntjac are very vulnerable to road accidents. Is there a trunk road nearby which they often attempt to cross? Vehicles account for hundreds of muntjac every year.

When stalking on our ground in Lanarkshire I found several sets of red deer slots. Although none have been seen in our forest they are obviously present and it will only be a matter of time before they are seen/shot. The main forest is a block of 4,500 acres of mainly Sitka spruce and I wonder, if a colony of reds started living there, would they push the roe numbers down or would the roe resist such intrusions being a browser more than a grazer like the red?

The question of red/roe competition is debatable. One can't be too dogmatic about one species being exclusively grazers and the other browsers. Obviously if there is a real lot of the bigger species, they will use up all the available browse and the roe will suffer, but there are lots of places where woodland reds and roe co-exist quite happily at moderate densities. I have in fact seen a young roe buck following a stag around for whatever reason, and this has been noted by other writers. It can partly be a matter of the habitat being more suited to one than the other. The different deer species have varying habitat preferences. Muntjac and roe like thick cover, while red and sika prefer older stands of timber, so in a modern plantation there is a period after planting when roe predominate but after ten years or so their density gets less while the wood may hold increasing numbers of red, sika or fallow. If your block of conifer forest is getting into the pole stage with very little undergrowth, it would suit the reds quite well for cover between expeditions to the hill to forage, while the roe being more static might find it less amenable to their lifestyle. Sitka spruce is pretty un-palatable, so they have to rely mainly on what they can find along the rides.

I hear that there are a number of wild boar breeding in the wild these days. Are they likely to find and eat roe and muntjac fawns?

In Continental Europe where deer and boar co-exist, nobody seems too worried about fawn losses from boar acting as predators, although they would undoubtedly act as scavengers, eating any carcasses and probably killing any wounded, ill or moribund deer they find. They have good noses, and might well discover and eat very young fawns of either species which were not agile enough to escape.

2 ASPECTS OF STALKING

Stalking Motives and Mistakes

It was one of those sultry days on the hill when the stags had not yet broken out and a great herd of them lay below us just basking in the September sun. An occasional half-hearted roar promised better things to come. Above us the towering heads of the Cairngorms, below us nothing too obvious in the way of a gully to lead any nearer to the outliers. The head stalker and I lay in the last of the long heather with little to do except hope that something would happen – like a not-too-obtrusive blue anorak on the distant mountain track – to start them into some sort of motion towards better ground. A silly thought struck me, so turning slightly to my companion, of whom I was rather in awe, I said 'Has it ever struck you what two grown men are doing playing at Cowboys and Indians in the heather?' There was a long pause, then 'Yes – but I'll not often be telling my gentlemen so!'

It is true, isn't it? – that we cherish our illusions. Maybe the 'enemy' aren't likely to shoot back if an incautious movement gives our presence away, nor does dinner depend on the hunter's return laden with spoil. It probably came from Sainsbury's days ago anyway.

What do we get out of stalking? For sure it hasn't too much to do with reducing a large animal to an inconveniently heavy heap of potential food. When we talk about the joys of stalking, even with fellow-enthusiasts, it is mostly to dwell on the incredible pleasure and privilege of being out in lovely places and at times when the countryside retains some of the tranquillity and unspoiled beauty of a century or more ago. The birdsong of a May morning; the untrammelled hills in their glory; the beeches in their autumn splendour. We rejoice in the sight of a rare bird, flowers with the morning dew on them, but above all the rewards from being able to watch the deer about their daily lives in the half light of dawn and dusk, or in the glory of sunrise.

Being completely honest, is that the truth, or just the picture which we like to paint of our maraudings? It is certainly true of the dedicated watcher,

40

whether of birds or deer, and how much I respect them for their unselfish dedication. But how many of us would make the effort was it not for that powerful rifle on the shoulder and all the additional excitements which are inseparable from carrying it? Would our preoccupation with deer ever have begun without that hunting instinct which is so strong in most stalkers? Who among us, faced with the chance of a shot, has not wrestled with a sudden fit of the shakes compounded of shortened breath and pounding heart beat? Buck fever is no disgrace – *provided* that it can be controlled at the critical moment to allow straight shooting. I have seen captains of industry who thought nothing of sacking a thousand employees at the stroke of a pen reduced to a jelly by the sight of a pair of sprouting antlers. Admit it: stalking is desperately exciting at the crunch and if one loses that pinnacle of excitement then as a hobby it soon palls.

The paradox that we love the deer we stalk makes indigestible material for the less sympathetic. Were it not for the real affection which stalkers have for their quarry deer would still be languishing in their former status as vermin, to be snared, shotgunned and generally treated as big rats, a plague for farmers, foresters and gardeners. Nor would we have the benefit of an increasing pool of knowledge which comes from the intense observation of deer at all times of year and in different circumstances contributed by successive generations of stalkers. Excellent courses are now available all run by experienced deer managers.

Maybe we should mature a bit as experience builds up. Certainly a beginner can be excused (sometimes!) for taking the wrong beast through over-enthusiasm, but one ought to grow out of that pretty soon. Going for a big trophy is fine *provided* that it forms part of a planned, balanced shooting plan, and that shooting plan is meticulously carried out. If you do the dog-work, slogging away to get the right number of does in the winter and there are a reasonable number of mature males in the herd, you deserve the occasional trophy. Those who have limited time and only want to shoot trophy bucks must pay the price to allow somebody else to be paid to do the rest. That price is likely to be both high and entirely justified.

Going North

For anyone who wants to stalk but can't afford the red carpet stuff, the choice lies between finding someone who wants help – real help – with the doe cull, or alternatively going north where antlers are smaller and prices more affordable. Stalking big conifer blocks can be a bit daunting, but the fringe of the moor can provide some exhilarating sport. An evening's stalk along the top fence of any typical hillside conifer block can be rewarding and may disclose quite a few otherwise reclusive bucks drifting upwards from their usual haunts, presumably to get a breath of cooler wind or relief from the midges. From time to time I have encountered roe that lived way out in the heather, and those not the fugitive yearlings I expected. Though they may see very few people in the year, or perhaps because of it, these hill-living deer are often extremely shy, appearing to use their eyesight much more than totally woodland-living animals. Stalking them can be a real challenge as they have to be approached with the same technique as hill red deer, and when disturbed do not dodge behind the nearest knoll before relaxing, but once out of sight take to their heels and all one sees is a series of bobbing white backsides in the far distance.

Some years ago I was put firmly in my place by a roe buck which appeared while we were loading a stag on the pony far up the hill on Glenfeshie. As the roe specialist I was urged by the stalker and gillie to do a demonstration stalk. Nothing loath I set off, performed a highly scientific stalk and, needless to say, missed him – not only once but twice. If you get the chance of a hill buck, don't scorn it – but if you have an audience don't miss it either!

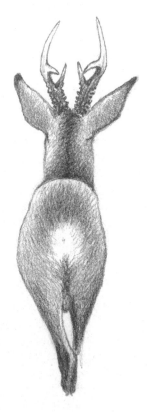

Through the medium of scent which we find so hard to comprehend, and from daily observation of mankind, the deer in a wood which is regularly stalked know the form. They know you, the stalker, as an individual, and as one to watch. You smell differently, dress differently and have a different vehicle from the farmer, the gamekeeper and the chap who goes jogging so inconveniently at five in the morning. Above all you behave differently. If you are always careful to stalk upwind you may see deer, but by the time you have done your morning's outing, every deer will have been alerted to your presence, the route you took (with reference to the prevailing wind) the time of arrival and of departure. Remember that you can't avoid leaving a widening wash of scent behind you. Do the same stalk very often and you won't see more than the odd idiot yearling. They have you outsmarted.

In the face of this acute observation of ourselves, it behoves us to try, at least to some extent, to pay them back in the same coin. So just sometimes, don't be in too much of a hurry to grab the rifle. Have a good look with the binoculars. What was he doing? Where was he going? Above all what was he thinking? Then you might not get so obviously outsmarted in the future!

Eyes Have They and See Not

Nobody would ever think of himself as resembling the idols of the heathen, but it's easy enough when you go out into the country to observe lots of people who behave like them. They are looking so hard for a television-type image of what to expect that they never notice a dozen songbirds in full throat, step regardless on the very bee orchid they went out to find, or fail to remark a group of deer feeding in a field 'because there are always animals (cows) in fields'. Other people are easy to criticise.

How do we, as stalkers and nature-lovers, rate in the heathen–idol stakes? What do we really understand about deer? Do we even get the maximum pleasure out of each stalking expedition, learning all the time from what we see, not just watching, but drawing inferences from their movements and behaviour. They may seem unpredictable, but how much is caprice on their part, and how much blind ignorance on ours?

I had a session once with a scientist who was tracking roe as part of his PhD study. His notes were immaculate with every time, location and detail of what he saw written down, but pure 'science' can have its limitations. It was boring and pointless. In the end I rudely interrupted his explanation by saying 'If you saw one roe on top of another, you'd record it like that. You wouldn't dare put down that they might be mating!'

Of course meticulous observation and recording is vital, but so is that intuitive leap of interpretation, when the motives of the animal can dimly be understood. And yet scientific training can frighten the student away from any flight of comprehension beyond what he actually sees, or, more sadly, what some other scientist has already had published.

Among stalkers, one of the troubles is that we are very often in a hurry. There is the doe cull to complete, an angry forester to placate, an anti-deer landlord to be convinced that he doesn't need a keener man. Although stalking rights are in demand, there are still too many stalkers who are greedy and take on more land than they can manage properly, and this means haste again.

As soon as we see a deer, we are immediately involved with problems of positive identification, calculations about how to get in range and how the wind suits. What the deer are actually doing, apart from walking away, is easy to disregard. Yet put at its lowest level, comprehension of the deer mentality means that it is just that much easier to predict where they will be for given weather conditions, what they are likely to do when alerted, and so on.

A good stalker doesn't just know what the deer are doing, he knows at least to some extent what they are thinking. Make a small mistake in a long crawl; the beast is suspicious. Is he going to relax again; stand but become increasingly jumpy, or take off if you can't stop him first? If you have never studied the set of the ears in relation to alarm, the significance of nose-licking, stamping or barking, you are still in the kindergarten stage of real stalking.

These things cannot be learned in haste. In fact it is doubtful if they can really be learned with a rifle on your shoulder and dominating your thoughts.

Now that the buck and doe seasons for roe nearly or actually meet, depending on what side of the border you inhabit, we have virtually lost that valuable time in early spring when deer are easily observed on the fields, but used to be out of season. There was leisure to sit down and watch them; to speculate where particular bucks would settle for the summer; to observe how many fawns per doe had survived the winter; whether they were actually eating the winter-sown crops, or whether the position of their noses while grazing showed that it was the newly-germinated weeds which they were taking. Of course if you aren't really pushed that is still perfectly possible, starting your buck cull just that bit later.

Maybe a high seat provides the best compromise. The rifle can be laid aside. Because you are still and probably above the track of any revealing air currents rather than an intruder in the wood, life soon starts to ebb and flow round about. If there is nothing to shoot there will be plenty to learn from quiet observation. Even if no deer appear, there may be other sights and sounds to enjoy. Other animals may well have something to teach us about being betrayed, for example by the hurried exit of a series of pigeons flying up. A blackbird 'pinks' for a raptor, but gives a different alarm note for a deer. All important stuff for the competent stalker to recognise.

If you think that this sort of detail doesn't apply to a really experienced stalker and nature-lover like yourself, try going out on your own ground with an expert in another discipline – no matter what. A bird man lives in what amounts to a different world to our own. A geologist will have plenty of revealing comments on the relationship of landscape to deer browse and cover. Doctors, vets, farmers, all can produce illuminating sidelights on deer as part of the whole countryside. One of the most fascinating days I ever had on the hill in Scotland was in the company of a diminutive girl botanist.

She explained (leading a garron the while) how to recognise the differing soil types, from acid peat to the mineral soils left by melting ice 12,000 years ago, the principal species making up each impoverished plant community, the resistance of some to change and the potential of others. We did shoot a stag that day, somewhat unexpectedly and at close range, but I am sure the stalker himself would have agreed that it was secondary to the main interest of the day.

We can't all spend long days at leisure on our stalking ground, but nobody in England is so far from a deer park open to the public to grudge spending the odd couple of hours there. Deer which have long been accustomed to the presence of the heedless public shrug off their natural shyness and can be seen living a reasonably normal life. So much can be learned and enjoyed in a park if one can only resist the urge to get too close. Photography has its place, but like stalking with a rifle, getting into position for a good exposure involves purposeful behaviour which the deer recognise. Even if they do not move away, they will be on the alert, and this ruins the value of the outing if you want to learn, and not just take snaps.

Take a good pair of binoculars and a cushion; choose an unobtrusive but commanding position – and stay there! If it is the latter part of the year; take the trouble to let the keeper know, or you just might find yourself in the firing line.

Sitting under a gnarled old oak tree recently, I was watching a herd of fallow deer, mostly does and fawns, about their domestic lives in the park which is their ancestral home. As stalkers you see a lot of deer in the course of the year, or the chance is there anyway, but how much time do you spend actually looking at them? How often is it a matter of 'There's one! – Is it a buck? – Is it a safe shot?' If so – Bang! Do you wonder what it was doing, where it was going, let alone what was it thinking about? I am deliberately exaggerating, but in stalking most of us are under pressures of one sort or another. One can always plead the damaged trees, the fading light or what-ever but examine your conscience a bit and see if there isn't a grain or two of truth in the scenario.

Looking at park deer in the lazy summer days is a good exercise for training the stalker's eye, besides the pleasure and interest of being in such a pleasant remnant of medieval England, as most parks tend to be. The deer may be semi-tame, but all the latent instincts and behaviour patterns are there if you look for them. Their reactions to weather and time of day; mother-young relationships; response to a distant, or a suddenly-appearing threat; certain individuals' dominance and how they maintain it. Maybe their management and culling is in your hands. In the thin coat of summer and with the entire herd standing or lying at leisure in front of you, how easy it is to make a mental Hoffmann Pyramid – yearling – yearling – four adult does – that's an old one, she ought to go, and so on through the group. Try to analyse what characteristics led you to your assessment: line of the back – saggy tummy – droopy ears – long nose and so on. It's going to be a very different job next winter when they are all bunched up in the middle of nowhere because they know full well you are there with a rifle. The trim lines of summer are hidden in a thick layer of scruffy hair and you have to make decisions, and make them fast! Some of the mental pictures you formed those months ago will stick and prevent at least some of the gross errors we all commit. Always remember that a good shepherd knows all his sheep as individuals and he doesn't achieve that by counting them as they rush by.

With males of course it is easier – at least within one antler-growing season, but even then really close observation *at leisure* pays dividends. At stalking courses I used to suggest that stalkers would benefit from using one of those little books which have three silhouette heads on each page: left and right profiles plus straight-on. All one had to do during the census month is to draw in the antlers, with the ears as a guide to length. Place, date and time underneath, of course, with your estimate of age. Even if drawing doesn't come easily, it's not too difficult to make some sort of effort, even if the result wouldn't get you into the Royal Academy. The main thing is that it teaches one to look carefully: how far above the ears are the tips? Are the back points long? Are the brows set on low, or high? If the buck gives you a decent chance, those characteristics will be burned into your memory in a way that would be impossible for an untrained eye to retain just by looking at him through the glasses. Having fixed him, estimated his age and maybe given him a name, he will be immediately recognisable even if he turns up at a distance. Best of all, if he is shot later, you can compare your estimates with the much more conclusive evidence available from a careful post-mortem.

Everyone thinks of going to a deer park in the rut, and obviously there is plenty to see at that time which might be hidden in woodland, but from one end of the year to the other there's always something to ponder over, and often something to make you smile. In Knole Park I saw a cheeky magpie tormenting a resting fallow buck. He would fly on to the buck's neck and peck vigorously for flies or other goodies. Eventually it obviously tickled, and an angry toss of the antlers would make the bird fly up, only to repeat the torment the next minute. If that sort of thing doesn't raise a giggle, you are truly like the idols of the heathen:

> Eyes have they, but they see not;
> They have ears but they hear not;
> Noses have they, but they smell not.

I am not sure about the last, however.

Forty Acres of Stalking

Small modern houses and trophies do not go very well together, and sadly a good many of mine, once treasured and personally dusted had to go in the last move. Sometimes I wonder what graphic stories about each one are even now being woven by some Bavarian hunter for the amazement and envy of his fellow sportsmen. Of course some favourites have stayed: my first buck (a better one than I deserved), another with spectacular brows which I shot from the back position and which took an agonising forty-five minutes to find, and a big gold medal which ought to have gone with the rest, as he came more or less by chance and fell to rather a poor, hurried shot. However, what should turn up the other day from a cobwebbed corner of the garage roof than a rather thin six-pointer with a good shape, marked laboriously on the back of the shield:

No. 6 'Radish Great Buck'.
Radish Plantation, Devon 14.8.1954.
.22 Hornet. 46 ½lb clean.
Length 9 ¼". Span 5 ¾" Round both Coronets 9 ⅜".

Not really a very Great Buck, I know, but it was only the sixth I'd ever shot, and that with the now-illegal .22 Hornet. Why should this unremarkable, if good-looking trophy have survived the holocaust? Partly, I suppose because Radish Plantation, all forty acres (16ha.) of it, was my first bit of stalking where there were more than occasional deer and this was the best one I got there. More, perhaps, because it was the fruit of a vast amount of youthful enthusiasm and effort. Mainly because I remember even now how elusive he was, and how often I had been within an ace of getting him, only to be foiled at the last minute. Because of that he was, and is still, an old friend; a souvenir – as all the very best trophies must be – of early mornings and evenings snatched away from work, frustrations suffered, experiences shared with friends, difficulties finally overcome.

What fun that place was! I wonder what it is like now, and if anyone stalks it these days? Then it was just a tangle of scrub cladding both sides of a little valley with a clear stream running over dark-coloured pebbles down the middle. There was one track and whatever clear bits were left by the sporadic operations of a log merchant who took my minuscule rent, as I suspect he insisted for all his takings, in good folding non-traceable pound notes. He had a pig which regularly got out and confused my amateur efforts at tracking.

Access was laboriously slow – good training in real still-hunting – but there were lots of roe; no doubt any gaps caused by my stalking were filled in from neighbouring woods towards the Dorset border. This in delightful contrast to the country round my home fifteen miles away, which they had only just reached in their westwards colonisation, and where bucks were scarce indeed.

Clearing the stream of brambles gave stalking a new, barefoot dimension and by wading up it I surprised one or two bucks who until then had not been troubled by my incursions. One entry in the diary reads 'Went up the stream, now clear all the way to the boundary, and met an eel.' There were also some small, wild trout.

Probably I thought in the flush of excitement that that buck was bigger than he really was. Certainly the morning he finally rode home (as my bucks did in those days) resting between the mudguard and the bonnet of my pre-war Austin Twelve car was something of a triumph, and I don't think it would have been quite the same if, like the gold medal head hanging above me now, he had been an unknown stranger fallen to a quick shot.

Details of those long-ago days grow dim and without my early stalking diaries, written in a juvenile hand in exercise books since bound together, I would not have remembered quite what a triumph it was, nor the exact details of our intermittent acquaintance through one long summer which added such a spice to that day of 'sunlight after a heavy thunderstorm' in August when the urgencies of the rut, perhaps, finally lowered his guard.

He had been there in full velvet when I first looked round the place in February. Later, creeping up the bed of the stream on 4 April I saw a tree violently shaken and getting closer saw what to my eyes was 'a magnificent buck, threshing antlers, scraping and rubbing shoulders. His head very long and regular with a good span, quite clean. With a doe he crossed the stream in front of me and went quietly up into sunlight among the birches of the Top Wood.' He was christened Radish Great Buck on the spot. Why didn't I shoot then? The diary gives no guide. After that meeting he failed to show himself for a couple of months, though I suspected his presence in spite of my frequent visits, or because of them. 31 July saw me there once more, this time with Stephen Powell, whose father Bill Powell many older wildfowlers will remember with affection. This time the Great Buck was chasing a doe first one way across our front, then back again. Again he was spared a shot but left both of us with some moments of emotion.

On 14 August I had had to wait until work in the office was over at five-thirty to draw a deep breath of relief and satisfaction at the entrance before setting off across Top Wood (all the smallest features had acquired names) which was all stones and impossible to stalk over, sneaking down a hedge line to sit overlooking the minute clearing where two little streams joined, and let things settle after my noisy approach. What a temptation it is to press on when nothing shows up! But if you only have forty acres altogether, impatience like that would soon have had me out at the other side! It was good discipline. This time patience was rewarded at eight o'clock by the appearance of the Great Buck himself. He moved about in the bushes for what seemed like ages without presenting a decent chance, but just as he was finally moving off he hesitated clear of twigs and my shot went home at the base of his neck. The buck went down and never moved. As usual with the Hornet the bullet had passed through but lodged in the skin on the far side having used up all its modest power.

After recording the details, my diary entry finishes 'I do not expect to have a more enjoyable day.' Looking back down the years I have been lucky enough to have grander days, mostly because of the generosity of many wonderful friends, but in sport each experience is complete in itself and may not be compared with another, however enjoyable. I could have shot him on two previous occasions but forbore for one reason or another. Having had the patience to wait for the final good moment no doubt added enormously to the warm glow of that evening so long ago. It is there now.

Stalkers' Birds

No. This is not about that sort of bird, though I have friends who have actually gone stalking on their honeymoon: pretty risky, or even suicidal before any formal nuptials! Better to sneak up on them – *'Layin' low and saying nuffin'* – making sure the knot is firmly tied before the full horror of the stalker's life is revealed. Or that's how I managed it anyway!

Turning to birds two-legged but feathered; how much do we really appreciate the wide gamut of bird-song which contributes enormously to the background of a morning in the woods? Some years ago Jack Charlton very courageously allowed himself to be filmed in a TV series showing the best face of a variety of country sports. With some he was obviously already adept, but stalking had not happened to come his way before, and I was involved in trying to get him his very first buck. We had a marvellous piece of country for the purpose and all went well, though the events of those two days would make another chapter.

We started through storytale woods in the early dawn of a May morning and were finished by breakfast time, all but some fill-in shots which would be done the following day. Yorkshire Television provided a first-class team to do the camera and sound work. When we were relaxing during the day, the sound engineer said 'Would you like to hear the tapes we made this morning?' This really was a revelation! I can honestly say that I had noted the challenge of a cock pheasant sometime during the session, but concentrating as one has to do to make stalking successful (let alone when the stalker and Rifle are trailed by a producer, a continuity girl, two cameramen and a sound engineer!) I had no idea at all of the sheer volume of the morning chorus. Two hours at full blast then slowly tapering off. As he so graphically put it 'It's like five of Ludwig Kogh's best recordings, all superimposed on one another!'

Most of us would be alert and concentrating primarily on entering the wood without disturbing its tranquillity. Such are the demands of constantly spying for the slightest indication of a deer, planning where your next foot needs to be placed – between *that* stick and missing *that* crackly leaf, (besides attending all the time to what that unreliable so-and-so beside you is doing with his rifle) that very little attention can be spared for admiring the fowls of the air. Only safely ensconced in a high seat can one relax and enjoy the wider delights of the woodland that we have the privilege to be in.

Maybe other stalkers are more relaxed over their excursions, or possibly a more open terrain allows them to take in a bigger panorama of nature. Much of my early stalking was done in very thick woodland indeed, but even there the presence or actions of particular birds stick in the memory, not all of them on the plus side. Woodpigeons are definitely a liability. One of my trusted clients came back from a solo outing with nothing to show. 'How did it go?' 'Oh! The woods were full of newspapers, flapping out of the trees and scaring the deer!'

He was right – indeed they do. Then on another occasion I was slumped in a high seat deeply asleep when a pigeon decided to perch on the front rail by my nose with a great flapping of air brakes! Why I didn't fall out I can't think. Black mark to pigeons. Blackbirds, nicely though they sing, can also be a deer-scaring pest. They have a special cry, a series of ascending notes quite different from the alarm with which they greet an owl, which signals two things: to a man that a deer is on the move nearby; to a deer just the reverse. Sometimes you can profit by it, more often you pay! If your stalking technique is good enough, the blackbird stays mostly in credit.

The sound of a spotted woodpecker drumming is a true harbinger of spring in our south-country woods. Hear it and know that the good days are all ahead. The same goes for the first cuckoo. At the other end of the country, what stalker out on the moorland fringes cannot respond to the wild trilling of the curlew; it never fails to lift my back hair, though with delight rather than fear. One early-spring dawn I was threading my way through some frost-laden scrub in Moray when a totally new booming, bubbling noise started not too far off. Southerner that I am, it took me a minute to realise that this was a blackcock on his lek, but I shan't forget it.

Henry Tegner in his book about Northumberland roe *The Buck of Lordenshaw* wrote with affection of the blackcock's song, linking it as I do with the wide heather moors and birch-covered slopes of the Border north-wards and the sporting roe which inhabit them. Maybe I'll never hear it again as blackgame sadly become more and more rare, yet they used to be widespread and plentiful. I have seen them myself on Exmoor, and Gerald Springthorpe told me how a small party of cocks still came from goodness knows where each spring to lek in Cannock Chase when he was Ranger there. No doubt they are long gone, poor old bachelors, for there were no more grey-hens for them to impress with their booming and posturing.

Another picture from the north, which I treasure, was the sight of two magnificent cock capercaillies sailing out of an old Scots pine tree at the top of the Kildrummie Woods in Aberdeenshire, where I was stalking. I forget whether I shot a doe or missed it that morning, but the occasion was unforgettable.

Hill stalking, of course, brings in that knowing character the raven. It is always said to be good luck if he comes with you (keeping a calculated distance nevertheless!) in the foreknowledge that you will have a gralloch for him sometime that day. Sitting idly spying with a professional stalker one day, three of the big birds left us and swooped across the glen to where they had spotted a car pull in to a favourite picnic spot. In no time they badgered the wretched tourists into parting with their sandwiches by flying round and round their heads with loud croaks. They would never take liberties like that with an armed stalking party!

The grand sight of an eagle, too, makes a stalking day. They never seem to catch anything, for all their effortless circling, but no doubt it happens, though I suspect he is more of a carrion eater than his admirers would like to admit. Some white-tailed sea eagles were released on the west coast of Scotland in an attempt to re-establish them. Out stalking I caught sight of one. Broader-winged than the golden, and from that brief impression, less elegant, but still something memorable to make the day.

Another white stone in the book of stalking memories was the wood near Kursk in Russia, where my stalking was accompanied by flocks of that most lovely and colourful bird the bee-eater.

Back in the southern woods, summer stalking always used to be plagued by the buzzing of innumerable flies which seem largely to have vanished these days, leaving only the biters to invade my hatband. Without them the insect-eating birds are having a hard time. One wood in particular was a famous place for nightjars, which swooped and clapped their wings over my head in the gloaming as I stalked the rides. Once I spent a short summer night in a rather palatial Forestry Commission observation hide in the Midlands, intending to rise at dawn, do a morning's stalk and slip off home. A nightjar had different ideas: around midnight one alighted on the roof of the hide and sounded off like a burglar alarm above my head. No more sleep that night! Even then I couldn't put the nightjar on the stalker's black list. He is too scarce and too beautiful.

Another lovely bird which I associate with many evening stalks is the roding woodcock. Curious squeaks and grunts signal his regular circling just at that last tinge of afterglow when an old buck can be expected to show himself, the animal and the bird turning a woodland glade into a living picture needing a master like Poortvliet or McPhail to capture.

So, like you, I value and enjoy the birds we see and hear about the woods – but if there is one thing that's certain, it's that if you try to bird-watch and still-hunt at the same time, you aren't likely to bring home the venison!

A Disastrous Stalk

Disasters shouldn't happen to anyone stupid enough to go stalking and then write about it. Perhaps one does try to present what is best in sport, or at least to gloss over some of the more dreadful things that you try to forget and can't. Believe me, they still happen! Most stalkers are far too conceited about their stalking, so it does us all good, every now and then, to have a good laugh at ourselves or writhe at the recollection of some past catastrophe.

The stalk for my very first Scottish roe was an unforgettable occasion when an old friend, Jeremy, was acting as my guide, not the other way round as had been the case when we stalked together in Wiltshire. We drove up through the Dunachton woods in the dawn that magical morning and watched a cock capercaillie displaying on an anthill under the delicate birches. As the sun rose, we spied a group of roe feeding out on the heather. There was what looked like a good buck, and not too far off for a shot. In those days I had not tumbled to the fact that Scottish roe had shorter ears in proportion to their heads, making estimation of their antlers difficult, nor that judging distance in the open when stretched in the heather was equally tricky. Suffice it to say that I over-estimated one, and under-estimated the other. The inevitable consequence was that the buck, to my horror, went off with a broken fore-leg.

'We'll have to go down to the house and get a dog,' was all Jeremy said, but it was then five in the morning and our landlord, whom I had never met, was a notorious late riser.

I can see now the boulder on which we sat *for two and a half solid hours*, chewing the cud of mortification and waiting for the first possible moment when I could knock on the door and announce to a perfect stranger 'I'm Richard Prior: I've wounded one of your bucks'. Talk about a sinking feeling – I was about two inches high when we finally got there.

Confession may be good for the soul, but the cheerful welcome and hearty breakfast was a great deal better for mine. Our host Andrew, bless him, even seemed excited at the prospect of a hunt.

We tried his rifle (which I remember was six inches left and a bit high!) and set off with a labrador and two white terriers to the scene of the crime.

There was the usual search, with my heart in its boots. Then, down below the heather in the woodland fringe we heard encouraging yipping noises. The other two set off at a gallop I couldn't even try to attempt, so when I eventually puffed up, there was the buck finally out of pain, two very pink, gory and frantically excited terriers, and Jeremy holding up in triumph the top two inches of one antler – he had arrived at the battle ground just as one terrier latched on, bringing the buck crashing against a tree and breaking off a whole point. This flew into the air, and he made a brilliant slip catch of the piece.

A trophy to remember, but not one to be proud of.

Be Quick!

There is a book, long out of print, called *Oh Shoot! The Confessions of an Agitated Sportsman.* Many of my experiences as a professional stalker could go into a book under the equally heart-felt title of *Don't Shoot! The Confessions of an Agitated Guide.*

Roe, we know, are alert to the slightest movement or unusual sound in the woods. For the most part we try to challenge their finer senses by stealth, but that's not all there is to woodland stalking by any means. Of course, we usually go too fast and too far during a woodland stalking outing. More bucks are walked past than are seen, and more missed through haste than are snatched by quick action, let alone all the considerations of safety, identification and the rest which dictate a deliberate technique. Sometimes, however, a bit of sharp work may be called for.

There are moments, perhaps more than we realise, when the actions of our quarry, once spotted and interpreted, dictate pretty prompt action: to anticipate some decision which one can see the beast is about to make, or merely to be in position to take a deliberate shot at the critical moment.

Stalking alone, in a state of absolute concentration verging on trance is the summit of the art. Such complete identification with the natural vibrations of the wood cannot be achieved in the company of a friend, no matter how skilled or compatible. Or a dog. Nor can it be achieved unless your own mental and physical state allows it. The aftermath of a frantic week at the office; harsh words with Herself before leaving home, or the imminent prospect of financial trouble are insurmountable obstacles to the highest flights of stalking awareness. So are sore feet or a trickle of rain down the spine.

Better to spend a couple of sessions in a high seat, and let the local wildlife circulate past while your tensions have a chance to drain away. But don't take your laptop, your mobile phone and your troubles up there with you!

That is not to deny that there is a case for stalking in company. Sharing the magic of a woodland morning makes one more aware of the variety of marvels which might pass unnoticed without a companion. It can also be the occasion for surprising revelations about your own technique compared to that of your companion.

There is intense pleasure in seeing a newcomer to the sport filled with excitement and enthusiasm. Only in this way can the thrill of your own first buck be recaptured. One hopes that it will be a typical, but run-of-the-mill trophy, leaving plenty of higher peaks for him to conquer in the future. The number of vast and ancient bucks which have fallen to complete novices is legion.

I had the chance to stalk on some completely new ground in Scotland with a friend whose only previous introduction to stalking had been on the open hill. If the weather, the birdsong and the surroundings were marvellous, the roe were determined to pull our legs. An ideal-looking expanse of woodland produced only does, in spite of all our efforts. The first buck to appear next day was so beautiful and obviously young that neither of us had the slightest urge to shoot him. A real Male Model – and he knew it! The next two were such scruffy yearlings that one had to look closely even to make out the pedicles. As for antlers, I don't know if either had any at all. The sort of bucks that one would normally knock off with satisfaction as good management, but hardly the thing for his very first.

On our way home, there was the Male Model, posing again. Knowing we meant him no harm he took no notice as we admired him through the glasses and finally through the scope, discussing at length where, in this attitude or that, we would have placed the bullet. There never was such a dead buck still living!

As time began to run short, the luck began to turn. Or you could say that by then we had started to learn where to look for the roe. A chorus of barking from a rocky, scrub-covered hillside revealed the presence of at least two bucks. Both were small in body and modest as to antler, but none the less what we were looking for.

In the long Highland twilight we attempted an extended stalk, balancing concealment with the need to get within range before the dusk started to turn everything grey and uncertain. This was where the other face of roe stalking began to show: the risk had to be run of moving swiftly. Needless to say the dusk won. I loathe taking a shot when it is so dark that the muzzle flash blinds you momentarily, and would not suggest that any beginner should take such a risk. We left him, backing away as from the royal presence, though truth to tell he was but a labourer among bucks.

Next morning he was there again, and looking a good deal bigger with the better light. His territory on the opposite slope included a group of scrubby trees and a large boulder. On our way in, we bumped a yearling which set off towards the buck, who would inevitably chase him off before returning to the centre of his ground.

This time we needed a different kind of speed. First, of course, to get in range and then to anticipate what the buck would do, and to be waiting for him – sitting comfortably with rifle half poised – to take advantage of that good chance, however brief.

The inevitable happened: with a brief flurry of aggressive barks, the territorial buck put down his head and fairly raced the youngster off up the slope. Now was the time for us to hurry down to the firing point while his attention was diverted, forsaking all caution. After two days of unremitting stealth, it is difficult suddenly to change into top gear, but we made it.

There were two possible locations for a shot. One as he came back down the same track if he happened to hesitate in an opening, and then again when he came back to the boulder which marked the centre of his territory. The snag was that the two could not be commanded from the same point. A very hurried shift of seven or eight yards would have to be made while the

buck passed from the track through a few bushes and out to the boulder.

Looking back, of course, I ought to have explained the need both for preparedness and speed. As it was, the buck did stop in the opening, but my pupil was not ready for him, nor did he move quickly enough to take advantage of the interval while the buck was hidden by the bushes to shift position and settle in again for a steady shot. Ah well! Bad marks for the instructor, and no trophy.

We probably say so much about making no noise, and no rapid movements that any beginner is convinced that the whole thing goes on in slow motion. A lone stalker scarcely realises how much he varies his pace to suit the ground; how by getting into the mind of a deer he anticipates when to freeze and when it is safe to move: when extreme patience will bring the animal back eventually to within easy shot, and when a rapid cutting-out movement can pull all sorts of chestnuts out of the stalking fire. You never won at Granny's Footsteps without choosing the moment for a sudden dash.

Stalking red deer, especially on the open hill, is totally different. Except for travelling stags at the beginning of the rut, a beast spotted in the morning will like enough still be in the same area an hour or two later – and you will probably be able to see him.

The nervous, active roe is always on the move, and in one step can be out of sight. Nor is it likely that you will be able to take a prone shot. On open ground the herbage is usually too high for anything lower than a sitting or kneeling position. In thick woodland it's a matter of 'standing up and shooting it out like a man' – with whatever stick or other aids you can conjure up and with a fair share, one hopes, of the legendary but totally fictitious accuracy of a John Wayne.

There's another thing about stalking on strange ground, with or without a companion – it just shows how differently roe behave under different conditions and how very little we really understand about them.

A Long Shot For a Big Buck

At the start of a new season the thoughts of most stalkers turn to the prospect of birdsong-filled woods in the early morning; of the heart-stopping sight of a big buck lingering just too long in the sunlight before sneaking off to cover, or of the chances which may offer in the weeks to come. Or may not. After a few years' experience, there will be thoughts, too, of past dawns and of bucks shot or missed. So often it is the funny things that happened rather than the major trophies which stick in one's mind; friends or clients who were with you and their triumphs and disasters. Even so, there is nothing like gazing reflectively at a nicely-mounted trophy hanging there to bring some scene into sharp focus, no matter how many years have passed in the interim.

Many visitors bringing trophies for measuring have admired the heads in my study (there are only two). One is a heavy gold medal, but the other which really draws their attention is lighter in weight, but has unusually long curved brow points. Turning over photographs the other day I came across his portrait, taken just after I had found him. Draped over a low tree stump to try not to make him look too dead for the camera, he still gazes over the Devon coombe which had been his home.

On 22 April that year, following a call from someone suffering from deer damage, I went to a place called Widworthy and arranged to have the stalking there at a rent of £1 for each buck shot. It was 1956. There was a fine bowl of woodland running down to a boggy patch at the bottom with a long strip of hillside back towards the farm. At that time it was in the process of being cleared and replanted. Now, as I look across from the main road, it is a forest. No doubt there are many fewer roe there and maybe the quality is not so high as it was in those early days. It would be interesting to know. The roe had not long spread from Dorset and they were enjoying the benefits of new ground – and possibly the presence of only one dedicated roe stalker in the whole of East Devon! At that stage it was an ideal place and in a short walk that afternoon my hopes were soaring. I saw a small buck with a doe and another doe farther on. Most of the area was pretty bare, but with useful bits of cover still left.

Nothing more could be done until next weekend when, during an evening expedition, I just saw two does (or the same one twice) but there were encouraging signs of a buck fraying and 'some disturbances in the bottom'.

A week later the chance came up for an early-morning outing and at five o'clock with a southerly wind and a beautiful clear sunrise in prospect, all looked set fair. A little valley fog would clear as the temperature rose. There was a doe feeding on the near side of a belt of birch trees and I got fairly close to make sure of her as it was still gloomy. Passing her, I went on up the hill where there was another doe feeding in a grass field next to the road-side trees.

After a good spy and finding nothing, I turned downhill again and crossed the swamp, which proved a soggy and squelchy undertaking. Towards the upper end there were encouraging signs of roe: scrapes, bushes peeled, and slots. I was delighted to see one mountain ash stem still green where a buck must have frayed within a very short time. A doe went off, no doubt alarmed by the squelches, was joined by another and both made off at high speed up the hill. Still no buck! I sat down and had a good spy with the glasses, then seeing a fox on the field opposite doing a bit of honest mousing I got out the telescope and had a look round with that. He was doing stalks and cat jumps in some tussocky grass.

Almost at once I spotted a roe sitting in the birch bushes above, and looking again, the hindquarters of another, more concealed. The first was a young four-pointer buck. The other came out from the trees, but stayed motionless with his head behind a tree. He was a hundred and seventy-five yards away and almost invisible to the naked eye with the effect of the now strong sunlight and shadow on him. By lying still and fiddling with the telescope I made out his brows which gave the impression of a long curved single spike. Then he moved his head for a moment and I could see two beams with apparently perfect tops.

With fallen trees and a liberal sprinkling of stones I did not think stalking him would be possible, so I adopted the classic back position of the target shooter with my neck wedged comfortably into a stump, and taking care I didn't blow my feet off, I took a very deliberate shot with the .22 Hornet, aiming high on his shoulder – and apparently missed!

The buck moved slowly back into the bushes and I had two more shots in desperation – both misses! Oh dear. The small buck broke past me but no monster followed and I could see nearly all the slope above. No sign. I got up and very carefully advanced to where I thought he was. Still no sign. I combed the entire birch clump and surrounding country. Nothing: not a vestige. How flat, dejected and furious with oneself can one be? I walked back to pick up the telescope, considered the landscape and decided he must have gone into a small patch of foot-high scrub birch sixty yards away. First time through – nothing. Second time – and there he lay! Shot through the heart, lying totally concealed in the greenery, moulting hair everywhere – but lovely! I took pictures, scarcely believing the turn of luck, loaded him into the rucksack and staggered up the hill. He seemed awfully heavy. In fact he weighed fifty-eight pounds clean – and his antlers, as I know now, on the borderline between silver medal and gold – 27.4cm (10¾in) long on the best side. That was one buck I didn't mind paying my £1 rent for!

Funnily enough when I sent a picture of him to Herbie Fooks, one of the great men of stalking at the time, he replied saying that the buck was far too young and should not have been shot. I have a sneaking suspicion he was jealous! He had had no chance to see the teeth, which were well-worn.

Like any trophy, the memories are precious to me alone, but as ever there is a moral. Don't take long shots with an inadequate rifle, and don't give up looking if you have the slightest suspicion that a beast might not have been missed. That was a very long three-quarter hour search in ever-deepening depression and doubt. If I hadn't kept on, his bones would lie there still.

Roe Bashing

I went to see a stalking party at the local hotel:

'How are you getting on?'

'Well, on the first day we walked ten kilometres through the wood and saw lots of roe. Edward saw a very good buck and we know where he is living.

'On Tuesday we walked fifteen kilometres through the wood, but they didn't seem to be out that day, maybe the weather was not good, but yesterday we spent all day in the woods and walked twenty-five kilometres, and they all seem to have vanished! What has happened? Have the poachers been in?'

Of course put like that, the answer is obvious. The problem was to curb over-enthusiasm without spoiling their enjoyment. For one reason or another, most stalkers feel under pressure sooner or later. Maybe the buck of a lifetime slipped away in the dusk and just has to be there the next morning – or if not, the next night, or the next, and so on. So you 'bash' the place, and surprise, surprise – he fails to turn up. That is why he has lived long enough to be the buck of a lifetime!

Few amateur stalkers in the South have enough ground to take a full week's stalking without making the deer frustratingly elusive by about Wednesday. Better to take long weekends with a week or two between, and let them settle again. If you have to take the week, restrain yourself and just sit. Umpires do it for a fortnight at Wimbledon, so you can too. Stalking can be tiring, but success is not measured in miles covered, very much the reverse.

Again, maybe the forester is going up the wall because you haven't shot enough does to satisfy him. As the end of the season rushes on, you take a few precious days off, and haunt the best places morning, noon and night until you and the does are due for a set of ulcers. Nothing could be more unproductive.

Early one spring I was lucky enough to visit two places near home where the roe are not touched. One could see, so clearly, the daily rhythm which is natural to the species if they are not harassed. Small family parties of deer were out at all times of day, either feeding quietly, wandering about, or lying in some sunny corner chewing the cud. There was even a band of ten, serenely occupying the middle of a field of oil-seed rape, while a tractor and sprayer trundled up and down behind them. It would have been easy to assume that here, at last, was a genuine herd of 'field roe' as one sees pictured in Poland. In fact, an hour's observation demonstrated that there was no cohesion in the group; as the tractor finished its work and the sun went

60

down, the group fragmented: a doe with her fawns wandered off in one direction; a buck in another, until just three were left in possession.

They were, in fact, reacting to disturbance by farm operations by moving to an area where they knew by experience that they were unlikely to be disturbed. If the disturbance had been in response to regular stalking, their reactions would have been different, but comparable; an apparently calculated alteration to their preferred habits. The heavier the pressure and the more often repeated, the more fundamental will be their reaction.

We think of roe as crepuscular animals (which sounds more impressive than saying they move at dusk and dawn) but the picture I have sketched above is much more typical. The dusk and dawn thing is itself a response to human activities. For many years after we started stalking roe, instead of blowing them up in end-of-season drives, the accepted technique was to stalk from first light to breakfast time, and from after the cows were gathered up for evening milking until it became too dark to shoot.

The stalker is, of course, not the only disturbing factor, though the most worrying, so to some extent the rule to stalk early and late still applies. However, any tractor driver or forest worker will tell you that the deer tend to show up these days after the working day has begun – or just when the stalker has gone home to breakfast! There is no coincidence in this, just a straightforward survival technique evolved by a successful and receptive animal.

All right, you say, let's stalk them all morning. It may work the first couple of mornings, but you are not dealing with a creature prepared to go the way of the dinosaurs. By the third there will have been a quick meeting of the Survival Board, and a new work schedule will be in operation. Push it too far and they will first become nocturnal and then likely to push off to less disturbed parts of the woods.

Later in the year, unless the woods are particularly well provided with undergrowth, the deer are likely to be concentrated in areas of better feeding or are forced out on to the nearest farm crops. Daily bashing of these places will produce a healthy crop of very shy deer. The next stage is to get help and try some moves, with or without a dog. The rule for this is: *never try a manoeuvre more than once a year.* If it goes right once you are lucky, just rest content and don't try it again that season, no matter what the pressure may be. Invent something different. Moves, except in special cases, are no substitute for stalking, only a supplement to it.

In Scotland there is the additional temptation of authorised night shooting. Yes, you may be able to get a few extra deer in this way, but except in the case of a recently-fenced enclosure in which some survivors linger, it is no way to effect a real reduction of deer doing damage. If there are enough in the area to be doing significant damage, night shooting will do no more than cream off the easy ones and render the rest so shy that they will take to cover at the first murmur of an engine or the flick of a light.

Regardless of legality, be aware of the effect of night and day disturbance on a roe population. If you are concerned, as all stalkers should be, with damage done by deer to forest crops, take thought to the likely consequence of this sort of harassment. If limitation of damage is the object, remember that shy deer will rarely venture out to feed and so all their browsing will be inside the plantations. It is likely, therefore, to be more extensive and serious than if they could move about normally. With red and sika it is even worse, because they are very likely to start the highly detrimental and long-term habit of bark stripping.

If you are merely concerned with maintaining trophy quality among your bucks, the cardinal rule is that good bucks love a quiet life. They are the first to shift under the stress of repeated threats, especially if, time after time, they get sudden wafts of the alarming, pig-like scent of man without decent warning, or worse, if they are hunted out by loose dogs.

I remember one wood which was virtually emptied of roe because the local farmer exercised his dogs by the rough and ready method of leaving the back door open at night. Another where the stalker found, after some frantic end-of-season moves with dogs to get enough does, that in one small area next May four promising territorial bucks had been replaced by nine yearlings. From Ritz to Coffee Bar is a short step. Hit hard at your does and yearlings by all means, but let things calm down afterwards. Don't bash them the whole time.

Varying It

Once a season I spend an hour at the local shooting school. One year it was so disastrous that the Instructor turned to me: 'I know you *can* shoot, Richard – I've seen you!'

At other times if the easy clays start to powder and one starts to feel a small glow, he shouts up to the trapper 'Vary 'em!' and you know a mental effort will be needed to cope with targets that are going to arrive at differing heights and angles. It is much the same with stalking the roe. Mopping up a few unwary bucks can be easy, but then if the 'luck' seems to be running out, it's time to sit down and think how your technique might be varied to suit the circumstances.

We try all the time to match our wits to the sharp senses (about seven of them at the last count) of our quarry, not to speak of the weather conditions, the unpredictable behaviour of the general public and all other variables. Joggers are now a problem in some places. One of my problems has been crouching scientists silently making notes in ditches just where I might want to lodge a bullet. From time to time we all feel that the tapestry of life is a bit rich, but one just has to sit on it and take care nothing splits.

The open farmland stalking I have enjoyed in the last few years is a lot different from textbook woodland stalking. For one thing, the coverts planted for pheasants are very small, maybe with just a feed ride in the middle. They are much used by the deer, and a heavy browse line allows them to see your legs if you walk through the middle, while if you skulk round the outside you are silhouetted against the sky. The only chance is to find a beast feeding or resting in the open, or sunning itself under a hedge. If the deer are not too heavily stalked, this can best be done during the day. Otherwise your presence is constantly betrayed by pigeons clattering in hordes off roost.

With roe one often has to be quick and decided in making a stalk. Recently I seem to have had a series of very long waits, having to remind myself at intervals that it is better to be in shot of a beast and waiting for it to get up, than spooking it through impatience and having to look for another.

My mind goes back to last doe season; always a desperate time because nothing much can be done while the pheasant shooting is on. It is not that stalking disturbs the birds, provided one keeps right away from release pens, but frequent driven days makes the deer (and gamekeepers) nervous and irregular in their habits.

With good farm tracks it is usually possible to have a general spy from the car. Tractor and Land Rover traffic is a normal and harmless activity, so an unobtrusive tour up and down during working hours has little effect.

I try to choose sunny days, I tell myself, because the deer are more in evidence and maybe more relaxed. On such a day in February, as the frost was coming out of the ground after a cold spell, a reconnaissance up the spine road just before mid-day was blank. However, on the return trip I saw that a party of roe lying in a strip of game cover had risen to their feet to assure themselves that I was harmless.

By the time I had backtracked, they were lying down again but I could still see the face of one doe surveying the valley. If I could reach a line of big bales sheltering the release pen, by lying on top of them I would have a reasonable if distant shot, about 120 yards.

Why can I never learn to dress up at the farm before doing my spying trip? No boots, no padded jacket, and perhaps no time either. Just grab the rifle and binoculars and get your best trousers muddy with a cold and flat crawl. Up on the bales – there she still is – and get your breath before she gets to her feet.

Was that doe laughing? She sat there looking me in the eye for a full hour without moving a muscle. I adjusted the rifle for a deadly shot as she rose. No action. I glared through the sight in case, being thoroughly rested, I could risk an assassination. There was a fence between us and Murphy's Law dictated that a strand of barbed wire bisected the vital area. To hit something the size of one strand of wire at any range is very difficult; to hit a deer on the other side of that single strand is just impossible. Every time a coconut. Twang!

In the end I got so cold that something had to be done, so I lobbed a small stone. The doe stood up to order, except she was facing me and unshootable. Then, without a second chance the whole party took off into the open fields. It would have been easy to shrug, pick up the rifle and decamp, but it is good to let disturbed deer get right out of sight before getting up, so I waited while they regrouped on the far skyline. After, several minutes of indecision there was obviously something of a leadership crisis, a moment of milling about and they all came streaming back past me. As they paused to duck through a fence, I had my revenge on the same po-faced old doe.

What to do now? The idea trickled in that the other chalk valley has a little jink in it at the top so that you can't see everything from the track, although you think you can. By now it would be sunny and sheltered.

A short expedition up the farm boundary opened up the jink and what did I discover but four pairs of ears, just where they thought nobody could see them. Right: make plans – wind: easterly. A bit tight for an approach up the nearest game strip, but it might be possible. Pause to confirm their exact location, which can look very different from another angle. Back down, load the rifle, fix the bipod and set off. It's going to be a flat crawl, Scottish style. Through the remains of a game crop, flinching at intervals at the noisy departure of already-paired grey partridges. Nice to see them – somewhere else!

Fixing my points of reference I walked out as far as possible until the ears were visible again (not quite where I thought they would be) and then submitted to the clammy embrace of winter-sown oats liberally strewn with flints. On and on. I never have been much good at crawling. The trouble of downland is that it always seems to be domed. Imagine stalking a buck on the top of St Paul's Cathedral. From any angle he would be constantly on the skyline, with a risk of hitting the Stock Exchange if you fired. Equally, if you crawl he is hull-down and to get enough elevation to shoot you have either to be very near or very much in sight, probably both.

I identified a pair of female ears and hunched slowly towards them, trying to look like a cowpat. At thirty yards I could see her head and neck but even with the bipod legs fully extended there was grass and probably a stone perilously close to the bullet's path. It's easy to forget that fatal inch of difference between sight line and trajectory in the heat of the moment.

Waiting again, and wondering if she would suddenly take off, or oblig-ingly lift her head for a better view of this suspicious cowpat. No action. In the end her head had been motionless for so long, locked on me, that I knew she would go soon. One between the eyes was the only solution, and maybe justified at that range, head on. Sideways head shots break jaws and create misery for all concerned. At the shot she collapsed, and the rest of the party started up, but roe-like, hesitated for one quick look. Another doe was broadside and an easy second shot.

With bucks, of course, the problems are different. By May there will be little to see in the roe-high crops, so one has to try to get some yearlings early in the season and hope for better fortune with one or two seniors immediately after harvest when their summer's cover has suddenly gone and they tend to be disorientated. With straw burning a thing of the past we see more deer out stubbling, and for longer. The countryside certainly looks and smells better after harvest.

New Ground

We take a lot of our own stalking technique for granted, especially when we are out on the same ground most of the time. It is only when you start trailing around after a guest that you begin to realise what a highly-developed technique there is for approaching and looking around a ride corner or how much your pace varies according to the different needs for vigilance as you traverse bits of your own wood. In the total concentration of stalking solo little refinements of technique become automatic and unnoticed, so taking a friend out can either be quite an eye-opener if you are sufficiently objective, or merely exasperating.

On familiar ground I am sure that our pattern of stalking becomes far too fixed. For a given wind you start at *that* gate, take *that* ride, and probably end up for the last half hour at *that* high seat. The joke is that the deer are far more aware of this than you are yourself, and they act accordingly. Have you ever heard a stalker say 'My bucks just seem to disappear after the first few days of the season!'

Or course there are enormous advantages in knowing your ground and the habits of the deer on it. One day towards the end of the doe season we had a fine afternoon after a succession of dreary days, wet and windy. Although my stalking lies twenty-five miles away, it was a pound to a penny that one group would be lying out on the winter barley in a dip in the ground which was out of the wind, but just right for the afternoon sun. Last time I left it too late, and they were just packing up, like a family party at Blackpool towards tea time. Leisurely, but carrying their deck chairs, and definitely out of range before I got near. An hour earlier this time, and all that was needed was a quick spy to confirm they were there and a long muddy crawl to get up to them. On this downland shoot I find a bipod invaluable. With the legs extended it gives enough clearance for a shot over straw, early cereals or even stubble turnips high enough to give cover for crawling.

After a succession of blank outings on this farm, the pressure was on to show results. On a long crawl I find the greatest difficulty is to keep one's patience and not try a shot either at too long a range, or with the risk of bullet deflection through the herbage. This time, self-discipline won, and those extra ten yards brought the whole unsuspecting party into view. One fair buck, which inevitably had chosen the highest position and had been in sight throughout the stalk, two does and a doe fawn. One doe rose to stretch, and paid the price. The fawn had a 7mm through the neck before it realised anything was wrong, and the other doe only ran a few yards before standing to look back and offering a perfect target. Then the work started! Half a mile of sticky plough to negotiate up to the nearest farm track, and always the appalling decision of whether to make two journeys with a fair load, or one with an overload. As usual, I stuffed two in the rucksack, dragging the other.

I am sold on the 7 × 57. It seems to do the job with the least fuss or deer-scaring noise. That is even more important than looks! Even so, one does take pleasure in a good-looking rifle. If I stalked roe in Scotland I would certainly go back to a .22 centrefire, probably the .222. Many stalkers are overgunned. When loosing the .275 off at roe I am often forced to remember that W D M Bell considered that it was all he needed for elephants – and he shot more than a thousand of them.

Where the deficiencies start to show is when you get off your own ground. I found myself chasing does in Inverness-shire. Nothing, but the poor old crystal ball to indicate where a doe might be; when to hurry on and when to really start spying. It was a good mental exercise, let alone an ego-shrinking one. Miles of conifers in late thicket, and pretty different from Downland Wiltshire.

The loveliest bit consisted of rolling heather hillocks, with scattered clumps of birch. In principle one only had to peer over each successive hillock and spy the unsuspecting roe on the reverse slope. There were two snags; the deer were windy in the extreme, and the area was infested by a mass of sheep. One was probably the result of the other. Anyway, when you bumped a roe, it took off for the middle distance, usually emptying the next few hillocks at the same time. After two attempts on rainswept afternoons, I realised that one needed to go there in the morning, with the sun at your back and the wind in your teeth: when the deer were enjoying the first rays, and less likely to scoot off. One lives and learns.

Later on, I had a couple of interesting days stalking roe and sika in the vast newly-afforested blocks of Argyllshire. There I had the pleasure of going out with professional stalker Stewart Marshall to show me the ropes – and the deer. Where the trees are still young, but mostly high enough to hide a deer, spying was really hard because of the lack of scale. One did not know the size of object to look for, and almost every time when Stewart pointed out where a roe was feeding, it looked twice the expected size, and was not nearly as far off as the wide open views suggested.

In his forestry country, there are furrows like dykes to jump, not to speak of dykes like young rivers. I began to feel my age – about a hundred and fifty! A thicker stick rather than my woodland wand would have helped. Stewart thought nothing of jumping those peaty drains with a sika stag on his back. They have a monster rucksack made for the purpose called a 'Sikasack'. Better him than me!

Having listened to the weather forecast which dismissed the west of Scotland with one word – Dreadful – I only had a camouflaged waxproof to wear. Later I acquired the woollen Swanndri which is just the thing for Sitka stalking. Pushing through gramophone-needle Sitka in the waxproof sounded like the London Philharmonic at full rip. It would have been better to be tweedy and damp.

Even so, we did make several successful stalks. Between the showers there was usually a roe to be seen somewhere all through the day. One was indicated by Stewart's Labrador from a considerable distance. When we finally located her, she was curled up like a fox under a tree, and pretty obviously asleep. I longed for my bipod to get over the heather without showing myself. The stick had to suffice. How the last doe of the day failed to register my painful progress I do not know. It was a longish stalk in full view, round the edge of a marshy pond. Granny's Footsteps is a game with roe I have always enjoyed, but ill-equipped as I was, every bit of bog myrtle, and every bushy Sitka spruce complained loudly at my passage. The last few yards meant a crawl through old heather, but even at that she only started to look a bit upset. I was too!

Perhaps this is why the Equipment sessions on my stalking courses always proved the centre of heated discussion. Is there some Admirable Crichton of the stalking world who, wherever he stalks, has just the right stuff, and immediately feels at home under all circumstances? What a detestable chap he would be. Probably never misses either.

Actually, the stalk was a lovely and picturesque end to a busy and, for me, unusual day. In that sort of tundra-like country, the lochan had much of the look of the Northern Yukon. The roe could well have been a giant moose dipping his bulbous nose for aquatic weeds. I wish it had been!

Black Weeks

Every stalker runs into his personal doldrums. Pretty often the Clerk of the Weather has a down on you and there is fog every morning for a week, or he gives you his personal rain cloud. Sometimes one just can't seem to shoot straight. At other times everything seems to be lovely – the deer have just got to be all out feeding – and they aren't. Do you write it down as valuable and character-building, give it up and go fishing, or try to puzzle out what is actually going on?

My own feeling is that one should try to single out the totally hopeless days for fishing or staying in bed, but attempt to rise to the challenge of the grey areas.

Eliminating the problems of shooting straight which any ballistic expert, and there are crowds of them at any deer meeting, can solve over less than half a pint, and taking it for granted that the weather is foul most of the time and there is nothing to do about it, what can be done in the other sector of the trouble scene – this business of just not seeing them?

Thinking about roe, one knows that there are bits of the year when the odds are stacked against us: farm land when the crops are high; late June in bracken country; after the rut; late November and early December.

Then there are the other, inexplicable, times when, for one reason or another, everything is dead; not a beast to be seen and you start thinking they have all been poached or something. Maybe they have, but it's unlikely that the lurcher boys got all of them.

Time is precious to us all, and no matter how we claim to love being out in the woods even when there is nothing to shoot, it does get a bit tedious if there is nothing to see either. The Catering Manager starts to get slightly edgy and may make some pointed remarks about the state of the garden. A degree of productivity is called for or the image suffers, so let us try to separate the possibles from the completely hopeless.

Thinking first about the standard 'Black Weeks' in the year: one learns to dread leaf-flush time in some of our South-country woods, or anywhere dominated by bracken when those mushroom-speed curled fronds are suddenly up to your knees. If spring growth is early, which is normal in these days of climate-change, and if you just have woodland in which to stalk, or the rest of your deer have vanished like Excalibur – mystic, wonderful – beneath a sea of oil-seed rape, there just isn't much to do about it but try to get the proper toll of yearlings in April and most of the adult bucks you want to shoot before the end of the first week in June.

If your stalking includes any fields, the deer may be coming on to them early and late either to get a change of food or in summer to escape the flies. Up to a certain point the crops will be low enough to allow the rather specialised sport of tramline hunting. Tramlines are the double wheelmarks left for successive sprayer passes through the crop. Deer use them, and so can the stalker! It is a curious thing that when deer are in cover low enough to expose the line of the back, they often get the idea they cannot be seen and permit liberties to be taken. Having located a shootable beast, perhaps in the middle of seventy acres (28ha.) of oil-seed rape or wheat, you choose a tramline which would take you in range, hustle down it crouched double, pop up at the critical point and go Bang. Sounds easy – it is only the popping up at the right moment and not before which can be tricky.

When that time passes, all too quickly, it's time to go fishing! If it's too hot for trout, it's just right for chub or carp.

Another lean time that leaps to mind is the post-rut depression. I don't think there is much doubt that when the last doe is satisfied, and the bucks know it, they flop down under the most comfortable bush and stay there, almost without moving, for days or weeks on end. We know they can do this because of the work of Dr Reino Hofman of Giessen University, who has shown that in roe the inner surface of the rumen varies in complexity between active and rest periods in the animal's life. Like tripe in a butcher's, the rumen is lined with small, finger-like processes. At busy times, such as when they are establishing their territories in spring, these fingers are dilated and thus increase the effective absorptive surface for nutrients. At other times, they partially collapse, reducing the surface area. This apparently allows a deer to continue to exist almost without feeding, losing little body weight provided it is largely inactive.

All right, it isn't much good looking for a buck after the rut for about three weeks. The only thing is, when did the rut stop? I have known bucks completely 'run' by 7 August, but remember one that was in full rut on 12 September.

As a very experienced fishing gillie said once: 'You must never tell your Gentleman that it is hopeless. Always say "It isn't very good just now, but there was a fisher here last year who caught a fifteen-pounder, and the water was just as bad!"'

In stalking, as in fishing, one hopes for a buck with his luck out to bring yours in. However, just trusting to luck isn't very satisfying. It's probably better to forget about the mature bucks in late August and go looking in the odd corner for frustrated and dispossessed yearlings who haven't had the chance to exhaust themselves with adult fun and games.

One often gets the same disappearing trick at the beginning of the doe season. Having decided to make a really good start, you go out full of determination and there they are gone. Not a sign. The deer farmers know all about the phenomenon and call it 'inappetence'. It is the same with fish, too. When the temperature drops you would think they have to stoke up, but it just doesn't work that way.

Something of an exception to this seems to crop up in some parts of Scotland, particularly where the deer have access to 'neeps', when the early part of November especially can be a most productive time.

It is true that November in Lowland Britain is the peak of the pheasant shooting season and the deer have good reason to feel harassed and out of their normal routine. I do think that if one has stalking on land where the shoot is important, you can show a little consideration to your landlord and the gamekeeper, holding back until the big shooting days are over. In any case, the deer will be more active by Christmastime or soon afterwards; the does are likely to be feeding in the fields on young grass or winter-sown cereal crops, and one will be considerably more welcome then, both to the farmer or farm manager and the keeper.

Early in the doe season I am also conscious that the fawns may not be fully independent of their mothers right at the start of the open season, especially in the harsher North. This is another reason for holding back unless it is imperative to take every chance of a shot because of over-population. In that case if you don't shoot them humanely first they are going to die anyway.

As a very privileged resident in stalking country, I can look slightly objectively, maybe, at those less fortunate who have to snatch what time they can for stalking. The temptation is to try to pick the likeliest places and go there as quickly as possible. Ten minutes sitting down, and you are already wondering if somewhere else would have been better. These things need to be recognised.

Cramming the maximum effort into a minimum time can produce another sort of 'Black Week' – every minute of each day is to be spent really winkling them out. No effort spared, no path unstalked, no high seat unsat-in.

In a couple of days or less, every deer knows that the pressure is on; that from first light until breakfast-time and from tea-time until dark it just doesn't pay to stir from the ancestral bramble bush. They aren't fools, and don't. Result: one 'Black Week'. Relaxation in these frantic days is not easy to achieve.

If you can't relax, try a course of yoga. Besides anything, a bit of levitation might help over those dry leaves. After half a century of trying one thing and the other, often with a startling lack of success, I've finally decided to go fishing!

The Perils of Pay Stalking

A lot of stalkers are involved in letting these days and not to put it too bluntly, some are getting in a horrid muddle in the process. Clients are going home dissatisfied by the service or the value for money they have received, while stories are rife of the awful things done or risked by visitors. The boot is by no means on one foot.

When woodland stalking started to be let there was an understandable reaction from the old guard who had been paying nothing for their sport and regarded it as a service to the landowner, getting some recompense for time and petrol by sharing the venison. A few did little but enjoy themselves, taking the odd buck and neglecting the does, but the majority were extremely dedicated, not only doing an honest job of management but spreading the word at a time when few owners knew or cared about woodland deer, apart from getting them killed by any method which came to hand. Many of the present generation of stalkers owe their expertise to the teaching of these pioneers. My first stalking lease was 'Four pounds a year, and a pint of cider to my brother whenever you see him'. No great return for that particular landowner and involving no massive obligations on either side.

In the early 1960s the Forestry Commission started to let roe stalking by the week, for a modest fee admittedly, but immediately it was necessary to introduce standards: of service to the visitor, and of good behaviour by him in return. Nobody wants to buy a pig in a poke, so the charges had to define what was on offer – in terms of outings, trophies, transport, professional support and so on. Early definitions soon ran into trouble defining what was meant by a 'good head' or a 'cull buck'. What was good on one forest might be pretty poor on another and quite likely qualify as rubbish to a visitor from abroad, hungry for gold medals.

Since the International Hunting Exhibition at Budapest in 1971 the CIC system of judging trophies had become familiar and even previous to that, the St Hubert Club had been holding its annual trophy exhibition in London which I and many of the active stalkers of the time attended.

As a way of standardising charges this system became accepted for the better trophies. While the fees remained low by Continental standards, a head could be roughly measured soon after boiling, an allowance made for drying-out and the score was used as a basis for the trophy fee. When prices rose, so that each CIC point made a significant addition to the bill, stalkers returning to Germany or elsewhere started having their trophies re-measured by the local committee and should the total come out less, then things began to hit the fan.

Various extra niggles cropped up fairly regularly. Loss of venison due to bad shooting, or for that matter, wasted effort on the stalker's part because his client missed everything. Days were lost, either because of foul weather or the fact that some estates do not permit stalking on Sundays. If stalkers arrived late on Sunday evening for their week's holiday, Monday morning's outing might be lost because a session at the target was, quite rightly, insisted upon. If one of these items is not on the price list, then the visitor has a legitimate grouse. By degrees my own list of conditions became more sophisticated, each one put in as a result of some avoidable misunderstanding. So far as roe were concerned, prices for skulls up to five hundred grammes were based purely on the cut skull weight twenty-four hours after boiling. Only above this was the CIC system used, and either the provisional score was agreed as a basis for charging, or the trophy was retained for the statutory three months' drying before it was measured.

Visitors are notorious for their habit of changing dates, or even not turning up, or worse still arriving with an extra friend, saying gaily 'they would share'. One client, when he turned up with his son, asked what his licence entitled him to. When informed, he said: 'The big bucks are for me – the little ones for Tom'.

So instructed, we trailed round as a trio. Each buck had to be examined to see if it was worthy of the Great Man, or if Tom could have a go. Naturally by the time this was decided, the intended trophy was already disappearing into the bushes. I stood it for three days, then took Tom out by himself. He first shot and gralloched a yearling perfectly, then we called a fine buck, which he shot equally well. The Great Man was simply livid. Later that week a monster buck came to the call and was handsomely missed by the GM. Turning to me in a fury he shouted 'This stick you give me is no good!' He was stamping with rage and to my private disappointment did just restrain himself from throwing his rather ornamental hat on the ground. The buck at this display was so surprised that he turned to watch from forty yards, but when I tried to point out that it was still in shot, he didn't appear to hear what I said.

Few guests can be relied on to stay still. Having been put safely in a high seat for the evening, they take it into their minds to stray like ill-trained gundogs, thus spoiling the chances of other stalkers, or even being downright dangerous through shooting in unexpected places or wandering clean off their ground. We have seen it all, and while the last sanction is to be 'fully booked for next season', things can get so bad that it may be necessary to fall back on those conditions to bring some sort of discipline back during the week. To do this, one has to insist that when they send their money in advance (well in advance) of their holiday, they return a copy of your price list and conditions with a declaration that they have read, understood and agree to abide by them. Is this too militant? I don't think so.

Of course the obligation is there to give any visitor a good run for his money. Bad luck or bad weather can produce a dreadful dearth of deer, which should iron itself out in the course of five days, whereas a two- or three-day holiday doesn't bridge enough time. Also we are trying to offer a real holiday with some pleasant memories at the end of it, not just a dash out, bang and dash back sort of scurry. On the other hand, if a single-handed stalker offers more than five days of stalking a week he is condemning himself to complete slavery which is not sustainable through the season without serious risks to his health. I had a most considerate Belgian stalker who came for his first visit at the tail of that sort of busy time. If we sat in a high seat, or anywhere else, I was immediately asleep. On the Wednesday of his week he said 'Richard I am a bit tired, I don't want to go out tomorrow morning.' Bless him.

Sometimes one has to be mindful of a client's health. I had had a heart subject one week where every stalk had to be planned downhill. Quite an undertaking. It was a relief next week to welcome a guest who looked fitter. He was armed with a formidable double 9.3mm express which in due course he discharged at a good buck – and missed it. With steely calm I told him to try the other barrel. All was well and we went to view the slain. To my horror I noticed he had gone a nasty colour. I hastily said we would sit down and admire his buck. 'It is your heart?' I asked after a time. He replied ' No, it is just the emotion!'

Although one remembers clients who failed to measure up for one reason and another, they have been pretty tolerant of my shortcomings as a professional stalker. Days can pass without sight of a decent buck; stalks all too easily come unstuck. Coming round a hedge corner, I saw a buck within shot. Motioning my guest to advance, I knelt down beside him and put my fingers in my ears for the shot. Time passed – no shot. Eventually the buck walked off, so I said 'Why did you not shoot?' So he replied 'I kept asking you if I should shoot and you said nothing!' Oh Dear.

A lot of trophies come in for

measuring which have been really badly prepared, even by stalkers thinking enough of themselves to take out clients, and that is thoroughly un-professional. From first to last the client should get the impression that he is in good hands, and that his interests and foibles are catered for as far as possible. If you have done all that and then spoil it all by not handing over well-prepared trophies which he will be proud to show his friends, they will not clamour to join him next year. He himself might not come back and I wouldn't blame him!

Downshifting and the Stalker

Pooh Bear and Mahatma Gandhi, among others nominated by my newspaper, share the distinc-tion of being 'Downshifters'. As I understand it, this new term applies to those who have abandoned any thought of being 'Upwardly Mobile' and are content to enjoy the simple pleasures of life: a bowl of rice, maybe, or a windy day in the Hundred Acre Wood. That got me thinking about life in general and the stalker in particular. Are we all a lot of downshifters hankering for a simple existence down among the deer?

Anybody who takes other people out stalking gets every opportunity of observing the personality of successive visitors. A lucky few seem at ease from the start, but more are care-worn and take the pres-sures (and even the laptop) of big business out into the woods with them. It is understandably difficult to unwind the tensions of city life in a matter of hours, but some manage it and others don't. If you have been running, mentally at least, all week, it is not easy to think and look around every time you move one foot in front of the other. But that is woodland stalking – you do it, or you don't get much luck. As Henry Tegner wrote 'Two steps forward and then one back – that's the pace'. Maybe relaxation will come after a day or two of birdsong and bluebells and certainly success in doing so can be measured in improved stalking technique and in the overall enjoy-ment to be had from the holiday.

A handful of my visitors could be seen making an instant metamorphosis when they arrived. Downshifting, if you like, at the slam of a Mercedes door. Even in business they were probably just that bit more talented than their pressurised colleagues who were never able to shut off steam. Competition is the breath of commerce no doubt, but it has no place in the woods: in fact the least suspicion of it is inimical to the pleasure to be had from stalking, let alone to success. Worst were the keen types who always clamoured for the first week of the buck season. It was no good my saying that late May was always better because the weather was warmer; they were pathetically worried that all the best trophies would have been shot before they arrived. Competition between two stalkers could also be annoying, resulting in too much movement over the ground, bad judgements, buck fever, hurried shooting, or undue concentration on one place because a good buck had appeared there on the first night. Even with good and well-matched stalkers the luck has a way of running one way against the odds, only to change and favour the other equally unfairly. They just had to have the patience to wait it out, even if that took several holidays. This competitive spirit seemed to be at its worst between couples both of whom were stalking. And especially if they were unmarried. One such, a very beautiful girl too, was obviously aware of the side her bread was buttered. We were sitting companionably in a high seat one summer evening when a good buck came out which I told her to shoot.

'Oh no! I cannot!'

'Quick shoot it!' I whispered urgently, 'You won't get a better!'

'No! No! It is bigger than the buck that Jacques shot!'

I took the point.

Two stalkers used to come to me regularly who were something of a comic turn; their attitudes were so different, not to speak of their respective stature. One was small and fiery, willing to make every effort to succeed, but like a cat on hot bricks in a high seat if nothing seemed to be going on.

'Could we not go and see if that buck we saw . . .'

'Surely there will be a big buck in the other clearing . . .'

In total contrast, his friend was huge and had real abilities not only as a patient stalker, but as an archetypal downshifter. He had a lovely belly-laugh too. Although really pleased if a good buck came his way, he set out purely to enjoy himself and if it was warmer late in May, that's when he wanted to come. If a yearling came out which needed shooting, well, he would be amused to shoot it for me. As a result, of course, we always seemed to encounter one trophy buck after another, and that was after all the keenies had come and gone in the shivering weeks at the beginning of the season. His success did rather grate on his companion, who was sportsman enough to conceal it though his anxiety was apparent, which made his chances of success all the slimmer. Under those circumstances one tries all the harder for the unlucky stalker but even if superhuman efforts did produce a major buck for him, nervousness made a sure shot all the more difficult.

My own downshifting was done long ago at the age of thirty-two when I dropped a business career to do something I really cared about. I had always dreamed of having time to stand and stare, straw in mouth. Not that stalking has much of that about it as I soon discovered. Making the change also needed serious adjustments to my lifestyle. The lack of human contact was strange to start with, even allowing for the welcome absence of stress inseparable from a business life. Then it was infinitely refreshing! Shortly after that I was amazingly lucky to marry a wife who had herself to make even greater sacrifices. Life in a tiny cottage in a damp ditch miles from anywhere was bad enough, let alone with a husband who was out most of the night, but who had to sleep all afternoon. If my downshift was voluntary, hers was imposed, and all the more difficult.

However, it was work I loved and I have never regretted the move downwards, if that was what it was. Funnily enough, to the Upwardly Mobile my lack of ambition was often a matter of ill-concealed contempt. Fun had to be something snatched from the real-life matter of making money and I must have seemed to them little better than a street musician. One very high-powered director could not bear it any longer, and took my wife aside to tell her how wrong it was for me to *enjoy* my work. In his vocabulary work must be a struggle, a fight with one's competitors, a scaring but rewarding process from which to wring enough money to maintain an impressive lifestyle including taking expensive stalking holidays in England. But to take pleasure in it . . . ! Wrong and dreadful. I won't tell you his nationality.

So the lesson I draw from all this is that to enjoy the Hundred Acre Wood, whether or not you are lucky enough to live there, it is essential to relax and not to worry about who is going to win at Poohsticks.

Tactics and Confessions

One of Bernard Shaw's pithy sayings is reputed to have been 'Parents should not be an example, but an object lesson to their children.' Over the years I have tried to tell a good many would-be stalkers how to go about roe stalking, but Oh Goodness! If only they knew the number of times that I have failed to take my own advice! As I get slightly worn round the edges, things seem to get even worse. One tends to park the vehicle in a commanding position for a general spy of the countryside (with the heater going) rather than footing it. When a stalk offers, is there a short cut rather than a long crawl? Worst of all I notice a definite temptation to take shots that would – maybe

– have been possible twenty years ago in the flush of constant practice and youthful nerve, but which now should be firmly and definitely passed up for something more certain.

My stalking latterly was more on farmland than in thick woodland. Comparing the two, open downland stalking is very different, and in many ways more demanding. One local farm is typical: ranges are longer and the chances extremely thin of finding a shootable deer actually offering a safe shot. All too often the roe are silhouetted on a horizon only interrupted by the tower of our church. And don't they know it! When I took it over there were more than fifty resident roe on a thousand acres round which there was a fence, which might not seem too bad until you know that there are only two little woods and some hedges. The rest is open farmland. Forty does had to go in two hectic winters, with a smaller number of yearling bucks accounted for each summer, before the numbers came down to a manageable level of around twenty winter residents.

The result of this could be seen in a restored reproductive rate, the disappearance of large groups of field-living roe, and a return to the sort of territorial behaviour which we think of as normal for the species. Even so, quite a number spend most of their time living in the hedges. Because they are left quiet most of the time and not over-stalked, they are not as jumpy as deer that are subjected to constant harassment. Looking back at the last doe season that I enjoyed there, one stalk sticks in my mind as an example of the sort of tactics one needs to get at roe living principally in the fields.

Towards the end of February one starts to get that useful half hour or so after the last tractor has rumbled home, when the deer are anxious to get out for their evening feed. Compared with the early morning it is easier to get about the farm; one does not have scores of sleepy woodpigeons clattering out of every clump of trees to mark the stalker's progress. In the dusk of a mild February evening I had come a long way round to gain the wind and was doing a careful spy. (Not out of the car this time!) A trio of roe were lying in the lee of a thick hedge. Blessings on a superb pair of binoculars for picking up their earth-brown shapes, and more blessings for their definition which allowed definite identification of one good buck already with nearly full-grown antlers and also two does. For once there was a good earth bank behind them, but no way to make a direct approach. A quick re-check of the wind made it clear that I would have to retrace my steps nearly back to the car, and start again hoping that the light would hold up long enough. It was one of those occasions when speed rather than stealth was of the essence – up to a point. Not only would it be dark soon, but they could be relied on to start feeding out into the crop at any moment, where the chance of a safe shot would soon vanish.

Hot and flustered after my half-mile dash, there was a long shelter belt to negotiate with a parallel strip of dead artichokes which gave cover but would have to be negotiated somehow before I could poke my nose, and barrel, over the lip of the little valley where the deer might still be found. Getting more or less within striking distance, I found that cross-tracks had luckily been made in the artichokes as pheasant flushing points, even though a wilderness of dry stems were still scattered about. I hate crawling! Fifteen yards of misery followed, with alarming snicks and cracks the whole way, no matter how I arched myself over the remains; kneeling as an alternative on a series of razor-sharp flints.

Of course, when I peered out the deer had gone, but a despairing spy round disclosed them, still in contention about eighty yards away, hull-down. The legs of the bipod on my rifle were already extended but, as usual, one side was higher than the other and had to be shortened with appropriate contortions. Even then, there was a jagged skyline of flints between me and the nearest doe. Patience! Another yard or two uphill and the shot will be 'on'. Does she come uphill? Of course not. Frantic humpings, regardless of sticks and stones, to a friendly molehill – one doe looking distinctly alarmed – more adjustments of the legs in those last seconds before the balloon goes up, and a clear broadside at last. One lying still, the other two inevitably posing with the church tower once again firmly behind them. That will do for the evening.

Nearly at the end of the doe season, I had an emergency call from a farmer friend who is trying hard to establish some very promising little coverts out on the downs which should produce some testing pheasants – provided my four-footed friends don't eat all the trees down to ground level! Why are they always my deer?

This is real wide-open spaces stuff, every acre of which is marked with sweat and abrasions from the days when I used to stalk it regularly. Spot a party of roe four hundred yards from any cover, angle round until you are in the eye of the sun – then start crawling! An hour later you may be nearer the place where they were, but . . .

On the first outing the whole place was deserted. Mild, damp weather, good wind, everything quiet – but no deer. Amazing. Later it emerged that the keeper had spent most of last night lamping the place for foxes. Ah well, you can't win them all. However, luck is often with the persistent. I walked round what cover there was, and eventually put a doe and a doe fawn up. They hadn't seen much of me, and hesitated after the first run. A rest on the nearest fencepost made sure of both.

I couldn't return until nearly the last day of the season, but a spy from the farm road disclosed three roe actually in one of the ravaged plantations. Safe to shoot if only one could get near, but how? They were in a wide valley near a clump of tall bare beech trees with a small release pen in one corner surrounded with big straw bales for protection. Not a vestige of dead ground or cover to use after the first hundred yards. I did the easy bit, and by then they had totally vanished. Had they seen me and decamped? Surely one would have seen them go across the empty acres?

Nothing to do but advance and spy, advance and spy, pace by slow pace. Half an hour drags by. A movement in the clump turns out to be a hare, then another. No deer. There is the ear of a third hare in the grass – or is it? By this time I am in plain view, trusting to camouflage clothes and slow movement in case the deer are still there. Another spy of the hare – it moves its head – it is a doe lying down, within a hundred yards but with a tangle of beech branches in the way and difficult to see anyway.

Inch down the slope when she is not looking. Granny's Footsteps. Branches out of the way, lie down, bipod legs up, what now? That is where things started to go wrong. If I had waited, she would have started feeding again quite soon, but I felt confident, and those stones were desperately uncomfortable. I drew a most careful bead on her neck – and missed it. She got to her feet, hesitated in full view long enough for a second shot. At that, a doe appeared between two beech stems; was it the same one, or another? There was no time to deliberate in case she was wounded, so a third 7mm bullet winged its noisy way. Because of the beech trees, I could see no sign of the survivors running off, and there was no sign of anything lying in the trees. Nothing to do but approach the scene with rifle ready, and see what had happened at the sharp end.

One roe, and one only, was plain to see. Had I shot at another? There was one large patch of hair which could have been the same one – or was it a second? The only thing was to search. Fortunately the ground under the clump was pretty bare – nothing there – and the grass in the plantation only ankle-high. Carefully walking up and down between the tree shelters I could see no sign of deer or hair or blood. Anything lying on either side of the plantation would have been immediately visible even hundreds of yards away. There was another small plantation at right-angles to the first – nothing there either. Back to the dead doe, which didn't have enough bullet holes in her to account for everything. Well, if there had been another, I missed it. Back to the farm with the carcass hoping nobody had heard all the noise. One does like to do a neat, workmanlike job, and this morning's barrage definitely was not. However, the niggling doubt was still there, so I owned up and told the sorry story. My friend promised to walk round the plantations and have another look.

He found nothing, but a week later telephoned to say that the doe had been found. Shot through the heart, she had dashed fifteen yards, jumped the big bales and finished up dead inside the release pen, where I never thought to look.

Four morals: don't try fancy shots; never give up when there is any doubt; don't stalk without a dog, or the use of one; and don't suppress the horrid truth when something has gone wrong.

My immortal soul must be better for the confession. It still doesn't feel very good.

The Rut and Calling

Calling roe is the high peak of the year for many stalkers, but trying to get it right, specially from a distance, is just about as chancy and frustrating as expecting ideal snow conditions on a week's skiing holiday. The weather, the vagaries of individual deer, the state of the moon and unexpected human activities in the woods all affect just when the rut is likely to start, when in the day a particular buck will rouse and chase his doe, or whether there will be much going on at all. Of course the does will find a buck and mate, but some years the courting business is protracted with wild chases, barking and squeaking in all directions while another year everything gets settled in the bushes apparently without ceremony.

The mental picture is of big bucks plunging through the bushes in instant response to the call, and this can happen. Sometimes. I remember taking a Women's Institute party out one afternoon to visit the woods and just as an illustration, demonstrated how one might call a buck. Within seconds a buck appeared regardless of the presence of a dozen ladies in summer frocks all exclaiming. Never a better exhibition! When I've been trying hard to lure something out for a visiting stalker it has sometimes worked – but never like that!

In most parts of the country rutting activity starts towards the end of July, activity peaking about 5 to 7 August and dying away round about 12 August. It is now clear that the doe only has one oestrus each year, so she is determined to mate successfully. In the early days she will stick to the buck she has selected and mates with him, often repeatedly. However, towards the end of her season this apparent monogamy breaks down and she may accept the attentions of one or several other bucks. Perhaps she wants to make sure of becoming pregnant. This explains the 'blue cabarets' in which hectic rutting by one or more does and several bucks may be witnessed. This is also the time when calling is most likely to be successful.

The whole business of stalking is pretty much of a mystery to most of us, and I hope it goes on being that way! More of an art than a science, you could say, and nothing in stalking is more of an art, less of a science, and a fair mystery into the bargain, than trying to call a roe buck.

Some stalkers consider it unsporting to lure a buck in rut by playing on his overstrained urges. Others consider success in calling an old buck to be the epitome of the stalker's art, just as a dedicated pheasant shot delights in his ability to tackle really strong, high birds in good style.

With the arrival of visiting stalkers from the Continent, we have learned a lot about calling in the last few years, but anyone thinking that it is a new sport in this country would be mistaken. It is interesting to consult the Patriarchs of roe stalking: Millais, 'Snaffle' (the pen-name of Guy Hardwin Gallenga, not the artist 'Snaffles'), Frank Wallace and Henry Tegner on the subject.

Millais, in *British Deer and their Horns* did not mention calling at all. 'Snaffle', who learned his craft in several European countries, disapproved: 'To my mind, it is not sport at all; and the only time that I have used the call was when I was in camp in the Herzegovina, and very short of meat.'

His argument was that it was too easy: 'In a week or so every buck on a shooting can be brought up for inspection.' However, one notes that on the occasion when he was very short of meat: *'Of course* [my italics] no roe buck appeared, perhaps the call was not of the correct pitch. At any rate, the only living things that did come were mosquitoes, and they nearly devoured me.' Present day callers will sympathise.

Frank Wallace wrote nothing about calling, although he had enormous experience of roe stalking abroad. I remember him describing going out calling roe with a keeper near Lake Constance, but suspect that he, too, felt it was unsporting.

Nearer to the present day, Henry Tegner wrote of his initiation into the technique by a Herr Tauchnitz on a roe forest near Vienna:

Evening after evening we would go out together to a likely clearing in the woods in the hope of luring a roe to our piping. The only things he managed to lure out of the forest, to come peeping at us, like two fairies out of Hans Andersen's tales, were a roe doe and her fawn. No buck with massive antlers did we see. We peeped, grunted and coughed – or at least that was what it sounded like to me – until my ears became attuned to the softer nuances of the instruments.

No doubt Henry Tegner's daughter, my old friend Veronica Heath, would be able to recall how far her father progressed with his calling in later years. It was Tegner who first wrote of the Great Ridge buck which was taken by calling. This beautiful head 28.4cm in length, exhibited at the Düsseldorf International Exhibition in 1954, was shot by Frank Sykes in 1939. Tegner stated that the buck was called by Captain Patrick Sykes, but regarding this detail there seems to be some doubt. Major Tom Whitehead, who stalked for years in the Great Ridge always claimed that it was he who did the calling. When I asked Frank Sykes about it shortly before his death he was unable to remember who was with him at the time which perhaps is not surprising as within a month of that roe rut the world was at war.

When Major Whitehead's son, Nicholas, came in with a trophy to measure, I was fascinated to hear that he had been reminiscing with his father about calling. Apparently in his youth Tom lived in Germany, on the Dutch border. He learned to call roe there with a whistle well before the First War. Later he moved to central Europe, probably what is now the Czech Republic, where they only knew how to use a beech leaf. Eventually he brought his skill to this country, and even comparatively recently went out calling in the Wiltshire woods. He can almost certainly claim to be the pioneer of calling in this country and should have his due place in the annals of roe stalking.

In spite of occasional cries of 'Unsporting!' those early accounts highlight the fact that calling does not always work, no matter how skilled the caller. Maybe the call one is using is 'not of the correct pitch' yet tomorrow, under apparently identical conditions, it really works. So does a 'silent' dog whistle – sometimes! Apart from the doe-in-season squeak, and its close relative the fawn-in-trouble squeak, very few stalkers have ever heard the cries they attempt to reproduce. Few really bother to enter the mind of a roe buck to set him up, rather than blowing hopefully.

The time of day is important, and it is interesting to note that Henry Tegner went out 'evening after evening' without success. Few bucks will come in the evening; the best time is between 10am and 3.30pm, maybe Herr Tauchnitz wanted to give Henry some lessons in calling but not too many of his bucks.

The curse of language often gets in the way of a free exchange of ideas with knowledgeable visitors, but given goodwill and enthusiasm on both sides one picks up a point here, another there, and in the end a degree of success starts to creep in.

To those who attended his practical calling schools, the visit to this country of Dr Istvan Bertoti from Hungary was a landmark. Wherever he went, Dr Bertoti seemed to be able to charm roe out of the ground, and that with half a dozen stalkers grouped round him. He did say that the tone of the call is critical. I was curious to see that he used Faulhaber calls, which are generally less popular over here, in addition to some home-made whistles.

One point he made was not really taken in, yet it may be a keystone to the success or otherwise of your calling. That is, never call until you are reasonably sure that there is a doe in season in the area. It stands to reason if you think about the world of scent in which roe live. A buck could not fail to be aware of the pheromones given off by a doe on heat anywhere near, yet lots of stalkers try a call or two well before the rut gets going, just to see if anything happens. All they are doing is educating their bucks, who after such a lesson will be pretty reluctant to respond later on.

Someone bought a call from me, and when I told him that, he said 'Oh, that's all right, I'll go and practise in my neighbour's woods!'

I do not think personally that calling a buck with a whistle is unsporting. Educating another stalker's bucks is pretty dubious. What is undoubtedly unsporting is to use calling – or any other technique – to shoot too many mature bucks.

Perchance He Sleepeth?

I've always had a sneaking sympathy for the priests of Baal in the Bible who made a horlicks of their calling demonstration. I have done the same myself. The fact is that calling anything, whether a god from his personal Olympus, my dog when she's gone rabbiting, or a roe buck out of a bramble bush is a tricky business with a high potential failure rate. The fact is you have not only got to sound like an animal, if that's what you're trying to call, but think like one as well.

I went out stalking once in Austria with a jäger who at first I took to be a unilateral transvestite, but after a while the reason for his rather opulent bosom turned out to be an enormous conch shell. From this he produced the most amazing roars and bellows before returning it again to his tunic. It left a lasting impression although we didn't see the stag.

Calling red deer on the open hill in Scotland is practically never tried and most people agree that under those conditions, there is little need for the method which could, in any case, be considered rather unfair. Nevertheless, the odd deep grunt has made many a stag hesitate, turn, or get to its feet, thus converting a critical moment into a fatal one. In the woods, straight calling on the Continental pattern is certainly a legitimate means of bringing a stag into range and is not nearly as easy as it sounds.

Red deer, of course, are not the only species which can be called although some are more difficult than others. Fallow are very tricky and the most one can hope for is to get a stand buck to cross from one side of his stamping ground to the other. Sika, on the other hand, can come well to a whistle, an art which was developed by Eric Masters at Wareham. Even now, only a few people are any good at it. Eric used to take his whistles out of squeaky toys, driving the staff of the local toyshop nearly mad trying everything until he found one with the right pitch. Roe sometimes come at the drop of a hat, but muntjac calling is still in its infancy. Charles Smith-Jones, in his excellent book *Muntjac – Managing an Alien Species*, says that they will come to a roe call, probably out of pure curiosity. They are vocal little beasts and I see no reason why a calling technique should not be worked out for one. There are certainly people who are knowledgeable enough these days to understand muntjac mentality and dream something up.

We tend to say that successful calling depends on understanding the behaviour patterns of the species, so with the herding deer, like red or sika, we imitate the challenge of another male. For the solitary roe, techniques for which are probably best understood in this country, we try to reproduce the blandishments of the gentle sex, but are we just accepting tradition? Admittedly, our calling technique falls far short of the expertise of some Continental stalkers and it would pay us to brush up on accepted technique that we know would work if we were good enough. However, I am convinced that there are not only refinements of technique, but entirely new ideas which are well worth trying.

Take the roe buck for example. We know the doe attracts a buck to her and attempts to keep him from being seduced by other does. Even so, a good barking match with the territorial buck can sometimes get him cross enough to show himself, that is provided you use the challenge bark, *boh! boh! boh!* and not the alarm bark, *baagh-bo-bo-bo!* We add to our effectiveness by choosing female squeak or male bark as appropriate.

We know that red deer live in a matriarchy. The hind is by no means a hapless prisoner of the stag, but exercises choice when accepting a mate, no doubt breathing sweet nothings into his ear as she does so. Anyone who has spent time in a deer park knows the wide repertoire of bellows, squeaks, moans and grunts which make up day-to-day speech among the herd. Maybe we could bug a particularly attractive hind and get her particular sweet nothings down on tape. The effect on the stags should be the same as a sultry night-club singer on a fort-full of legionnaires. Unfair? Maybe – but it could be fun! And what about the 'Buck Lures' advertised in American hunting magazines?

The whole question of the fairness of calling does not depend primarily on the method, but on what you do about the beast when he finally emerges from the woodwork. The actual difficulty of calling may justify shooting the odd buck, or conditions may be so thick that it is, in fact, one of the few ways of getting on terms with animals which are scarcely ever seen at other times of year. If you can cap the skill needed to call with the skill needed to take a sensational photograph, the result will be a real and memorable trophy. The buck himself will be no worse off once he has recovered from the shock of finding not a delicate doe, but a stinking photographer. He may, however, be very difficult to call again.

Although the pitch and tone of your roe whistle is important and will make the difference between consistent or occasional success, time and place are vital. It is not usually much good calling before 15 July or even 20th and things go very quiet again a month later, although both dates in Scotland may be delayed by as much as a week.

Hot, still weather seems to make the roe responsive. One sees more actual rutting activity in warm weather although it doesn't matter too much whether it is dry, or damp and steamy. Unfortunately, we often seem to get a period of cool, windy weather round about the beginning of August and although there is no doubt that rutting continues, one does not see much of it and few bucks come to the call.

Do not ask a buck to emerge from his favourite thicket. He may do if he is mad enough, but it is too much to ask. For preference choose a place where a buck is known to live and where, by standing up against a tree you have fair visibility all round but where the buck does not feel unduly exposed. If you can spy one out in the open fields, preferably without a doe, he can quite likely be called back towards cover, and it is interesting to be able to observe his reactions to the call, so that when you are in thick woodland the process can be visualised.

Having decided on a suitable tree against which to stand, scrape the leaves and twigs away with your foot and then stay still as death for five minutes. The first time I went out with a stalker who did this, I wondered at his disregard of the usual rules of as near absolute silence as possible, but then I was amazed at the number of times a buck emerged before he ever called at all. The penny dropped later: a rutting buck in his chosen territory hears what might be a rival scraping and fraying. Of course he is bound to come and investigate. Simple, once it has been pointed out! If he does not respond you have to fall back on the accepted techniques, a high rhythmic squeak to suggest a fawn in difficulties – this should bring first the doe, then the buck behind her. Failing that, the lower and hoarser pee-pee of a doe in season, and the two-tone pee-ay of a doe pursued by a buck. There should be a decent interval between the different voices but having reached the last, one can make an increasing amount of noise, always remembering on a still day, that a buck may hear it a long way off and take ten or fifteen minutes to come and see what the form is. Calling is not a hasty business. When everything works it can be exciting. When it doesn't, which is all too often, one feels frustrated and ridiculous. It is much worse, of course, when someone is there, although one hopes he will not taunt you like Samuel did the priests of Baal – and say 'Cry louder, perchance he sleepeth!'

Dogs Good and Bad

A reindeer-herder presented me with a pair of furry slippers: 'What sort of fur is it?'

'Dog. In Siberia we have two sorts of dog: Good dogs – and slippers!'

Probably to our loss in some ways, we tend to have a distinctly more tolerant attitude than that to the peccadillos of our pets, though sometimes I must admit I have felt like murder.

A dog has been with me on nearly all my woodland stalking expeditions, mainly as my insurance policy against the inevitable moment when you have had a shot and the beast has disappeared, either obviously wounded or just somewhere in thick cover, probably dead. One of my Labradors was a paragon: responsive, obedient, a pleasure as a companion, and knowing the stalking game better than me. All I can say about the others is that they had their points, good and not so good! Which means I'm not much of a dog trainer, but struck lucky once. None of them would do the fancy tricks that other stalkers' deer dogs displayed. They didn't bark dead, take me to a fallen buck or even point very demonstrably. They would track and pull down a wounder and follow a blood trail, which was fine provided I could keep up! The saving trick was to keep a collar and a small bell in the roe sack which was put on if work was required. At least one got the general direction.

My first Labrador was a hopeless gundog – headstrong and totally cloth-eared – but he was good on deer and after a season or two stalking with me every day got to know his job without being told. I went out with him once to a farm where a red stag, frustrated in the rut, was chasing heifers and generally creating chaos. I didn't want to kill the stag, but mounting a dilapidated combine, decided to put two shots from the .30-06 at his feet. The stag was totally unmoved at this barrage, so I dispatched my trusty hound after him. This solved the problem. Fergie, having been gone ten minutes or so, came back with a disgusted look on his face which so clearly said 'I can't believe it! An animal that big – and you missed it!' Who says dogs can't talk.

The real pointing breeds can be a marvellous help in thick woodland and their body language is infinitely clearer than with a Labrador. One can come to depend on them too much, in fact, forgetting that they can only react to anything upwind. If you happen to be stalking across the wind, there is one whole side which has to be left to your own scanning.

In Continental Europe there is a very keen following of those who interest themselves in deer dogs, holding training sessions and field trials for this special purpose.

There are primarily two distinct disciplines in which deer dogs are trained: either you have a dog with you while stalking to point deer by scent and then to find dead or wounded deer soon after the shot, or if a deer has been known to be wounded or lost, breeds with very keen noses are employed to track and find them even after hours or days.

For the first category the HPR (Hunt – Point – Retrieve) breeds are favoured, especially the German shorthaired and wire-haired pointers, the Weimaraner and the Hungarian Visla. Deer work is an integral part of their heredity as well as in their formal training although they are multi-purpose breeds. For long-term tracking and finding dead game, the Hanoverian and Bavarian bloodhounds are outstanding. Slightly separate from this are the Scandinavian elkhounds, which are used to locate elk (moose) and bring them to bay to be approached and shot by the hunter, or afterwards located if the shot was not immediately fatal.

Teckels, working dachshunds, are very useful in tracking wounded game, generally being used on a long leash. Being small, one can carry them up into a high seat, but they rely on hunting ability rather than speed to account for anything which is still mobile which a longer-legged breed might run down.

Most of these alien varieties are already well established in this country, but many stalkers in Britain use our own gundog breeds, of which the Labrador is the most common because of their trainability. I have known some English springers and Border terriers which were good at the job. All regular stalkers should own a dog trained to deer, or at least know someone locally who can be called on at need.

If the choice falls on one of the HPR breeds or a Labrador, deer work does not prevent your dog being a steady and valuable small-game finder and retriever as well. I once asked a police dog-handler about training Labradors for finding drugs and explosives – was it necessary for them to specialise on one or the other. He looked disdainfully at me and said 'You just order "Seek plastic!" or "Seek pot!"' Straight answer to a silly question. He went on to explain how his dogs were also trained to empty themselves on command. 'You can't go looking for a bit of grass or a lamp-post while the burglar runs away!'

My daughter took up the challenge with the current bitch and it worked perfectly. Not that I wanted her to chase burglars, but it was handy before or in the middle of a car journey.

There is a very advanced technique called the *Bringsel*, and I have a photo of a Labrador in Denmark which was successfully trained in this complicated idea. It takes a lot of patience! The dog has a collar to which a wooden toggle is attached. When a dead buck is found, the dog swings the toggle into his mouth, almost as a substitute retrieve, coming back to his handler and then returning to the beast. His handler told me the main trouble in training a Labrador is that the dog is too keen to please his master and brings anything back to him whether he found the deer or not!

Alternatively, you can teach your dog to 'bark dead', staying by the dead beast and barking until you come. If he is used for game shooting as well, this could be an awkward habit, in which case buy either a falconry bell or a small-size (two to three inches high) tourist cowbell which can be attached to his collar when there is a beast to find. You can usually get there in time before he loses interest in the beast!

I have seen beagles used in this country and in Sweden to move roe, but they are extremely difficult to control, even for this which is natural to them. I can't see one acting as a stalking companion. You may start out looking for deer, but after a bit it's more likely you will be looking for beagles for the rest of the day!

There was a comical affair one day when we were trying to catch roe in nets for marking and tracking at Chedington in West Dorset and an enthusiast turned up with several basset hounds which would be ideal for shifting deer out of the bramble thickets. Nets were spread, the team was briefed and stationed and the hounds were loosed – but that was all. Silence. I only discovered later that the basset hounds found nasty prickles in the undergrowth and padded safely but ineffectively round the paths. Maybe they tripped over their ears too, but they never reached my end of the wood.

I did dare to ask a rather forbidding Head Stalker in the Highlands if I could take my dog out on the hill. It was the paragon. There was a long heavy silence, then he asked 'Will he sit?' (knowing mine was a bitch). So I said 'Yes!' 'Will he cry?' – 'No!' (Hoping for the best). 'Then he'll not be like the Laird's dogs then!' Luckily nothing went wrong, and I knew that she would crawl alongside if I let her. She learned that herself by trying to move unobtrusively when 'Sat', hoping I wouldn't notice.

Typical Questions on Stalking

I have a problem getting enough does in the winter. My stalking is also an intensive pheasant shoot and I can't get on the ground from October to the end of January. Even then the deer are dispersed and wild. Under the circumstances, couldn't I do the same as they do abroad, and shoot yearling does in September? I am quite confident enough to pick them out from the adults.

You are up against two problems: one is the law, which does not permit you to shoot does in September. The other is a question of public relations. Although you may be able to pick out the yearlings, other stalkers see you shooting does out of season for no apparent reason and may feel they can do likewise. Farm staff and country-dwellers round about hearing of your activities will react to what they see as orphaning fawns. What goes in one country may be definitely bad news in another. Men with guns have a bad enough press without making it worse.

90

Aspects of Stalking

A stalker friend has shown me roe slots in soft ground, and tells me that one can see the difference between buck and doe. Is it possible? I couldn't see any difference!

Unlike the bigger species of deer, like red or fallow, there isn't much difference in size between roe buck and doe, so an instant opinion is not likely to be very accurate. However, if one can see a good length of marks, mature bucks do tend to splay their forefeet out slightly which can sometimes be seen. Females, except when heavily pregnant, tend to 'register' fore and hind feet more neatly when walking than bucks.

I know that a shotgun should always be unloaded when crossing a fence etc, but with the greater safety of a bolt-action rifle, does the same apply to stalking?

The straight answer is YES. The obligation to unload is part of basic safe behaviour, no matter how inconvenient or noisy. It is also an integral part of the syllabus of all stalking competence tests. Fail to unload faced with a fence to cross or a high seat to mount, and you will fail the test! Besides any other consideration, it is essential to demonstrate at all times that we are responsible and above all safe firearms users.

During the last doe season I took what I thought was a careful shot with my .270 at a doe. She hunched and staggered off about fifty yards into some woodland. When I followed up there were only a few blood drops and when I put her up in some bushes, she went off again and I didn't find her. What ought I to have done?

It's a miserable business when you lose a beast, and you are right to question what you did. Of course it's easy to say 'take more trouble with your shooting in the first place' but we have all done it. Second, was your rifle properly zeroed? When did you last check it?

When a deer 'hunches' like that, it is usually hit dead centre – in the paunch or liver. That's why there wasn't much blood. Under those circumstances it's better to wait at least half an hour for it to die, or at least stiffen up. Sometimes that is difficult. At all events, it must be painstakingly re-stalked with even more care than you would take with an unwounded animal. Having lost it, you must sink your pride and let people know round about – keepers and farm men – in case they can spot it and contact you. Ideally, all stalkers should either have a dog trained to deer, or at least know someone to contact locally who can help.

When I go out stalking, how many rounds should I have with me? I always seem to go out looking like a bandit, weighed down with ammo and then if I'm lucky I get one shot. What do you do yourself?

One has to allow for times when things go wrong. Also what you expect to be doing. In the summer buck-stalking you probably hope for the one, but a good morning's doe culling in the winter might account for three – or half a dozen if the size of the cull and means of transport allow. The same thing applies on the hill. Every stalker, too, if he is truthful, has the occasional disaster no matter how careful he is with his shots. A wounded animal may require more than one shot to stop it, and stopping it should be only second to safety in deciding what you do.

The situation has changed a bit recently, as one is no longer allowed to leave a few rounds reserve in the car for emergencies, and few of us live so near our stalking that we can dash back to the house in case of need.

While I worked as a professional I had a leather case with ten rounds in it in my pocket, plus another with six which lived in the roe sack. That served well for roe. For stags on the hill, just the ten never left me short. Even then I had a spare couple in my bag in case the main supply dropped out during a crawl!

I've always enjoyed my stalking, but age is catching up on me (I am nearly seventy-five) and I mostly just go out for a roe in the evening and sit in a high seat. I'm careful not to take difficult shots and mostly hit what I aim at. Do you think I'm stretching things and ought to give up?

I do sympathise with your problem. This is something which you have to face objectively; nobody else can decide for you. The first question should be: is your sight clear enough not only to see a beast through the scope, but to spot movement which might turn out to be somebody walking in the woods? Second: how steady are you? Are you sure, or only relieved when a shot is successful? If the latter, it's probably time to think about enjoying the pleasures of watching the deer without taking the rifle. There is a great deal of pleasure in spending a summer evening in a well-placed seat, but do make sure that your seats are completely sound, and very easy to get into. We were more agile once! Whatever else, can I suggest that you never go out alone without a mobile phone? The older we get, the easier it is for some sort of accident to happen. It doesn't have to be turned on till you need it!

I have some farm-land stalking in Somerset with small woods scattered about. Mostly roe but some fallow and muntjac. I use a .308 Winchester. Shots half the time are at pretty long range where one may have to crawl into range, but in the copses it's short-range work where one has to be quick, specially with the muntjac. Do you recommend a stick (maybe two tied together) or a bipod? Or just take regulation prone shots in the fields?

Personally, I have always used a tall stick, my height up to eye level. This will give you the height and stability to shoot in and over cover in the woods. It is pretty quick if you carry it in your left hand (assuming you are right-handed) slinging the rifle on your right shoulder, muzzle-down. It can be brought up to the shoulder with the minimum of movement and your left hand, holding the stick with three fingers, is ready to receive the fore-end. Out in the fields there is so often enough straw, growing crop or stones to make a classic prone shot impossible. A bipod with telescoping legs is invaluable for this sort of work, but they are slow and click loudly as you pull out the legs, so only helpful for long shots. You are likely to have enough time to get the bipod out of your roe sack and clip it to the rifle. I prefer the sort which allow you to correct for tilt without fiddling with the legs.

I really am confused about the best times to go out roe stalking. Up here in the North, at midsummer it is hardly worth going to bed at all if one is out until dark and out again at first light. Then after a few days I'm too tired to get up at all!

It's no good getting so whacked that you either go to sleep in high seats or just blunder about not enjoying it. Added to that is the very real risk of driving a car in the early hours when sleep can hit you without warning.

Of course there are occasions when you are after a particular buck and his routine makes an ambush at first or last light the only solution. However, looking over my stalking diaries the tradition of first and last light as the most likely times does not have much foundation. On cold mornings the deer are likely to wait until the sun is up, and then relax on warm banks and sunny corners. If there are many pigeons about, it is better to let them leave, so that you can move about the woods without a constant clatter. Deer are not fools.

In the evening there is usually more movement towards dusk, but when a buck looks shadowy, it's better to leave him. Even though he is fairly clear in the scope, the muzzle flash will blind you and leave you with a beast which is difficult to locate. The most successful stalkers in my experience are those who, though keen, take a relaxed attitude to their sport.

In his excellent book *Deer Management – Quality in Southern England* Dominic Griffith quotes some revealing statistics. From a sample of 2,000 roe shot, ninety per cent of all bucks in the morning were shot between 5.15 and 8.30 with a peak about 7.00. Only two per cent were shot at first light. The corresponding figures for evening stalks: ninety-one per cent were shot between 19.00 and 21.30 with a peak about 20.0. Eighty-seven per cent of does shot in the morning were between 6.30 and 9.00 and ninety-four per cent of evening-shot does were between 15.00 and 17.45. Of course, these are south-country times to be adjusted for higher latitudes, but the facts are worthy of thought.

As the corn crops get higher, I am lucky if I can see more of a deer than the head. Is it best to try for a head shot, or guess where its body is and aim down to that?

Head shots taken from the side almost always result in a broken jaw, which is agonising, but not fatal in the short term. If the beast is looking away, or straight at you, and you are very close and sure of your shooting, that is more likely to kill it on the spot. If the beast is hull-down in vegetation aiming off is pointless. You can't really tell where the vital organs might be, and in any case a bullet's path through growing crops is unpredictable. Often the best solution is a portable high seat which commands a much better and safer view for several more weeks. Once the crops have grown that high, try to ambush your deer as they come out of the woods and before they disappear into the green jungle.

Whenever I go stalking I get covered with ticks crawling up my legs and elsewhere. What is the best method of getting them off, and is there any way of stopping the invasion?

Ticks need a drink of blood before each stage of their life cycle, and crawl up the herbage when it is moist then they wait for a potential host to pass. Putting out a hooked claw, they come on board. You may also pick them up from carrying or dressing deer. They are active from late spring to autumn. Besides various animal diseases, they carry at least one disease which you need to know about. If a tick bite develops into a red spot larger then a ten pence piece, go and see your GP and mention Lyme disease.

Pulling them off runs the risk of leaving mouthparts embedded in your skin, which then fester and can be quite a trouble. It is better to paint the beast with nail varnish or something similar.

The worst collector of ticks is the traditional breeches stocking. Trousers are less of a magnet. Tuck them into your boots when the ticks are bad.

What is the best weather to go out woodland stalking?

For most of us – it's when you get the chance! Joking apart, some weather is unpleasant and some downright dangerous, so you do well to ask. Fog is the very worst, not only are deer dimly seen, if at all, but you can't be sure of your background for safety. When in doubt – don't!

High wind makes deer nervous and skittish; rain and cold wind together makes them miserable. Look in sheltered places, under hedges, in the lee of bale stacks, anywhere, in fact, where conditions are a little less desolate. A sudden storm can produce a lot of movement as deer shift to better cover.

Freshly-fallen snow has a disturbing effect on deer. Your best chance is to look under dense conifer stands where the snow is thinner and deer may be attracted by fallen needles or broken-off branches of good browse. After a day or two there may be more movement, but if the snow is crusted, walking about is like treading on cornflakes and it's better to go to a high seat overlooking any place which catches the early sun. After a cold night they may be slow to move, but when the sun rises they like to run about to get warm. In your chilly seat you may want to do the same!

We all visualise lovely summer mornings full of birdsong, and lovely they are. Roe will probably be about fairly early but may lie down a couple of hours after dawn only to move again if the flies get bad just when you are thinking of breakfast.

Curiously, a warm drizzle, winter or summer, can be really good. Deer seem deliberate in their movements and take less notice of a shot.

Clear nights with a full moon are often followed by mornings when there is very little deer movement. They will probably be resting, but may be on the hoof again later in the morning.

Last November I gralloched a sika stag and while doing it, grazed my finger. Later it swelled up and the adjoining one too. I was prescribed antibiotics which reduced the swelling after a time but are there any particular poisons or diseases which I might have picked up?

Everyone knows that a stag, red or sika, smells awful during and after the rut but in the excitement of a successful shot it is easy to forget that we are trying to produce food fit for human consumption under somewhat adverse conditions, to put it mildly.

Stags soil, that is wallow, in a mud bath. The first effect is to blacken their coat and thus appear larger and more formidable to an adversary. They urinate in the wallow, and on themselves, so that they are covered by a stinking layer of mud and manure. One imagines that this may be attractive to the females he wishes to lure onto his rutting stand, no matter how vile it may be to our noses. Any open cut or abrasion lays a stalker open to a fairly noxious cocktail of infectious agents. In addition if he is unlucky enough to have an allergy to deer hair or blood he will suffer more than he would through breathing in the fumes.

So of course you did right to get medical help, and it is unlikely that there will be any long-term effects. The significant deer-associated Lyme disease is not spread by contact but by tick-bite, and while isolated cases of other diseases such as TB are reported from time to time, training in proper gralloching techniques should alert the stalker to look out for suspicious abnormalities.

All stalkers should, of course, keep up to date with Tetanus jabs.

Rudimentary first-aid for cuts should be carried. A temporary but quite effective dressing can be improvised from a clean handkerchief, a polythene bag and a strip of adhesive plaster to keep it in place until something better can be done with a kit in the car. On the open hill there is usually a stream handy in which one can wash, but not in woodland. Both for protection and in the name of hygiene it is advisable to wear gloves during the gralloch. I favour reasonably strong domestic rubber gloves rather than medical examination gloves which tear easily in the rough work of handling a heavy beast. Evening stalking frequently involves a gralloch in the dark. One can get tiny head lights now and using one could avoid quite a serious cut.

I would like to know if anybody could offer me some advice on obtaining permission to stalk on land. I have enrolled on a BDS stalkers' course and am also a member of BDS and BASC.

As I don't have the land to use, I haven't been able to apply for a Firearm Certificate (FAC) although I do have references willing to complete the forms for me. Previously I was a trainee keeper but the job ended approximately fourteen years ago and the contacts I had have moved on and away.

I realise that landowners aren't going to let just anybody shoot on their land. I also don't expect to get this help without having to pay for the privilege. Saying that, I am not in the position to go out and purchase the stalking rights to land, which I have seen advertised as an option.

It's a Catch-22 position – people won't help if I don't already have a FAC, and I can't be in the position of having the FAC without somebody's help!

You have made a good start by enrolling on the BDS stalkers' course. That shows that you are willing to go to trouble, and will have a basic knowledge. Attending local meetings of both BDS and BASC is also a very good way of getting to know the enthusiasts.

Getting local contacts is obviously the first start, and with your past background in gamekeeping, you might go about getting to know likely people by offering to beat or otherwise help on a local shoot. Living as you do in country where fallow deer are numerous, it may be easier to find someone who needs help with culling in this way. Competition is fierce for roe stalking which makes that more difficult to get into.

To learn, one sometimes has to pay. There are plenty of hard-working professional stalkers who offer doe stalking at very reasonable rates. If you contact one of them (a list of members of The UK Association of Professional Deer Managers is available from their Secretary, Rose Cottage, 381 Easebourne Lane, Midhurst, GU29 9BN) and make definite arrangements for stalking he may be able to help with your Firearms Certificate application. If you prove yourself with him over a few visits, an offer to help may prove acceptable. There's a lot of heavy work to do with fallow deer!

I often get barked at when I am out stalking roe in the summer. Can one tell if it is a buck or a doe? Or for that matter, is there any way one can interpret the noise to one's own advantage?

The nearer we get to the rut, the more bucks tend to bark aggressively, and indeed one can take advantage of this display. It is important, however, to know something of the language. Both bucks and does bark, and although one can assume that a gruff tone must be a buck, that is not necessarily the case. Like people, some does have deep voices, and some bucks are rather squeaky!

Most important is to distinguish between the alarm bark – a long-drawn *baaah!, baaah!*, often accompanied by stamping, the erection of the white target, and a bouncing run off. Nothing to be done – you have either been spotted or winded. Even then, not all the other deer round about will necessarily take notice of it.

If the bark is the aggressive *boh!, boh!*, then there is a chance of improving the situation. Stand still, and the beast may show himself as he circles to discover what he has glimpsed or heard, usually circling to get downwind, when all is lost unless your adversary is completely daft or steamed up with the rut. This is a situation where unobtrusive clothing, including gloves and even a face veil give an advantage, as the buck knows where you are, even if he is uncertain whether you are a rival or an enemy.

The other thing is to reply with as near to a similar bark (but slightly higher in pitch) as you can manage. This takes practice, preferably not in a public place! There is just a chance that a duet will commence, with a thin chance of your seeing him before he sees you. If you are with somebody, there is a great risk of laughing, or being laughed at – but it sometimes works!

I can't find out if it is legal to stalk deer on a Sunday. Nobody I have phoned gives a straight answer. Can you help?

There should be no question about this: you can shoot deer on a Sunday, assuming that otherwise you have the right. The Game Act 1831 lays down that it is an offence for any person in England and Wales to kill or take any *game* on a Sunday or Christmas Day. The misunderstanding arises because at that time deer were not considered game, and were not included in the definition. However, by the time of the passing of the Game Licences Act in 1860, deer were included. Thus the anomaly exists that you need a Game Licence to stalk deer at any time while there is no restriction on Sunday shooting. Exceptions modify this to the extent that a Game Licence is probably only needed to stalk on 'unenclosed ground' but for the nominal cost of the annual licence you are well advised to have one anyway and avoid any arguments.

The position in Scotland is different in that there are no legal restrictions on shooting on Sundays, but there is a strong tradition that one should not do so. In fact all stalkers should be considerate for local feelings on this subject anywhere in the country. Sunday is a day set apart by many people on religious grounds and to others it is a day for quiet relaxation. Field sports are under the microscope these days and we all must do our utmost not to annoy others, or now everyone is terrorist-minded, give anyone cause for alarm either from loud gunshots or unnecessary displays of arms, clothing or dead game at any time but especially on Sunday.

You weren't very polite about a skull I sent you for measuring. The thing is that I only have short weekends for stalking, and the keeper deals with my heads. He maintains that the best thing is to leave them in the rain until the skull is clean, but as you say, this does leave them a bit brown. Is there some way I can bleach them?

Incidentally what is the best way of mounting them on a shield?

I would hate to be lacking in good manners, but not only was the skull brown, but exposure to the elements has taken the natural colour out of the antlers. It's a pity with a trophy which could well have looked well, a pleasant reminder of a good stalk.

There isn't much to do with that skull unless you paint it with white matt emulsion. Any attempt to use bleach just etches the bone away and leaves a mess.

When you next get a buck, cut the head off as soon as possible after shooting and put it quickly in a bucket of cold water which soaks any blood out of the nasal cavities. Then it doesn't take long to boil up a saucepan (not aluminium) with a tablespoonful of washing soda in the water while you skin the head roughly and give the skull twenty minutes' or so boiling, keeping the antlers clear. Most keepers have a pressure washer, and it wouldn't be asking him too much to jet off the cooked flesh with that. It's the quickest method and quite effective. This will ensure that the bone is reasonably white. Then he, or you, can cover the bone with a thin layer of cotton wool and soak it in domestic strength hydrogen peroxide overnight. Then you will have a trophy to be proud of.

I don't like to see the heads of screws spoiling the frontal bone. There is a good anchorage for a screw from behind, between the eye sockets. You can buy shields with fairly complicated fixing devices, but a simple wood-screw does the trick very well. In a few months it will need tightening as the skull shrinks slightly. Don't fill the skull cavity with plaster if you intend to have the head measured later on.

Aspects of Stalking

My European stalking tenants do not seem to have a bit of consideration for the deer. They shoot them anyhow, just to get a trophy. When I complain, they say that they are paying a good rent, so why should I worry. Besides the loss of saleable venison, I do care. Do I have to grin and bear it?

No, you don't. The demand for woodland stalking is high despite the strong pound, and there are plenty of European sportsmen who care just as much as we do about the way game is shot. In fact many are more careful about the treatment of shot game than is usual here. There should be a clause in the tenancy agreement about sportsmanlike behaviour, if nothing stronger. If the offender is a guest of the tenant; a quiet word saying that he is not welcome another time is enough. If the offence continues after a couple of warnings, then a new tenant should be found as soon as possible. Such behaviour does the good name of shooting generally no good at all and the mud will stick if you do nothing about it.

I have a few paying guests each year for roe stalking. They always want to take their trophies home, so how do I get a quick assessment on medal status so that I can charge them fairly?

Except for really big heads it is very much better to avoid the CIC formula for medals and charge on a basis of skull weight twenty-four hours after boiling-out. Besides anything, it avoids arguments afterwards! Start at 250 or 300 grammes and go up in 50 gramme steps to 500. At that, the head will either be gold or silver, and it's worth getting it properly assessed, even if this means posting the trophy on to your client afterwards. It isn't going to happen that often!

It is terribly important to state your terms and conditions as clearly as possible, and get all clients to sign and return a copy with their deposit. You will find some ideas in my book *Trees & Deer* (Batsford).

So far as current prices are concerned, much depends on the standard of sport offered, and where it is. If you are a genuine professional stalker, then it would be helpful to apply to join the UK Association of Professional Deer Managers, so that you can exchange ideas with others in the same field.

I am starting to take visitors out stalking in association with a local sporting agent. In the woods one can't walk two abreast, so should I go in front or behind the client?

This is a knotty one! If you come behind the client and you see a deer first (which is likely) he will go blundering on and nothing short of a shout will stop him. On the other hand if you go in front to get over that difficulty, you don't know where the muzzle of his rifle is pointing, or if he

99

remembered to put the safety catch on. That is an uncomfortable feeling. I prefer to see what's going on, even if one temporarily loses contact with a client occasionally. It is worth telling him before the stalk that you will say 'Stop' at the critical moment. That's less likely to scare a deer than hissing or whistling.

Typical Questions on the Rut and Calling

*W*hen does the roe rut really start? I have seen serious chases in May this year, and two bucks came to the call on 5 July. Is this exceptional?

Rutting activity does vary greatly, not only from year to year, but from one area to another. I think you can disregard the chasing in May which is probably showing a buck's interest in the changed scent of a newly-fawned doe. Later in the summer the start of rutting depends on the presence of a doe in season. The pheromones she releases will excite bucks in the area around her while farther away nothing may be going on elsewhere. The earliest I have called a buck is 4 July; the latest 12 September.

I found what I think is a 'roe ring' last September. It was a more or less circular track in some old rough grass. Are the deer likely to use it again next summer? Why do they do it?

Roe rings are, as you say, narrow paths trodden by buck and doe in July and August, at the time of the rut. They can be circular, round some object like a bush, figure-of-eight, or quite irregular in shape. Their purpose is obviously part of the courting process, though does with their fawns have also been seen to use them.

In some places roe rings have been known to be used in successive years. In *British Deer and their Horns* J G Millais wrote of roe rings at Cawdor in Scotland which he thought had been in use for centuries. This may just have been that it was a place loved by roe where conditions did not change much over the years. I have not personally come across a ring which was used for more than one rut, and they are often in corn fields and other places where farm or woodland work changed things from year to year. It is certainly worth having a look towards the end of next July to see if they are being used again.

I haven't had much luck trying to call roe. Can you give me a few tips?

The main thing is not to start calling until you are certain there is a roe doe somewhere around who is in full rut. All the local bucks will be on their toes.

Best weather: hot and thundery, or warm and damp. Worst: cold or windy. It is often better to delay calling operations until late morning, especially after moonshiny nights because the roe will have been active in the small hours and take a snooze round dawn before the next romp. At all times remember that people may be about and may be attracted to your calling.

I have bought a roe call and hope to try it this rut. The instructions are very precise about how many 'fieps' and so on, but it doesn't say what are the best places, or how long to go on trying.

Roe calling is an art, not a science! The best places tend to be where you know a suitable buck has his territory and where you can see him coming without either standing in the open like a traffic cop, or where he has to come completely out of cover.

There are three basic noises you can use: the squeak of a roe kid, which should bring the mother hopefully followed by the buck. Then there is the similar but lower squeak which a doe emits when she is trying to attract a buck to her. Lastly there is a panic call, loud and high but ending lower, which may indicate a love chase in progress, attracting any other buck nearby.

The most phenomenally effective caller I ever met was a Dr Bertoti from Hungary, whom some older stalkers may remember. He used all three calls in that order, each one repeated ten or twenty times, then an interval of, say, five minutes before repeating it; another interval and he would change to the next type of call, finishing up with the loudest. Then a long wait before moving to another location. Bucks responding may take a considerable time to arrive, so it pays to be patient.

After breakfast to after lunch seem to be the likeliest times.

When I am out calling roe, or trying to, I am never clear about standing up (for visibility), sitting down (for camouflage) or sitting in a high seat. Someone told me the last idea won't work, and certainly it hasn't for me!

It isn't any good calling a buck and then not being able to see him! The only time I have needed to sit down is in coppice or similar scrub with a heavily-marked browse line so that one needs to be able to see below without moving. Otherwise in woodland it is better to stand to get all-around vision, remembering that a buck may circle to get the wind. Break your silhouette by standing up against a tree, and use gloves and a face mask. Camouflage clothes do help in this case because the beast knows exactly where you are, but minimum movement is the key, so keep your call on a string round your neck so that you don't have to fish about in a pocket to find it for that last encouraging toot!

I will get some stalking during the roe rut in July and hope to do some calling. I've planned to take time off about 20 July for a week. Is this about right, or should it be later?

A lot depends on the weather. Hot and thundery weather can bring the rut on early, but if it's cold you won't see any activity then. One can never depend on it. Normally rutting activity can start about 20 July or so, but the peak of activity is often well into August, say about the 7th. Calling tends to be more successful when activity has really hotted up, so if you can, put off your holiday until the end of the month.

What is the best roe call to get, so that I can be sure of pulling in some bucks? I have tried lots, and haven't so far had any luck.

Lots of stalkers these days are very successful with calling roe, and they use all sorts of different calls. How and when you do it is far more important than what whistle you use. There are some basic rules:

First, don't try calling until it is quite obvious that the rut is in full swing. Occasionally deer will come to a call outside the rut, but unless you are experienced enough to try sophisticated variations, amateur and premature attempts just educate the local bucks and make them ultra suspicious.

Second, know your buck territories! Calling is more likely to succeed if you are trying to tempt a territorial buck on his own ground. The exception to this is where you see a roe out in the fields and can get between him and his territory. It will be natural to him to go home if he is made to think something interesting is going on there.

Third, and without doubt the most important – don't be in a hurry. Books and magazines are full of accounts of bucks 'charging out of the bushes' and so on. Yes, one may do, but responding to a call may be a very leisurely business, so much so that when a buck does appear, it looks as if he is just there by chance. Don't believe it! After calling, a wait of ten or fifteen minutes in silence (which seems a very long time) can be surprisingly productive.

A lot of calls are pitched rather high and make a squeak similar to that of a kid calling for mum. This may bring the doe hurrying up, and possibly a buck after her. To imitate a doe in season, the squeak is lower and more hoarse. You can choose between calls that are adjustable to allow for this (such as the Hubertus) or fixed tone types which usually come in sets, like the Faulhaber. Most are blown. The Buttolo has a rubber bulb instead. It can be very effective, specially at long range, but all of them will work. It's the piano-player who produces the music!

I have read your books and those of Mr Whitehead, but do not find any mention of roe calling using straw. Every year I am successful in calling roe deer with a call made of rye straw. It is very easy to make – you only need a mature rye straw and a sharp knife to cut a reed in the middle of the straw. I learned about this rye call from an old Czech stalker. To use it you insert the straw joint [node] into your mouth, press lips round the straw and blow lightly. Is this not known in England?

There is always something to learn in the roe stalking business! The technique of calling using a beech leaf is generally known here, though most stalkers rely on some type of whistle. The leaf is stretched between the fingers as children do with a blade of grass. A single leaf only lasts for a few calls and one needs a supply of suitable leaves, preferably handed over the stalker's shoulder as I have seen it demonstrated, by an attractive attendant. Many years ago, one of my German clients did show me the trick with straw (I think he used wheat), making a slit about half an inch (1cm) long just above a node. One needs a very sharp, slim knife, craft knife or razor blade.

The end you put in your mouth has a node to seal it. The slit faces towards the node and the whole call is about two inches (5cm) long. Hold the end in your lips, not with the fingers.

Rye straw calls are very mellow, and can produce every tone from fawn to buck depending on the length of the slit. A little experimentation should produce good results by next rut!

3 RIFLES AND OTHER EQUIPMENT

Rifles and Questions About Them

My introduction to deer stalking came when one of the local farmers whose rabbits I was harrying said 'If you can get a deer, we'll share the venison!' In those days roe in East Devon were nearly as rare as hen's teeth, but the thought of Big Game was enthralling! Thus the roe bug bit me and I have never recovered. My .22 rimfire was obviously inadequate, but the great day came when I bought a Winchester Hi-sidewall rifle for the .22 Hornet. What to me were long, exciting, powerful brass cartridges are now illegal for deer as too feeble, but I killed my first roe with it and quite a few more.

I found both stock and fore-end flimsy, so re-stocked it with a fine bit of weathered oak from a field gate. You have never seen such a Monte-Carlo stock! Inletting was a much more difficult job than anyone could think, and I was proud of the awful thing. I sold it, restored to its original state, and got one of the early and excellent BSA Hunter short bolt-action rifles. Again in .22 Hornet because although they were chambering them in the much more desirable .222 for export, one could not get the ammunition. No doubt the Hornet needed care in choosing the range and point of aim, but looking back over the records, the kill-to-cartridge ratio was just as good as I achieved later with the .243. One failure point was that a shot in the shoulder ball-joint would stop the 50-grain bullet, the beast going off with a broken leg. Most often a chest shot would kill on the spot with the bullet lodged in the skin on the far side.

1963 not only brought the first Deer Act, which banned all .22 calibre weapons – but marriage. My wedding present from my new wife was a new BSA short-action in .243 calibre, the smallest allowed under the new law. I used it through most of my subsequent professional career. Goodness knows how many deer it accounted for, but in the end it wore out rather dramatically stalking stags in the Highlands. One day it was reasonably accurate – the next it was throwing bullets sideways. You could see the profile of each bullet on the target. When I had it checked, there was serious erosion at the throat and muzzle. The rifling on those barrels was cut into the steel. Modern ones are hammered and last much longer. Maybe it fired five thousand rounds, I don't know, but I had certainly made full use of my wedding present.

I have never been one of those stalkers with a cupboard full of rifles. Mostly, I suppose because I couldn't afford it, but also because once I have found a weapon to suit the job I prefer to stick to it. Over the years I have had the chance to try a big variety of calibres from .416 Rigby downwards, some briefly, others for long-term testing. As a second rifle, mainly for the bigger species, I acquired a Parker-Hale long-action in .30-06 calibre which was a wonderfully reliable friend, rarely losing its zero and handling a variety of bullet weights. I mostly used 130-grain loads for all but elk and boar, and 100-grain in the .243 BSA. When this latter wore out, I turned to the old-fashioned 7mm × 57 (.275) using 140 grain custom handloads. There are plenty of more modern calibres available, but my advice is to select something of minimum recoil (a combination of rifle weight in balance with the power of the cartridge) because it is easier to shoot straight if you aren't hanging on for grim death or flinching from the fierce set-back of some supposedly super magnum. Roe stalking is not, or shouldn't be, a matter of long shots. If the .22 centrefires were legal again in England, I would look seriously at something like the .223 unless bigger deer such as fallow were on the menu. Then, one might think about the .308 Winchester. There are many newer cartridges on offer now, but choosing a popular type ensures that you can always get cartridges without trouble.

Zeroing

'Get as close as you can – and then ten yards closer!' is a principle which we all admire but sometimes stretch in the field when the stops are out and you haven't got a trainee with you. So what one wants is a reasonably flat-shooting round, an accurate rifle and a range, formal or otherwise, where you can not only get the sights and bullet to coincide at a given distance, but to reassure yourself from time to time that all is still well.

In the case of chest shots, the vital target on a roe is around 10cm (4 inches). The average range in woodland is less than 100 metres. Even in fields, a roe at more than 150 metres is a very small target indeed and a shot at this range should only be attempted by experienced and confident stalkers. Modern deer cartridges if zeroed spot-on at 150 metres will be 2 to 4cm high at 100, and this will ensure that any shot within reasonable range will not need any allowance to keep inside the 10cm circle, given steady shooting.

Study of the appropriate ballistic tables gives you good information on bullet drop over a given range beyond this. Nevertheless, if there is the chance of using a range which allows practice at two to three hundred metres – try it: usually it is a humbling experience, and one which puts the 500 yard hit-'em-every-time boasters in proper context. You may also discover that manufacturers tend to publish figures based on longer barrel lengths than we commonly use, even if they are not responding to commercial pressures by a degree of optimism in their data. With a shorter barrel the drop at given ranges is materially increased. Nothing takes the place of careful zeroing.

Some nations pride themselves on their ability to take long shots successfully. I think especially of Alpine jägers who prefer a 350 metre chance at a chamois as more sporting, just as pheasant shooters in this country pride themselves on their ability of bring down 40-yard rocketers. One reads of fantastic shots attempted by some American sporting writers. I dare say some are there or thereabouts but maybe a tape measure is rarely to hand and the kills-to-cartridges statistics are conveniently omitted.

Questions on Rifles and Zeroing

I'm on a limited budget, but want to start woodland stalking. I have had the chance to buy a friend's rifle, but he is a professional stalker. How do I know if it's all right?

To start with, for Goodness' sake don't get tangled up with any beaten-up old gaspipe. It has probably had thousands of rounds through it and maybe a bramble poked up the bore once a year as maintenance. It may even have had a bit sawn off the muzzle, cutting away worn rifling at that critical point. Yes, I know that professional stalkers mostly take enormous care of their rifles, but they are not likely to part with one of those! If you do get tempted, negotiate on the strict understanding that it will be fully vetted by a competent riflesmith (and that does not necessarily include every High Street vendor of airgun slugs). Before and after the First War the .275 was popular for hill stalking, and very large numbers were turned out, especially by John Rigby the celebrated gunmakers. They were well-made and are still offered on the second-hand market. It would be an elementary precaution to check the serial number and discover the year of manufacture. A recent model should be something to cherish, but early weapons look back to the days of corrosive primers, and may be neglected-out or even shot-out. Rifles with scope sights were regarded then as cads' guns and totally unsporting, so those old weapons have low combs designed for open sights. If a scope sight is fitted, as it must be these days, the shooter has to crane his head into an uncomfortable position to allow for the increased height of the line of sight. Put up a modern rifle and your natural head position should line up eye and scope at the first intention. If it doesn't – look for a different one!

For a first stalking rifle go for a bolt action, nothing else. American literature is full of weapon types which are unfamiliar, or even illegal under recent legislation. The Wild West was won with tube-magazine, lever-action Winchesters so the tradition lingers over there, and many variants on the theme are still offered; lever, trombone and auto-loader. However, for simplicity and accuracy there is nothing to beat a bolt-action rifle for the stalker. Even if you are left-handed, there is a good choice of models with the bolt handle reversed. The trigger should have a single pull with a creep-free let-off around 2½lb. Beware of Continental rifles with two triggers. The rear one 'sets' the front one, which then has an extremely light let-off. If you are not completely familiar with the mechanism they can be dangerous.

Single-shot rifles are attractive to look at and handle, but stalking often involves a quick follow-up shot, either to stop a wounded animal before it gets away, or to take a second chance in the moment of surprise before the scene dissolves. Box magazines give a rapid second shot if necessary, and they are easy to check as unloaded. Some are conveniently removable; some can only be unloaded by working the bolt, which is tedious. A swinging floor plate is a reasonable compromise.

If you intend to travel with your rifle in anything but a car, it is worth considering a take-down rifle. The long case needed for a one-piece is awkward and eye-catching as well as ankle-catching on an airport trolley, don't I know it! There was always a doubt about loss of zero when taking any rifle down and reassembling it, but the two designed for the purpose that I tested, the Sauer and Blaser were remarkably consistent. They have an additional advantage of having alternative barrels for different calibres, but maybe we are getting beyond the beginner's stage at that point. Inevitably they are expensive.

Weight is important. First of all you are going to carry the thing about on your shoulder for long hours. Second, the standard of accuracy needed for woodland stalking, though high, is not the same as that required by target shooters. Of course you need a rifle which shoots consistently without loss of zero, and certainly should give groups of an inch or less, but that does not mean that a heavy-barrel model is right for the purpose. As against these two points, beware of a delightfully light, easy-handling weapon, especially if it is chambered for one of the more powerful cartridges. The recoil will kill your pleasure in shooting, and may instil a set of flinches which are terribly hard to eliminate and which completely ruin your accuracy. The recoil energy of a .30-06, for example, is around 20ft/lb (as against 3.5 for the .222,

9 for the .243 and 65 for the .458 Winchester elephant rifle). Provided the stock is fully bedded into your shoulder the shove of recoil is absorbed by your body. The heavier the rifle for its calibre, the slower that shove. A very lightweight deer rifle recoils at speed, and especially if the stock is slightly short, the result is something similar to a hammer blow on your collarbone.

A lot of the variation in zero comes from movement between the wood-work and the barrel. Wood, no matter how well seasoned, tends to warp according to variations in humidity. Think of this when your rifle goes out into the warm rain of a July evening after months of dry seclusion in its gun safe! There are two ways out of this problem: relieve the barrel, so that there is a complete gap between barrel and fore-end, or abandon the thought of a finely-figured, lovingly-cherished piece of walnut and get a plastic stock. Relieved barrels have to be treated carefully; the channel tends to get jammed with pine needles and so on which completely nullifies the whole idea. Anyone with large hands needs to be careful, too, about gripping barrel and fore-end when taking aim; squeezing them together has disastrous effects on where the bullet actually goes. Despite the love which we all feel for an attractive looking rifle, I would go for a plastic job and know, in a business where there are plenty enough of them, that one variable in accurate shooting had been eliminated.

I only get a very few days' stalking in the year and don't have too much confidence in my shooting as a result. Can you make any suggestions?

What we should all do is to practise. I don't mean trying to crawl from one side of the lawn to the other without once lifting your backside – the neighbours might wonder, but there are plenty of ways in which you can polish up the technique so that when the chance does come to stalk deer, the possibilities of success are definitely improved.

A significant number of stalkers do make use of the range days which are regularly organised by BDS branches. There is nothing better for one's self-confidence than seeing a decent group printed in the bull. Quite apart from range work which builds up familiarity with your rifle, you know when the chance at a buck comes along soon after a zeroing and practice session that the rifle is spot on, and all that is needed is a little care in aiming, holding and let-off. Knowing this, there is much less tendency to aim at the middle and hope, which is what most people do if confidence is lacking.

I know that stalkers like to do things alone. Shooting on a range is a self-conscious business and one has a great reluctance to do badly in public. There always seems to be one of those know-alls monopolising the firing point, parading their enormous knowledge of ballistics to all and sundry. The jargon flies and it is all very daunting to the owner of one old smokepole. However, sooner or later the Great Expert will say that he never misses a deer and after that you can have a quiet giggle and take no further notice of the ballistic hot air machine.

I was told about one such that he was a 'Black Hat' man – that is to say that if you have a black hat, he's got one that is blacker! To the joy of that particular party of shooters, the man in question who claimed he could take a Kalashnikov to pieces in his sleep, subsequently failed his shooting test. Deep satisfaction was felt all round.

It was Francis Sell, that wise hunter of white-tails, who proposed, years ago, that the dedicated deer hunter should have an understudy for his deer rifle – a sub-calibre weapon, but as near as possible to it in handling qualities, design, sights and ballistics. With the short American deer-hunting season, there just is not the opportunity to sharpen up the many skills needed to bag a buck without the excellent practice which is offered by small-game stalking.

'Much off-season shooting is necessary if one is to develop the capacity for consistent hits on the big-game target . . . this means that the required shooting skill must come from the use of an understudy rifle, used in off-season shooting on targets other than deer.

'The types of firing to be done with the understudy rifle are those which will be required in deer territory – snapshooting, as is done in heavy cover, and more deliberate fire at longer ranges.'

In the free and easy arms market in which he lived, his suggestions were for matching each deer cartridge with one of the 'varmint' rounds; in lever action rifles, the .218 Bee with the .348, in bolt actions, the .22 Hornet with the .30-06 and so on. The Firearms Act makes our choice much more circumscribed but, depending on the sporting opportunities on offer, a world of extra stalking can open up.

Fox control demands considerable skill and precision with the rifle. Although stalking rifles are used at times, something of less report is likely to be more acceptable in relatively settled countryside. Ranges tend to be as long as with deer stalking, so a flat-shooting cartridge such as the .22-250 is effective and parallels such hardy favourites as the .270. The .222 shares trajectory with the .308 (146 grain).

Most of us will have to be content with a good-class .22 rimfire in bolt action for use against rabbits and, in fact, this is superb sport in its own right. Exactly the same considerations apply to getting to within fifty yards of a wary rabbit as to stalking a roe to twice the distance. Crawling, which might be thought eccentric on the front lawn, is often necessary to get within range. All the considerations of safety apply to the .22 (which has a bad reputation for ricochet) as to any deer rifle. Spying, thinking about the wind, making the best use of cover and avoiding noise all count with an educated rabbit, and you will soon learn to improve your shooting technique from gateposts and other informal positions.

In the end, there is nothing more revealing than a few shots with a .22 to show if you have developed a flinch! Try it.

What is your impression of the 6.5mm × 55 cartridge for stalking in Southern England?

This calibre has been a favourite in Scandinavia for many years, and is even legal in Sweden for use against elk. Factory loads use a 139 grain bullet at around 2700ft/sec and with muzzle energy of 2280ft/lbs These figures are very similar to those of the 7mm × 57 (.275 Rigby). Although I have not used one myself, I know several stalkers who are very satisfied with the 6.5 for everything up to reds. Despite the Swedish sanction, I would prefer something heavier if you have any plans to try for a big woodland stag, especially in the rut.

I have an old Parker-Hale .308 which I am fond of, but it has a dreadful, draggy trigger pull. It is the sort with a push-forward set trigger. I had it re-barrelled, so is it worth fitting with a new trigger?

I have had a similar Parker-Hale in .30-06 for many years and it has been the all-time reliable old hack, rarely needing anything done to the zero. The trigger is the same sort as yours, which I adjusted to a glass-crisp pull of 2¾lb. I only used the set trigger for zeroing, but it, too, could be adjusted not to be too explosive, but handy for that purpose, or a very deliberate shot off the bipod.

I would suggest, especially as you have already spent money on a new barrel and are fond of it, to take it to a competent riflesmith (not all gunsmiths come into that category) and get him to check the trigger mechanism. It may only need adjusting, or there may be some corrosion or other trouble, so it's not something to tackle yourself. Preferably be there when he tunes it to the let-off you like. After that, the rifle will need the zero checking, as the action will have been taken out of the woodwork and may need a shot or two to get everything back in place, and then after checking the tightness of the tang and action screws, a thorough confidence-building session on the target is essential.

If there is a fundamental fault with the trigger, you can then make a decision about fitting a new one, but somehow I think it won't be necessary.

Like you, I use a .30-06. I have to take roe at long range, so would like advice on a suitable bullets, also for red deer.

Without going too small in weight for such a large calibre when you may get either trouble with the bullet breaking up too readily, or puffing off in a modest wind, I have used a lot of 130 soft points which are flat-shooting and reliable. For reds I would go up to 150-grain, especially for stags in the rut. This means a change (and re-zeroing) when you go north for stags. If you need to compromise, some tests to find an all-rounder might be advisable as some of the 150-grain bullets are rather hard for roe and may penetrate without expanding.

I have had a few woodland stalking outings with a professional, borrowing his rifle and now I want to get going on my own. The trouble is I'm left-handed, so I find a bolt-action very awkward. Should I go for an American-type lever-action rifle, or can one get left-handed bolt-actioned rifles?

It's just as well to ask at this stage, and you might benefit a lot from one of the training courses which are available from The British Deer Society or BASC where you can talk to a qualified instructor about it before you commit yourself. I'm cack-handed myself, so I can sympathise! One thing is: how strongly left-handed you are (it varies between individuals) and whether your left eye is master. They don't necessarily go together.

The other thing is – do you intend to take up shotgun shooting as well, at any time in the future? Left-hand bolt action rifles are readily available, but if you decide to go for one of these, shooting off the left shoulder, then any shotgun you use has to be made or adapted to suit. Stocks can be bent, but it all takes time and money, otherwise your choice is restricted by what left-handed guns you can find.

If you aren't strongly left-handed, or if your right eye is the master, it may be worth persisting and learn to shoot off your right shoulder so that you can use any reasonably standard rifle or gun.

In any case, it's quite useful to train yourself to shoot a rifle off either shoulder. You may find yourself hiding behind a tree where taking a shot off your usual shoulder would reveal yourself to the quarry, while one off the other could be brought off without giving the game away. I shot my very first buck off my wrong shoulder because I had been lying down just right for a downhill shot, only the buck was watching me from above!

I do a lot of my stalking in semi-suburbia. Would a silencer be a good idea on my rifle? I gather one cannot eliminate the crack of a high-speed bullet.

There are a number of advantages in fitting a silencer, or more correctly sound moderator. The noise is very much reduced, though there is still, as you suggest, a crack. From the point of view of people living close or working in the vicinity, the stalker's activities are less obtrusive which is important these days. There may be nervous domestic livestock nearby which one is anxious not to frighten. In addition, if one needs to take more than one deer out of a group, as is often the case with does, the survivors of the first shot react very much less and may have difficulty in locating the source of the bang. Provided the sound moderator is fitted by a competent riflesmith and the manufacturer's instructions about maintenance are followed, accuracy is not affected.

The main snags are added weight and the alteration in the balance and handling of your rifle. A long-barrelled weapon might benefit from judicious shortening, always following your riflesmith's advice. The other point is the loss of its looks, which anyone is bound to feel who looks on his rifle as a work of art wedded to utility. Maybe we sacrificed them long ago when scope sights started to be accepted as standard. Only the Lloyd rifle made any attempt to integrate rifle and scope into one design. When push comes to shove, one's rifle is primarily a tool which should be as efficient as modern technology can make it. Under the conditions you describe, any artistic reservations on design should give way to serving the stalker to the utmost in the task he has to perform.

I notice when I take shooting guests down to the range 'to try their rifles' (but mainly to inform the professional stalker as to their abilities!) that many of them flinch. Some even shut their eyes when they pull the trigger. How can one tactfully get over this problem?

I developed a flinch some years ago when a series of primers blew back and it has been hard to cure. The only way is to convince the flincher of his fault, of which he may be entirely unaware. One way is to hand him his rifle on the range unloaded. The ensuing wave of the barrel when he pulls without a round in the chamber will be all too clear to everyone. If he is not prepared to take remedial action, all you can do is only to offer him shots from a high seat or at very close range. The proper way of going about it is to go back to the .22 rimfire, preferably using short ammunition with its negligible noise and recoil, and bang away until the habitual flinch is once again under control. It may take several sessions and several boxes of cartridges! Anyone who recognises the symptoms in himself would be well advised to review his choice of rifle. There's no need to use 'too much gun' for roe deer – more important to be sure of placing the bullet where it will do most good. Recoil not only concerns the chosen cartridge, though that of course is a prime cause. A short or poor-fitting stock may be doing the mischief, or that classic mistake of choosing a rifle in the showroom 'because it is so delightfully light to carry'. I knew a beautiful little Mauser in 7 × 57 which kicked like seven mules. The alternative if you aren't fussy about appearances, is to fit a sound moderator.

Arrogance and the Rifle Shooter

Like driving a car, rifle shooting is one of those macho things that no chap can admit to doing badly and keep his self-respect. There are car accidents, lots of them unfortunately, and a good many bucks arrive at the game dealer's looking like a colander. We can't blame women drivers for them!

When one looks at a target it's easy to 'tut-tut' over one or two shots which have slipped an inch outside the magic circle and start fiddling with the adjustments. Unless the whole group is as tight as ever but off centre, the only adjustment you need to make is to your own shooting position, trigger press, follow-through, or hangover.

Fatigue, mental or physical, can be disastrous: some of the worst shooting I have ever seen has been from good stalkers fresh (if that's the right word) from a hectic week at the office. Some of the most deplorable groups I have shot myself (and I consider myself pretty expert at producing them) have been made checking the rifle after a long car journey, or before trying to slip a bit of stalking into a slot between busy periods.

At a beginner's course I was trying to explain just how steady you have to hold the rifle to get the shots on the target. 'Imagine your rifle barrel is a stick a hundred yards long, and you are trying to hold the far end steady on the bull. Not too easy, especially in this wind! However, there's no magic about it – unless the sights are steady on the centre of the bull, there isn't a hope in Hell. If you can't do it lying down with a bag under your left hand, and with all the time in the world, how do you think you are going to hit a buck under the stress of excitement, with the crosshairs swinging on and off his entire body?'

Yet people who should know better still say 'I'm no good at a target, but give me a buck – and I'll kill it!'

Rubbish. All that is happening is that shooting on a target shows up what rotten shots they are, and a buck is bigger – if you count in the paunch and maybe the haunches too.

We are in a technological age and so tend to have an exaggerated confidence in our sophisticated gadgetry. A good scope allows us to see the critical spot we want to hit; the rifle, we know is capable of shooting to 1.5 minutes of angle, so if the shot doesn't land where it ought to have done it must be a Friday scope, or the barrel got bent coming up the motorway.

A generally accepted standard is to be able to put three shots at a hundred yards range within a pre-drawn four inch (10cm) bull. In a test the candidate is lying on a proper firing point and may use his rucksack or other normal equipment as a support. A piece of cake! Not so, apparently. This is the part of a test day where most failures crop up. Where is all that technology now? The rifle's pinpoint accuracy? The four hundred quid scope? The truth is that even under near-ideal conditions the human factor is the most potent, and the most likely to fail. A lot of people shy away from going for their competence tests because, as a few admit, they don't want to look foolish. The macho thing again. Let's go one deeper: a significant number know in their heart of hearts that their shooting isn't good enough to match up even to that comparatively modest standard. So they go on stalking in the same old way, mutilating the quarry they profess to love, even in some cases continuing to instruct new stalkers themselves. Can you beat that for arrogance?

In my book, the real macho types will go for perfection and not be content until, through coaching and endless practice on the range, they really can put the bullet pretty near the given spot, pretty nearly every time. It takes courage to admit your shortcomings and then do something about them. In my days as a professional stalker the rifle was on my shoulder every day. Even then, I had a range session at least once a month and shot two or three rounds zeroing for each one fired at deer. Constant shooting gave one easy familiarity with the weapon and confidence when taking a shot. It was all too obvious when lack of sleep took spots off that ability. There was another devil lurking in the background – over-confidence. I suppose everyone suffers to some extent; a long series of successful shots and one starts to believe that you are first cousin to Buffalo Bill. Gradually, the care you take with each shot starts to slide; you take longer and longer shots, or chancy ones in the half light, until there's the devil to pay, and a wounded deer to find – or lose.

Nearly every year it hit me, usually towards the end of the doe season. Without warning I couldn't seem to hit a barn door. Tests at a target were okay, rifle still spot on, but shot after shot a complete disaster. No lack of sleep to blame at that time of year; nothing and nobody to blame but myself. In the end I recognised the problem and took steps to set it right. The cure with me seemed to be to change rifles (being lucky enough to have two) shake myself mentally, have a session on the range and then take a good deal of care over the next few shots at deer.

Towards the end of my stalking career, when I shot a great deal less (and enjoyed each stalk a good deal more in consequence) and finding myself surprisingly old, it was no good taking that old self-confidence out with me stalking. One had to be extremely careful over every separate shot, easy or not. I needed more range work, not only for the essential practice, but to support that confidence that the rifle is 'on' which makes one aim carefully, squeeze carefully, and hang on after the shot is gone – what they call follow-through – to stop that fateful relaxation which, in fact, coincides with the trigger release and makes a bad shot inevitable.

Lots of younger stalkers don't have the luck I did and have to snatch an outing when they can. Youth apart, how difficult it is to remember that, for an office worker, the cards are stacked against pinpoint shooting: end-of-the-week strain, excitement at an unusual and thrilling chance, lack of familiarity with the rifle, lack of practice.

It isn't only your macho image which suffers after a poor shot, it is probably a buck too.

Scopes and Questions About Them

Consistent zero in a stalking rifle is something we all dream about – and rarely achieve! There are so many variables: warping due to changes in humidity; faulty bedding; excessive headspace; poor ammunition; all pointing to the advantages of a really well-made rifle and ammunition to match, but how many other problems can actually be traced to that awkward tube we clip on top of our rifles, spoiling the balance of a beautiful weapon? Many of them, I suspect. Screws work loose, particularly on a newish rifle. Some removable mounts, even really expensive ones, can have enough lost movement to affect the day-to-day zero. On cheaper scopes the lenses may shoot loose and a combination of budget price and a variable-power model makes a potential disaster area. Many of us will recall the popularity of one make of scope from the Orient which was amazingly cheap and remarkably consistent – provided you were lucky enough to get one from the 'Monday' production. If it happened to be a 'Friday' scope – Oh Boy!

So younger stalkers with a limited budget are well advised to put most of it into a good scope and mounts before thinking about the smoke-pole to go underneath. Today's mass-production rifles are wonderful value; the barrels are beautifully made and last a lifetime with reasonable care. Bench-rest accuracy does great things for the shooter's self-confidence, but in practical terms we have at least a four-inch (10cm) killing circle which gives some latitude at reasonable ranges. The main thing is to be able to pick up your target quickly; see it clearly under all conditions and place the reticle with confidence on a spot where the bullet will do most good.

I notice that quite a number of stalkers these days lumber themselves with heavy-barrel rifles, often surmounted by great bell-mouthed scopes with 56mm object lenses adding half a kilo or more to the weight they have to carry about. Are these really stalking rifles, or do these chaps spend more time lamping foxes? For sure I wouldn't have wanted to lug one of those cannons up the hill in Scotland even in my prime, or very far on the flat for that matter. I'd be too puffed to hold it straight. And why the vast scope? South of the Border we are strictly banned from shooting deer 'between the expiry of the first hour after sunset and the last hour before sunrise'. I would have thought that one should invest in a practical stalking set-up before launching out into such expensive specialist stuff, but then I'm probably old-fashioned.

The question of magnification needs thought. Until recently stalkers generally agreed that 4× allied to an object lens of about 40mm gave the best compromise for all-round use but in the last decade fashion has swung to 6×. What advantages does the extra power give? A bigger sight picture of the animal? Certainly it does that, but inevitably the field of view is reduced and any apparent shake is magnified in proportion. Better vision in poor light? Well, there we reach the realms of speculation. In technical terms increasing the power decreases the exit pupil (that is the light which can pass through the instrument and therefore its performance in bad light). The theoretical light gathering power is calculated as the square of the diameter of the scope's exit pupil. This in turn is arrived at by dividing the diameter of the objective by the magnification of the scope. So, for example, a 4×40 scope has an exit pupil of $[40 \div 4] = 10$. Light gathering power 100. A 6×40 scope has an exit pupil of $[40 \div 6] = 6.66$. Light gathering power 44.4. Some difference! However, there is another factor – the human eye. In youth and middle age the maximum dilation of the human pupil is about 7mm, and reduces with age, which is why our night vision slowly deteriorates. It is obvious that there is no advantage in having an exit pupil larger than that of the receiving eye and so the theoretical disadvantage of the higher power is cancelled out to some extent. Exit pupil readings larger than 8mm, therefore, offer no practical advantages and only increase the weight and cost of the scope.

Another factor in calculating what the eye actually sees is called twilight performance. There are complicated physiological processes involved in assessing this, but research has arrived at a formula based on the square root of the product of the diameter of the objective lens and the magnification. Thus for a 4×40 scope: twilight performance is 12.6, but for a 6×40 scope: 15.4. From this one assumes that the higher the magnification the better – completely the opposite of the previous theory! Naturally there is an answer which (as usual with anything to do with humanity) involves a compromise. Twilight performance is secondary to exit pupil diameter in that two conditions must first be met:

a. the diameter of the scope's exit pupil must not be larger than the pupil of the user's eye.
b. the scope's exit pupil must not be smaller than a certain lower limit which lies between 3 and 4mm.

Work it out for your own conditions – if you can! It certainly does look as if there are advantages for higher magnification in very poor light provided those two conditions are first met. But returning to my first point, as deer stalkers we are not only limited to the hours of daylight, but frequently have to walk substantial distances. Given reasonable luck we may not only have rifle, scope and binoculars to lug around – but a buck as well! Why add extra weight for some purely theoretical advantage?

Variable-power Scopes

With the popularity of vari-power scopes increasing as they become more reliable (if not less expensive!), some of the shots which they tempt one to make, rightly or wrongly, bring up one or two interesting queries.

Taking my own experience with an extra-low-power 1–2.5× scope for a start, the wide field seemed to make shots at moving targets temptingly easy. On the whole, like the parson and sin, I am against them! One slight snag was that the end of the barrel, and the foresight, if fitted, could be made out as a blurred image in the lower part of the picture. Of course the image would disappear if the scope were not mounted low on the action, but for consistent shooting I am a firm believer in mounting a scope as low as possible so that one's cheek is thoroughly in contact with the stock. Craning the neck to peer through a high-mounted scope is not only uncomfortable but disastrous from the point of view of consistent shooting. Cant (tilting the rifle one way or the other) is a source of needless inaccuracy exaggerated by high-mounted scopes, but even worse, during the vogue for high, see-through scope mounts, few stocks were ever designed to bring the cheek far enough up to give a proper position. Once the supposed need to retain iron sights and to see them through the scope mounts had passed, the only bar to really low mounting was the throw of the bolt handle and in some designs the operation of the safety catch. These problems have long been overcome and one can bring the lower edge of the objective housing of the scope down to within a whisker of the barrel, the only possibility being the appearance of a shadowy barrel in the sight picture.

Personally, in practice I have never been conscious of an image of barrel or foresight when using one of these scopes, even at minimum magnification. My own rifle was not, in fact, fitted with open sights at all. Being long sighted I never could see much through open sights anyway! Incidentally, barrel reflections which can be particularly annoying when using open sights may also produce a degree of flare in the scope. Modern technology has eliminated a lot of the trouble one used to get trying to shoot at a close angle to the sun and provided one can see at all, the flare does not affect aiming accuracy.

Turning to the other end of the range scale, most users of the high-power variables will agree that they are tempted to take longer shots. When I used a big 3×–12×, when faced with a distant chance it was enticing to wind up the magnification and happily assume that the enlarged picture made it as easy to hit as it would have been at the apparently shortened range. It is easy to talk about self-discipline, but who except a stalker knows the mental tensions under which he labours just at the critical moment? Possibly the modern trend towards fixed 6× scopes is a working compromise. However, there are times when it's handy and justified to jack up the power, not least for zeroing, using the scope to spot the shots, saving that tedious walk down the range every time.

Just to put the long-range thing into perspective, here are some figures of apparent distances when an object is viewed through scopes of different magnification:

Actual Distance	200m	100m	50m
	——— Apparent distance ———		
1.25×	160	80	40
4.5×	44	22	11
6×	33	16	8
10×	20	10	5
12×	16	8	4

(Statistics by courtesy of Zeiss)

Of course one essential element in shooting straight, but only one, is to be able to see the target and the bit of it you want to hit. Any experienced stalker decides whether to shoot or not partly by an instinctive analysis of the sight picture – the angle the animal is standing; any twigs in the way; how much the reticle swings as a result of uncertain hold, wind, shortened breath and (let's face it) excitement. No doubt high power helps to give a clear sight picture although there is the danger that twigs and so on between rifle and target may be increasingly blurred. One tries that bit harder when the target looks terribly small in the sight picture. It makes one put extra care into the shot and acts as a telling reminder of the vagaries of bullet windage over long distance which can be very important particularly in the lighter calibres, in addition to the loss of accuracy from a variety of causes which are minimised in the old-fashioned short-range killing shot.

There is the system of post reticles where if the body of, say, a roe fits between the ends of the two horizontals it is at such a range, but if it fits between the upright and horizontal posts, it is at another. Fine, if you have that sort of deliberate shot and the animal stands conveniently broadside, but when vari-power scopes came along they had to make the reticle appear to enlarge with increased magnification to maintain the range-finding facility. To my mind, the reverse should be the case – the crosswire should seem to become finer as power is increased, not the reverse.

I'm thinking of getting a new scope sight for woodland stalking, and as many of my deer don't come out until very late in the evening, I've got my eye on one with an electric dot reticle. Have you any experience of these?

Illuminated dot reticles are very popular abroad for shooting wild boar at night but when I tried one it had some snags, not least when the battery ran out just at the wrong moment! One should remember that night shooting is not allowed in England and Wales.

I did carry out some fairly extensive experiments with an illuminated reticle some years ago. It is easy to assume that having the crosswire illuminated would get over that exasperating moment when you can still see the animal through the scope (maybe it is a wounded beast lying in deep shade when the light has really gone) but the lines of the reticle have disappeared. Visualise the position: you can see a vague shape through the scope but the reticle bars are now a vague silvery colour and the fine crosswires have disappeared altogether. Just the moment to turn on a button and get your red spot. What happens is that when the spot comes on you lose all that slowly-accumulated night vision and all you can see is the spot!

My conclusion at the end of the experiments was that the illuminated reticle offered no advantages over a normal scope, given fine quality lenses. As we did not at that time have wild boar in any quantity in this country, the specialised needs for either low-power scopes for drives or for heavy reticles and large lenses for moonlight-feeding boar did not enter into my research. We now have several expanding populations of boar in the UK, but so far the question of the legality of night shooting them has not been raised.

Gadgets, Good, Bad and Horrible

I like to think that stalking is not as gadget-ridden as, for example, fishing or sailing, but is that entirely fair? You have only to glance at one of those Continental catalogues one loves to browse through, avid and envious, to waver a bit.

I had a turn-out of my 'stalking drawer' where things get stored which aren't of immediate use, yet might be just the thing – sometime or other – but somehow never quite get needed. Some I've bought or have been given over the years by fellow enthusiasts, some are home-made: badly by me, or cleverly by others.

As an excuse for poking around gunshops I used to ask if they had any roe calls. Usually the answer was 'No', but by that time I was in, and could have a snoop. Occasionally one struck gold and a wonderful and varied collection of calls accumulated; the best of them are ready for use in an old tobacco pouch. One extremely comprehensive set reproducing all the different voices of roe was made for me by a very distinguished stalker in Germany. Those were the basis for the calls which I later made and marketed myself. Another which took my fancy was a disc-shaped combined job. Blow into one side it attracted roe, opposite it was a 'mousepipe' for foxes and in the centre a 'hare-sucker' which I never mastered. The excellent Buttolo, which has called many a buck, was an early present from that doyen of roe stalkers, Andrew de Nahlik.

A leather-worker introduced me to cleverly-rolled buttons which are sewn on the shoulders of one's stalking jacket to stop the rifle sling slipping off. I put one on and it was terribly efficient – so much so that the sling might have been glued to my shoulder when, with a buck watching suspiciously, I tried to get the rifle smoothly into action. A smaller one would probably be fine. Incidentally, I have experimented a lot over the years to find an ideal rifle sling which wouldn't slip, rattle, or come loose at one end so that the weapon clatters to the ground unless you sense disaster quickly enough to catch it. The best solution I ever found was to decide the best length for that rifle, and then buy from a saddler a rubber-covered rein. This could be cut to the right length with enough allowance to go through the swivels and be sewn on with silent leather thonging. They lasted for years until the non-slip bobbles wore off the rubber. Then I was tempted on a visit to Litt's by an elasticated job with a nice broad piece to spread the weight over one's shoulder. It still tends to slide over the ruck-sack strap.

Thinking about slinging things round your neck brings binoculars to mind. When I was groaning under the iron fingers of my chiropractor (who doesn't tell me to stop stalking because he does it too) he said 'Why did you go around for twenty years with four pounds of binoculars on a narrow strap round your neck?' (Crack! Crunch! Ow!) The offending glasses were a pair of navy-surplus 7×50s which did do permanent damage to my vertebrae. Not only are binoculars lighter nowadays, but one can – and should – get a broad, shaped strap to hang them from. I still favour a $7\times$ magnification for woodland work. They are quicker to use.

I can't think how anyone stalks roe without a rucksack, but some do, and many are the devices I've seen used to sling (or to use the archaic term *hurdle*) a roe carcass for transport. Unless the thing is well trussed-up, at each step you get a crippling blow on the backside from the antlers and after a mile or so anything of that weight over one shoulder becomes torture. I had a belt made up on an Austrian pattern which converted to the straps of a rucksack, with the buck representing the bag hanging from a ring between your shoulder-blades. It was a bit fussy to get right, and nobody explained what you did on the way home about keeping your trousers up. In any case you don't want to stray down a public path these days with streams of gore dripping down the back of your jacket – a discreet sack is better on many counts. Some thought needs to be given to Her at the House too.

My first rucksack was made up by a tent-maker in Exeter and was far too small, narrow and deep. Again, the straps were too meagre. Others followed, slowly getting better and bigger. One morning the top ring on a commer-cial roe sack opened up when I was carrying a heavy buck, and produced something of a music-hall situation; the shoulder straps stayed in place, of course, so sack and buck pivoted violently and emerged between my legs. Finally I had an excellent bag made by a Scottish saddler/stalker, but even then I asked him to modify the strap on the quick release side. One needs about six inches fixed to the bottom corner of the bag, then a toggle-and-loop attachment.

Trophy-preparation has its share of gadgets. One of the worst is the saw which comes with a head-cutting jig. I never did have one that cut any sense. When one of my very old friends came over from Germany he showed me his solution. He bought an electric DIY jigsaw and fitted it with a power hacksaw blade. It just zips through a skull. Why can't one think of such an obvious thing? You can now get a clamp which stops the antlers disappearing into the boiling water, to emerge all discoloured. That's as good as the patent peroxide bath I got from somewhere was bad, clever though the idea might have been. I never could get all the skull into it, and always finished with the beastly stuff fizzing all over everything.

Quite why I'm not sure, but as time went by the accessories I acquired tended to be those which help one to shoot straighter. Is it a greater sense of responsibility, or an increasingly quavering trigger-finger?

For stalking in very open farm land, a long model bipod permanently attached to the rifle does help. It wrecks the appearance and balance of the weapon, adds greatly to the weight, but does allow a very deliberate prone or sitting shot over the inevitable bumps in the ground, combine straw or whatever.

The Lead Balloon Award for accessories in my collection goes to a long rubber tube which I bought in Budapest because it would keep the rain out of the eyepiece of my scope. When I jammed my eye, artillery-fashion into its beautifully-cushioned contours there was no possibility of that typical eyebrow injury from the scope, but trying it on the range gave me a set of flinches which would have been more understandable with a .700 Express.

What I need now is the All-terrain Bath Chair (with rifle rack, loading gantry and mini-bar). I hope somebody is working on the design now.

Shooting Off a Stick

Whether they care to use one or not, I suppose most woodland stalkers accept that a stick is normal equipment and think no more about it. We have all sorts of elegant variations from amazing hazel thumb sticks to garden canes and telescopic jobs to go in the rucksack till needed. Normal nowadays, but fairly recent so far as general use in this country is concerned.

Although accustomed to the invaluable three-quarter-length cromach for Highland stalking, I first met the tall, sturdy bergstock on my prentice expedition for a *Gams* (chamois) in the Austrian Alps long ago. One jäger showed me how, by borrowing his stick and crossing it with mine, an even more certain shot could be made. Many of its obvious uses in the mountains to steady my faltering steps across or uphill or to act as a brake going down did not apply in low-ground stalking. However, in thick woodland almost every shot at roe is taken standing and at comparatively short range when the steadying effect of a full-length stick is immediately obvious. Some modifications were needed, particularly dispensing with the steel spike (having regard to the many flints which litter the ground in Dorset), and substituting a rubber ferrule. Also being on the tall side, a prolonged search was needed for a ramrod-straight hazel stem long enough to come up to my forehead. Nothing is more fatal to success than crouching in order to accommodate yourself to a tourist-length thumbstick!

When my early paying guests started to come, some were used to the advantages of a stick but others were unused to shooting standing, I provided sticks and coached them in the technicalities of being able to get a steady shot off without actually dropping the stick or clattering it against the rifle. Some eventually brought their own, or booked one of mine for their stay. It was a Belgian who eventually turned up with two sticks of his own, bound together with rubber cut from a car inner tube. Since them the ideas have developed and some very sophisticated versions have appeared. There is no doubt that one can damp some of the gyrations performed by a rifle barrel by skilled use of a stick, and their almost universal use on St Hubert Club and BDS tests show that.

The problem is to avoid dropping the stick when presented with a shot. If you are right-handed the natural way seems to carry it in your right hand and have the rifle slung from the same shoulder. Think about it: you have to swap hands with the stick before unslinging the rifle. Even if you carry the rifle over your left shoulder, which some stalkers do, then you are still wrong-handed with the stick. See what I mean? Try getting used to walking with your stick in your left hand, with the rifle slung (preferably muzzle-down) on the right shoulder. A slick technique can be developed with practice, involving minimum movement and no noise.

When it comes to taking a shot, to use a stick effectively you need to stand rather more square-on than is normally taught for an off-hand shot, so that your two feet and the stick form a triangle on the ground, 'The Basic Tripod'. If your feet and the stick are more or less in line, you will have no lateral stability and wild shooting is the result. A split stick does help, but is slower in use and the two halves can rattle together at awkward moments. Don't go in for a fork at the top. You slide your hand up and down to get the right elevation, cradling the fore-end between thumb and forefinger while the stick is clamped with the other fingers. Dry practice at home is very helpful in developing a secure stance without having to think about it.

I have been known to disparage some of the ideas which have come from over the Channel, but in fact we have learned a lot from other nations whose traditions and experience of deer management and woodland stalking are much longer and more honourable than our own, so credit where credit is due.

High Seats

'Be careful how you go up that seat on the cross rides,' says the stalker – 'the top rung is dodgy!' Does that warning strike a familiar bell? High seats have been with us for many years now and not to put it too crudely, a good many of them may have been safe once but with the lapse of time are now death-traps.

Even if you fall out of a seat yourself and break your silly neck somebody is likely to be sorry, but if it's a visitor who does a backward somersault off the top of one of your seats it is unprofessional at best and at worst you may be liable for substantial damages. Spring is as good a time as any to make a point of going round your seats to check them before the busy season. To test for decay on wooden seats a penknife works well – push it into the uprights just at ground level where rot is likely to start. Jump on the centre of each rung (holding on as you do so), and bounce on the plank seat to simulate the restless weight of two men, one at least of whom might easily weigh twenty stone judging by some of my past guests! The thing is that while you yourself climb up a rickety seat with extra precaution standing on the ends of each rung, a visitor heaves his sometimes massive weight up by treading in the middle. If the distance between rungs is a bit much for him, he will put even more strain on them. One of my visitors, who was neither as young nor as healthy as he might have been,

125

broke the top rung and then the next on his way down. Fortunately the third was of sterner stuff and the demolition stopped at that point but it could have been nasty. He was very good about it, but such mishaps should not happen. That was before the regulation came in about wiring each rung, and just shows how necessary it is.

Sitting quietly with a client one evening, he remarked that there was a curious creaking noise from somewhere. Soon afterwards the plank we occupied folded in two, depositing us on the floor of the seat. There was a large knot in it which had failed with the extra burden. Lots of seats are made from material cut on site, but green timber cannot be relied on after the first year, though conifer poles which have had the bark peeled off can last pretty well except for that critical place 'between wind and water'. By contrast, timber which has been really well pressure-creosoted or chemically rot-proofed may last for years. It should still, however, be checked carefully as a routine twice a year, as the present Health and Safety Regulations insist on. Wooden rungs must be notched into the uprights and wired in place, not only up the poles, but across each rung so that the accident I have described should not happen. There should be rails to prevent accidentally falling out. Responsibility for design and maintenance is shared between owner and employee. The other liability which can seem a bit unreasonable concerns the passer-by who may be tempted to scale a high seat, to his injury. In these days when people are quick to sue – especially if they don't like the idea of shooting bambis anyway – any high seat which is past its sell-by date should be pulled down. So, too, any that have outlived their use, for example when a plantation has grown up and blocks the view. Take them away or break them up, but don't leave unnecessary temptations about to create trouble. Somebody once made a picnic fire in the top of one of my creosoted seats. I would love to have been a fly on the wall when they abandoned ship!

Metal seats too need maintenance. Even the ones which don't come to bits need painting and those which do have a nasty habit of rusting up the spigot joints without constant greasing. Steel tubes rust internally even if the outside is kept painted and this insidious damage is hard to detect. If the tube has no drain holes, water seeping in freezes and bursts it, usually at the most critical place near ground level.

When I first started making seats, they were made without conscious thought, to suit my rather lanky build. This led to complaints from visitors that sitting on a plank so high that their feet could not touch the floor became extremely painful after an hour or so. Added to that, if a buck did emerge they were unable to aim the rifle because the slits were too high! After a time, one learns. A comfortable shooting position makes for accuracy even among the buck-fevered. One year I had a rather excitable Latin who was desperate to get a big roe buck. Stalking was not possible for him, so we sat in a variety of seats through the week. Alas! Whenever a decent buck arrived, the whole seat started to quake, so bad was the chap's buck fever. I respected him because he recognised his state and refused to fire, but who would have thought that a seat had to be designed to be earth-quake-proof! In the end we had to enact a little charade. Seeing a big buck in a field, we advanced to a nearby oak, where I told him there was a little buck in the field which I would be glad if he would shoot. 'Just go up behind the tree, put up the rifle and slowly swing round the trunk until he comes into the sights – then fire!' This he did, the buck fell – and he wept like a crocodile when he saw how big it was. Had he seen it first, the shot could have gone anywhere! A little guile is sometimes needed with clients.

Of course, the lean-to sort of high seat has to use a solid support, other-wise in any sort of wind the tree's movement is enough to make straight shooting almost impossible. Like trying to shoot a ping-pong ball off a jet of water at a fairground. If a lissom tree just has to be used it's best to cut the top off just above the seat – but not before consulting the forester!

Another spring job is cutting away the branches which have grown into the field of fire. During the doe season everything may seem fine, but with the weight of new leaves the branches droop to a surprising degree. Sometimes it is helpful to sit in the seat and tell an assistant which are the offending twigs. Sometimes the branch in question is difficult to reach. I have a set of jointed poles with a pruning saw which slots into the end which is extremely effective for this, just as it is to clear branches by the river which caught my flies on the back cast last fishing season!

Sitting comfortably in a high seat on summer evenings is delightful: the life of the wood soon forgets your presence and there is always much to see before that master buck comes out. But comfort is the operative word, that and safety. Of course if it is too comfortable you may need an alarm clock!

Problems in a High Seat

We all do silly things at times, me more than most. A neighbouring landowner has a fallow problem and gets a good team together twice a year to move does. Two or three people who know the ground wander round wearing yellow 'Dayglo' jackets presumably surplus (or not) to the nearest road gang. Half a dozen Rifles are stationed in high seats which are strategically placed where the deer are likely to hesitate before deciding to make a definite move or linger having done so. My 'seat' was a platform between two slender oaks on which to stand, with a sawn rail as safety barrier and shooting support. It was reached by battens following the outward curve of the trunks. Getting up there with rifle and rucksack was like climbing the futtock shrouds of HMS *Victory*. There was nowhere to hang the rifle, and independent movement of the two supporting trees made one feel rather drunk after a while.

With a small team of experienced Rifles who take no risks with chancy shots, this can be a very successful method of coping with roe and fallow in large blocks of mixed or broadleaved woodland. None the less, it can be frustrating for the Rifles. One can be chilled and bored after an hour or more with nothing happening, then suddenly there is a flicker through the trees and the prospect of immediate action. Safety is the first consideration: you must know the location of neighbours, the areas where paths, flat ground or buildings make shooting impossible and the location of the movers who make their presence known by occasionally knocking on trees with a stick. Then the correct identification of the quarry – buck or doe; roe, muntjac or fallow, according to the orders. Only then – will they come nearer? Is it a clear shot through the twigs? Is there another deer behind the one you hope to shoot? The tension goes up like a space rocket.

About forty fallow had appeared within fifty yards of my high seat, lingered for endless minutes without offering a certain shot at an identifiable female target, and once more taken off. A distant bang indicated that one of my neighbours had had better luck in the visibility stakes. Time for a Liquorice Allsort to calm the nerves. (No rustling sweet papers!) Three roe, one a good buck in late velvet indicating his age, materialised under my seat. Their late-winter grey-brown coats were wonderful camouflage against a carpet of dead leaves. The roe doe cull was complete, and so of course they lingered about offering one duffer's shot after another.

Ten minutes later the binoculars translated another distant flicker into the legs, backsides and other bits of two or three more fallow eighty yards off, again in a tangle of hazel twiggery. I could see a doe clearly, standing broadside, a perfect chance, but only down at floor level of my platform. Lowering myself awkwardly, trust me to tip the rifle over the side – and down it clattered, sticking in the earth muzzle-down and then keeling over. Oh Dear!

Down the dreadful ladder to view the damage: muzzle plugged with wood and earth of course, but what else might be less easy to see. Naturally one ought to have packed up at that point and waited for the drive to finish. However, I found that my stalking knife has a corkscrew of less than .30 calibre, so down that went through the plug of rotten wood and earth. At the third attempt I could actually see up the barrel which looked like a rabbit hole. Blowing hard down it produced a shower of debris, some of which lodged in the action. There should have been a nice thin hazel stick to clear the rest, but Murphy instantly applied his Law. Nothing but a foot-long oak twig, rather knotty. After this it didn't look too dangerous to fire the thing, but where the bullet would go was anybody's guess.

Up the rigging again, and a bore-sighting test. More or less on, so far as I could see. I resumed my vigil, hoping that nothing would come my way, and it was kind enough not to. Lunchtime produced a cleaning rod, but no chance of a sighting shot. I had to trust to luck and short-range engagement. Once again my luck held and I departed shotless and thankful.

After a severe examination and cleaning I tried the collimator. More fool me – I hadn't recorded a reading after the last zeroing session. However, it seemed to say that nothing had shifted horribly. Two shots on the range showed a change of zero which needed no more than three clicks down which speaks volumes for the quality of the Pecar 4 × 32 scope sight which was fitted to it years ago, let alone the rifle. I had been lucky.

So – don't drop rifles out of high seats; but what should one include in the kit to cope with this sort of emergency? A pull-through? A portable cleaning rod? A collimator for on-the-spot checks? A parachute? Most woodland stalkers carry quite enough gadgets about with them anyway. Some basic kit in the car probably would be a good idea. Often the car isn't too far off, and rifles do get dropped, sat on, or have their muzzles filled with mud and snow. The main thing is not to press on regardless when you are not sure that the bore is clear, or when there is a doubt about the rifle's zero. It is like that old saying about proposing marriage: 'When in doubt – don't!'

Seeing this lamentable story in print provoked my host to send this poem:

PONTI'S LAMENT
I don't want to shoot a doe
What is to be done? I am full of woe!
This is a horrible high seat
That moans and groans and I feel sick!
How am I to escape this wretched hide
And get back to a warm fireside?
This is a mad plan exercise!
I should know! This is not how we stalk fallow!
Now if I drop my rifle into the ground
I will not be able to fire a round
Oh blast! a doe has shown her face
I'll fire a shot with good grace
Then with honour satisfied
I can repair to the fireside
BANG!
Oh no! Calamity has befallen this farce
I've missed her heart and hit her arse
I will now drop my gun and scope
And break it on the ground and hope
That my host will see my misery and pain
And never ask me to do this again!

My reply to this effort was not printable! We still remained friends nevertheless.

Typical Questions on Equipment

In several reference books I read that deer are colour-blind. If this is the case, is all this business of camouflage etc all codswallop? After all, Dayglo jackets and hats are required in America and they still seem to shoot deer. What's all the fuss – sales promotion by the clothes manufacturers?

First – deer are not really colour-blind, but it is thought that they can only distinguish colours at fairly close range. However, the construction of their eyes means that they are very quick to spot movement, and they see better than we do in poor light and mist. Don't we all know it! Think of what they see as a monochrome photograph, maybe slightly out-of-focus. Big blocks of bright or dark show up strongly against a contrasting background, and if that block moves the deer won't stop to ask. Similarly, your uncovered white hands going up and down with the binoculars are as good as a signal. No – broken patterns and unobtrusive clothes do help, but that doesn't mean dress like an insurgent especially where you are likely to meet the public!

I find that I can't carry out a shot beast (I shoot roe and muntjac) without getting plastered. I am thinking about getting a rucksack: can you advise me the points to watch when selecting one?

The main thing is to make sure that it is big enough! Mine is about 60cm wide by 50cm high with detachable straps so that you can wash the bag. The straps are wide to spread the weight; one side fixed, the other with a strap and toggle so that it can be secured when the laden bag is over one shoulder. The ring at the top must be strong! It needs a detachable waterproof liner. Get a spare if you can so that one is drying while you have the other. After gralloching fold the roe up with its head between its legs and dump it bottom-first into the lining. Then the whole package can be put in the roe sack without messing it up. The legs can stick up, but don't let the head dangle or it will drip over everything. Sling the bag on to one shoulder, then catch the loose strap, fit it over your other shoulder and secure it with the toggle. If the toggle is on the over-shoulder strap, the loop it fits into must be fairly long or you will have trouble catching hold of it. Keeping the whole thing reasonably clean is more important than might appear. I suffered for two long days stalking with a chap whose roe sack smelt as if there was still a dead deer inside it from last month. I suppose he was accustomed to the stink. I was not.

I do a bit of woodland stalking as well as my regular game shooting. Is it possible to get a breathable jacket which is really waterproof which will do for both?

Some shooting coats are not entirely satisfactory for stalking, either because of the difficulty of washing them easily (stalking tends to be messy!) or because they make deer-scaring noise brushing past twigs etc. Once punctured by thorns, one can get a permanent leak with the 'sandwich' type of construction, while the cheap and reliable waxproofs are giveaways among the brambles or in Sitka spruce woods. If you stalk regularly in these conditions, real wool such as the Swanndri is completely silent, fairly waterproof but gets heavier in rain. You might have a look at one or two makes which are made from Ventile cotton. Anything you decide on needs to be machine-washable, thin enough and plenty big enough to allow for cold-weather gear underneath without losing freedom of movement. It's better in the long run to have one for each sport. Compromises are often half-baked!

What is the best sort of footwear for woodland stalking?

One must be comfortable, so in wet conditions choose high boots which are really waterproof. Wellies may be tolerable if they are designed with real walking in mind but otherwise are far better avoided. Cheap ones are bad to walk in and noisy. Dew-drenched grass is also very wetting, but one can now get close-fitting lightweight boots interlined with a waterproof membrane (GoreTex is only one of them) with soles through which you can feel twigs and stones before they give you away. In heather, or tick-infested ground high-topped boots with the trousers tucked into them are better then shoes. Otherwise get some gaiters. They are also good in snow. Anything you wear must still be comfortable after hours of steady walking.

Please would you confirm the most suitable camouflage patterns for open-ground stalking, in both the East and West Highlands. To be tolerant of seasonal changes of hue, snow excepted.

Most of my stalking for stags and hill roe has been either on the west coast or in the Cairngorms. The first being primarily white grass and rock, the other heather – and rock. The estate tweeds reflect this, being on the whole respectively greyer or browner, often with a gold stripe and they do blend in very well, as they were designed to do. The problem is that wet tweed is heavy, and doesn't keep out the downpour as well as some of the modern synthetic materials. Nothing to my mind does better than tweed breeches, but with a lightweight breathable jacket. Some sort of disruptive pattern does give one an advantage, but it should not be too green or too dark. In the wet some get almost black-looking. It's worth having a look at some of the new camouflage patterns which are better for our conditions than the ex-army type (DPM) which was designed for deciduous woodland.

I have what is called a non-slip sling on my stalking rifle, but it has to be hitched up all the time to stop it falling off, specially if I have the roe sack on. Is there any cunning way you can stop it?

Your trouble is not the rifle sling, but the rucksack straps, because even if your sling doesn't slip off the leather strap, it drags strap and all off your shoulder. Two stages to get over the difficulty: sew a very small button on to the shoulder of your stalking jacket just below where the sling or roe sack strap sits comfortably. Not too big, otherwise the sling will hitch up when you want to get it unslung quickly. Second: glue some felt or similar non-slip material to that part of the roe sack strap where the two overlap. Car accessory dealers stock non-slip rubber which works well.

I take care to protect my hearing when I'm out with the gun, using ear plugs, or muffs clay pigeon shooting, but what do I do about stalking? One can't in practical terms prowl about the woods with muffs on, and the plugs would stop my hearing the sounds of deer moving etc. Are just a few shots a year going to do any damage? I am twenty-six.

This is quite a problem every stalker should consider. It's not just the Rifle's hearing which is at risk but anyone with him (including his dog) and especially the professional lying next to him as is so often the case on the open hill. I believe that every shot which you take unprotected has an effect on your hearing, but the damage is unlikely to show until you are in your forties. Short-barrel rifles and any fitted with muzzle brakes are the worst offenders.

Taking the easiest problem first: always ensure that your dog is firmly sat behind you when you take a shot. A friendly animal may wander round to the front, if only to lick your face! For standing shots it must be firmly at heel, not beside your feet.

For every zeroing session use your muffs and ensure that any nearby onlooker has them on too. Out stalking you may have the time to put in your earplugs before a deliberate shot but I doubt you will remember in the heat of the moment. I agree that non-electronic protectors would certainly inhibit a woodland stalker and the electronic sort are expensive. Those which are fitted to your ears are, of course, extremely effective, not only for stalking but for game shooting too. If you only have a very few shots a year, you may feel that it won't do material harm, but more than this and you must weigh the cost against future deafness. I didn't know the risks and am nearly stone deaf in the left ear as a result!

I have a super vari-power scope on my stalking rifle and don't see the reason for toting a big pair of binoculars (let alone buying them) when I can see everything with tremendous clarity through the scope. I got hauled over the coals by a professional stalker the other day, and felt a bit aggrieved, specially as he only had a pair of cheap 8x30s. Isn't this just a fad?

Just stop to think a minute – what is happening when you look at something through your scope? You don't take it off the rifle, so what you are doing is aiming a loaded rifle at an unidentified object, which may be a deer – or a dog – or a bird-watcher. Don't.

Apart from that, a decent pair of binoculars will increase your enjoyment of the outing. Stalking isn't all wanting to shoot something.

Typical Questions on Trophy Preparation

There are some old red deer heads on the gable end of this house and some roe on a shed. I would like to bring some inside for ornament, but they are rather bleached and the bone is covered with lichen. Is there any way of reviving them?

If the heads are really old and weathered, you have quite a job to make those heads look presentable at short range. If they haven't been there that long, there is quite a bit you can do.

If the antlers are just bleached (and it's surprising how quickly this happens, even while still attached to the original owner) then the colour can be restored by careful application of teak oil followed by a careful brushing with dark brown boot polish. Red deer antlers usually look better with the tips of the tines left white and repolished by rubbing with very fine steel wool, grading it off into the coloured part. If it is very well pearled, any colouring can be gently removed from the tops of the pearls, as it would be in life. Several years' exposure to sun and rain leaches away the wax from the antlers leaving them porous and you may need to replace this in addition to colouring and polishing. I have used warm boot wax for the purpose, but this is getting into artistry rather than restoration.

The skull part with the pedicles will also need attention. Often it has become brittle and porous. Scrubbing with warm water and detergent will make a start, using a fine wire brush to get lichen and bird droppings off. Bleach is unlikely to do much good at this stage, the stains have gone too deep. The most practical solution is likely to be a thin coat of off-white matt emulsion paint.

If the heads are mounted on shields, these can be stripped, stained and finished in the normal way if the wood is still sound.

A chum of mine shot what he thinks is a big roe buck in the rut in early August. Can you tell me what to look for to make a 'trophy' buck, and where he should apply to get a definite answer?

Beauty is in the eye of the beholder. The main thing about a memorable trophy is that the stalk should have been exciting. Some of the bucks I remember best had nothing much in the way of big antlers but something about the getting of each one stays with one for ever. That's a real trophy! However, it is interesting to know how a buck measures up against international standards and the days of having to exhibit one's precious head at a distant foreign exhibition are long gone.

There are one or two starting points for knowing if a head is likely to make the charts: first, the skull must be properly boiled out and dry. A skull loses about ten per cent of its weight in the first few weeks after boiling out. Don't glue it to the shield or fill the skull cavity with anything, as the nett weight is critical.

For a long time now, deer heads have been judged using formulae developed by the CIC (The International Council for Game and Wildlife Conservation), originally for large-scale exhibitions which were organised every ten years. It's not a competition so the award of a medal depends on the points scored, not if it is the best out of a number of others. In the case of roe the medal levels are: gold – 130 points; silver 115–129.9 points; bronze 105–114.9 points.

To be likely to qualify, a roe head (full skull less lower jaw) ought to weigh more than 450 grammes or if it is cut through the eye sockets, over 360 grammes. This is only a guide, as antler volume and beauty points have all to be considered.

Official Measurers are located as follows:

Dorset
Richard Prior (Wimborne) 01258 840 881
Charles Fenn (Weymouth) 01305 835 710

Somerset
Tony Dalby-Welsh (Shepton Mallet) 01749 343 725

Sussex
Barry Martin (Midhurst) 01730 810 270

Scotland
Allan Allison (Kinross) 01577 863 115
Alisdair Troup (Bridge of Allan) 01786 834 973
Iain Watson (I. of Lewis) (ian.watson@tesco.net)

Official measurers should be contacted by phone to arrange a convenient time and will quote the current fee for measurement. Medals are extra according to the final score.

4 MANAGEMENT

Stalker or Manager?

Many stalkers, myself included, who start out with stalking as an occasional hobby develop their passion for deer to the point when it is a part- or full-time career. 'Stalking' becomes 'Management'; 'Shooting' turns into 'Culling' and all this is admirable because nobody disputes that deer in this country need sympathetic management. There is general agreement that the methods we promote are the most humane way of achieving a balance between many different land uses in a small and over-populated country. The trouble is – how many so-called Deer Managers actually manage the deer in their care? How many of us deceive ourselves (and hopefully other people) by claiming that the deer in the area which we control are actually managed for their own good and for the protection of different crops? These days there are few districts without such dedicated people, but let us look at the results: vast herds of fallow does and fawns (I wonder why there are so few bucks?); muntjac spreading steadily; sika also extending their range; and as for roe – one can't plant a tree without either expensive fencing or equally expensive tree shelters.

A lot of paying guests come here from other countries and not all of them go back entirely satisfied. Should we wonder if our management is as good as we claim? Could we do better?

Until deer were worth money nobody cared much about their management or did much about it. Then things changed, at first for the better. We learned, and tried to practise, the new skill of looking after our deer, struggling against an over-population which seemed impossible to control or mis-manage by shooting too many. Then as the business of stalking built up, becoming a 'deer manager' seemed to offer a very attractive career for any dedicated stalker. Many give excellent value both to their landlords and to their clients, doing an honest job of frantic doe culling all winter and working all hours during the buck season to entertain their stalking guests. Unfortunately the truth has to be faced that the living which such a job offers is thin, to put it mildly, and while some grit their teeth and are resigned to poor commons, others have tried short cuts. It is these who are giving pay stalking in Britain a bad reputation.

Agonising about the Doe Cull

The road to Hell may be paved with this and that, but the wallpaper is definitely composed of doe cull plans. Plans which were made on the best management principles, finely tuned to achieve that delicate balance between a healthy deer herd and a happy forester, with a total which looked easily attainable long before the end of the season four months away . . . But were they achieved? Well – the keeper wouldn't let me on the ground – the weather got bad – I go pheasant shooting on Saturdays – and so on. We know all the excuses and have used them with elegant variations to justify not having done what we had planned to do before the end of February.

Fundamentally, most stalkers really don't like shooting does and I think this hasn't much to do with the fact they have no antlers. We are all charmed by the fawns when they appear and their mothers seem to take such good care of them through the summer that it seems hard to start banging them off regardless when November comes along. If we leave it until later in the winter the ethical objections to shooting visibly pregnant females get ever more pressing and repugnant. On this score I am reminded of returning one January evening to my landlord's house with a fallow doe, to be met by his wife who had a small baby. She asked the dreaded question 'Was it pregnant?' I flubbed about a bit but had to admit that it was. 'Oh! If I was going to be shot, I'd much prefer to be shot before the birth than after it!' So there is more than one way of looking at moral dilemmas.

Not only to have answers ready when awkward moments like that turn up, but to clear our own minds about the necessity for culling females, the whole thing must be thought through. Otherwise we are not deer enthusiasts or managers, but just killers. Perhaps, as the Antis would have us do, one should 'leave it to Nature'? What would happen if we didn't kill any does? So far as roe are concerned, we know that up to a point they are mutually intolerant, and dispersal should cure the problem. Dispersal? Where to? These days almost all suitable deer habitat is carrying its full population, so they have to group up and live in herds in the fields. Anywhere I have seen so-called 'field roe', in Poland, France or this country, all the adjacent woodland has been browsed to bits, so that food and safety can only be found in the bigger fields. A lot of growing crops are not especially good for roe, and anyone stalking big arable farms will be familiar with the unhealthy scouring which spoils the Persil-white of a roe's target. Poor digestion and unsuitable food lead to lost condition, a high parasite burden and a heavy mortality of young deer in early spring. Unless you have done something about it. Letting your deer die in a ditch in March is cruel, wasteful and what 'leaving it to Nature' is all about. We also have to think about the damage to farm and tree crops which the deer will do before 'Nature' clicks in with disease and starvation to cut the numbers down. The stalker is a compassionate predator; 'Nature' is not.

Then there is the question of orphaning fawns. Will the young ones have a better chance of surviving the winter if they have the benefit of their mother's guidance and leadership, at least until February? That is a much more rational question which needs to be clarified. Usually roe fawns are weaned by August, so there is not a question of dependence in that way, but in districts where a foot or more (>30cm) of snow can be expected most winters, mature does can break trail for their young and give a positive advantage. However, the worst weather is often well on into February, so are we to have a complete ban on shooting any does accompanied by last year's young? The only way a population can be kept in check is by limiting the number of breeding females, so if (as is usually the case) keeping the herd to a reasonable size is your prime task, then breeders and potential breeders (last summer's fawns) just have to be removed. Maybe stalkers who only have a few does to take out can afford to finesse and take the weaker out of a pair of doe twins. Even then – would it have died anyway? If so, you have done nothing but harvest some venison which would otherwise be wasted.

According to some, the counsel of perfection is only to remove old animals, the sick and non-breeders. First, it isn't that easy when a doe pops up within shot to tell if she happens to be old or ill. Second, although some will fail to become pregnant, such yeld years do not necessarily come towards the end of a productive life. Quite the reverse, quite healthy does may 'miss' occasionally through weather or other factors and resume breeding the following year. Then, so far as sick or wounded animals are concerned, one may appear by chance, but to pass up good opportunities of a shot in the search for a weakling is a sure-fire recipe for finishing up short of your quota at the end of the season. One doe on my stalking had a broken hind leg which stuck out sideways. I wasted quite a bit of time trying for her in vain, and every year she had twins. How she ever mated was a mystery, but was it so important to cull out that beast? A recent and obviously painful wound is another matter.

A good many beginners ask me how many does they ought to be shooting on a given acreage of stalking. That's the worst problem of all, given the well-known unreliability of census figures and the tendency of roe to drift back to favourite wintering ground, having been notably difficult to find all summer. If you thought you had the buck cull about right with a high proportion of yearlings to balance the mature animals, you can safely reckon to take a slightly larger number of does. That is a start. Before the weather

139

worsens it is worth spending some time in September trying to get an idea of the numbers of does and fawns to be seen on your ground. That at least gives a minimum number to work on. Then the severity of the browse line will help in assessing how much food is left to the deer for the rest of the winter. Always examine the lungs of shot deer to check for evidence of lungworm which is likely to get worse as a result of over-population. Also as the season goes by, the colour of the bone marrow will change from creamy white to pink or even red if food is very short. All these are signs that the doe cull should be stepped up. If a lot of deer start to die in March and the carcasses show that they were in bad condition, that is not a signal to reduce the cull next winter, but to increase it. It is also a signal that you did not do your job as deer manager.

It is not a bad thing to fix on the idea that doe cull targets should be flexible to cope with new information as the season progresses. However, they should only be flexible upwards. How many of us have started off full of enthusiasm in November to get a good start on the does, only to fail totally to find them? Where have they gone? Have the poachers scraped the lot? Panic – cut down the cull! So you forget about the does and enjoy your game shooting – or the telly – until 1 March. Then somebody rings up and yells that there are hundreds of the b . . . s on his fields. Where have they been hiding? Goodness knows. So you make excuses to break the law and shoot a lot of very heavily pregnant does out of season. That is when the job becomes really repugnant. In addition you know that it could and should have been done months ago. Don't fall into that trap!

Road Accidents and the Management Plan

Some of the finest roe antlers brought in to me for measuring are marked with the sad epitaph 'Found Dead – Road accident'.

How many animal tragedies does that terse phrase imply? Just one more casualty of our vehicle-dominated life. The true picture of the toll of deer killed on the roads ought to horrify the conscience of a reputedly animal-loving nation. But it would not, even if the full facts were published or even known. If the collision happens in front of the children, they cry and there is talk about calling a vet, but the fact that the front of the car is damaged is more important.

After one year of research on deer collisions, in 2004 Jochen Langbein's team recorded over 12,000 deer killed on our roads, and this is unlikely to represent more than a proportion of the real total. Knowing the actual loss of deer to the national herd would knock all our vaunted management plans flat.

To give a local example, the number of roe per year actually proved to have been killed on one fifteen-kilometre (10 mile) stretch of road in Dorset averaged one per two kilometres per year over more than ten years; nearly

140

one per mile per year. There is no reason to think that this road was any different from others, or more likely to be unusually dangerous to deer. Plus-up that figure for all the roads in roe-populated territory in Britain and the figure is staggering.

The deer manager is in a fool's paradise if he tries to claim either that his census is in any way accurate or that the reproductive success can be calculated just because he has maintained a reasonably stable density over some seasons by culling a certain percentage of the spring census. A careful stalker can assess the breeding potential by examining each female shot in the winter and counting the foetuses, but not all of them would go successfully to term, and a significant number of fawns die naturally before maturity. However, we all allow for this in calculating the cull, but how then can it be that even with this big road kill the herd seems to stay much the same size? Immigration may possibly be filling the vacuum created or, as is much more likely, we are seriously under-estimating the number of deer present. To be strictly practical, if you accept that your cull is keeping roughly the right number each year despite the loss from road accidents, accident statistics should be disregarded and not deducted from the normal cull.

The most annoying fact is that a large proportion of the deer run over will be major bucks, roe in particular but also fallow. Maybe muntjac too. Is this merely Murphy's well-known Law in full operation? If not, why does it happen? One can get an idea by looking at the statistics. In the Dorset study mentioned above the ratio of mature roe bucks to does killed was 13:8. Peaks are observed in May and July-August. According to a BDS study on the M6 and adjacent roads in Staffordshire, accidents involving fallow run to a climax in October. Quite obviously rutting lowers the male deer's vigilance and increases his inclination to roam. In addition, a major roe buck spends much time in late spring defending his territory and chasing out intruders, accounting for the earlier peak. One would assume that the cast-out yearling would run the greatest risk from a passing car or lorry as he is chased across the road. A very knowledge-able stalker gave me the answer. Yes, the big buck chases yearlings across any nearby road and they take their chance of being squashed, but a car driver may manage to avoid the deer he sees crossing, but fail to anticipate that another may be hard behind it. Exit one big buck. Even if the territorial buck gets away with it, then he is on the wrong side of the road and has to go back again, running twice the hazard of his smaller rival who is likely to stay on the far side.

Dealing with road casualties is a job which every stalker loathes, let alone being called out at night, often with the vaguest directions about the location of the scene. In the middle of the busy season a local stalker was roused out in the small hours to find a police car, a motor cyclist with a broken arm and a deer with a broken leg. Loading his .243, he said to the policeman 'Okay – Which one shall I put down first?' The motor cyclist's face was a study.

The current rash of glossy TV programmes about the marvels vets can perform gives false ideas to the uninformed about the kindest way of dealing with an injured wild animal. There is no real alternative to euthanasia but it needs to be quick, safe, effective, and unobtrusive if there is an audience. To be sure of dealing with any situation one probably needs a rifle and a shotgun, a good torch and a knife. And considerable tact.

The Pressures on Deer

I had a paper recently from my old stalking friend Dr Francis Roucher setting out his ideas on stress and the way deer might be affected. Zoologists, on the whole, have been chary of this subject, until of course the furore round the Bateson report on hunted deer. The common-sense view of that is that if you chase anything for very long, it gets tired, but that is not the sort of stress that Dr Roucher is worrying about – more the everyday disturbances which arise from the ever-increasing use of the countryside by the public.

We all know that deer are so extremely successful because they are very adaptable creatures, changing their whole lifestyles to make the best use of the modern world as they find it. The result is that hoofed game are flourishing nearly everywhere in Europe while many species of birds, for example, are struggling. Even in wilderness conditions deer have a pretty harassed life – they are, after all, a prey species at the mercy of wolf and bear, wolverine and eagle. It is reasonable to assume that evolution has seen to it that they are capable of living and breeding in spite of having to keep more than one eye on the nearest cover in case of an ambush. While we have introduced some new hazards – dog, rifle, jogger, motor car – into their lives for our own purposes we have at the same time eliminated most of their traditional enemies. In many ways life should be ten times better in our green and (in places) pleasant land. Maybe when we start worrying about stress we are creating a mental picture of primordial Elysian Fields in which the deer frolicked before the arrival of H sapiens. Nature is not kind; the lion doesn't lie down with the lamb – it eats it.

None the less, the various intrusions made by modern life into the natural habits of deer do affect them, either by changing their habits or seriously

142

influencing their ability to feed, rest and breed. For our own purposes we like to see animals, rather than retreating backsides, we enjoy the unobtrusive pleasures of still hunting, taking what needs to be removed with the minimum of disturbance, and we like to see a proportion of males showing the finest trophies. That real roe expert, the late Duke of Bavaria listed peace and quiet as one of the criteria for the growth of large antlers.

So far as woodland deer and roe in particular are concerned, one could divide modern-day disturbance other than actual pursuit into two kinds: things going on alongside roads and tracks, and incursions into the woods and places where the deer live and hide. The first sort may have an effect on feeding habits, timetable and so on, but the second if repeated or prolonged can induce at least temporary evacuation. Studies in Scandinavia on orienteering where large numbers of runners penetrate randomly into deer habitat have shown what disruption such events cause. Of course things settle down again, but after a series of such events the deer manager may find not only that he has a very nervous population to deal with, but that the mature males he has cultivated may have decamped giving way to numbers of juveniles. The biological effects of prolonged disturbance on condition, reproduction and antler growth are not easy to quantify in the wild.

Our own woodland deer have a reasonably tranquil life. They accept normal farm operations, recognise the vehicles and probably the individuals who never take much notice of them in their daily work. Even on pheasant shoots where each covert may be driven regularly through the season, the resident deer adapt quite easily. Some movement of fallow to outlying woods may be noticed, but roe and muntjac move one way and another through the day to avoid each drive. Determined and regular pursuit by poachers' lurchers is a very different matter. Another cause of serious stress is constant chasing by loose pet dogs. One of my stalking grounds was almost completely deserted by roe as a result of two Labradors being allowed to roam freely every night.

In order to cope better with thin times in winter, deer scale down their need for food by physiological changes to the rumen and by taking as little exercise as possible. It follows that if they are alarmed, flight uses up an undue amount of stored energy which is not as easily replaced as it would be at other times of year.

With the grazing deer in particular, quite innocent human activities can deny their regular grazing land to the deer and thus create damage elsewhere. Three severe cases of bark stripping come to mind. One involving red deer could be traced directly to the creation of a popular picnic site on what was in effect a deer lawn, another was an outbreak of bark stripping on beech by fallow which was almost certainly triggered by a changeover from cattle to sheep on the surrounding fields. When legal 'freedom to roam' in woodlands started in Denmark, the same problem followed, and it was curious to see that all the stripping (to conifers this time) was on the inner side of the trees, as if the deer were facing their enemy, taking out their hunger and frustration by stripping the tree behind which they sheltered.

Turning to stalking deer, my experience in parks suggests that it is not so much the actual shot, but purposeful approach which really alarms deer. So many times a Deer Society outing has been ruined by one selfish photographer stalking the herd to get his picture and inducing panic and bunching. In park culling, it is far better to have one or two desperate days in which the whole cull is achieved, rather than a policy of quiet sniping of a few at a time through the season. That is what makes the deer jumpy and less of a spectacle, which is one of the purposes of a park anyway, and may have an effect on their ability to make best use of the available food.

It is more difficult to apply the same idea to wild deer, partly because stalking is our pleasure. Some countries have very short seasons, and maybe this has a beneficial effect on the deer, but the necessary free-for-all can also be very dangerous! The cull would be likely to be fairly random – if time is short one would tend to shoot the first which gave a chance of a shot and it is only possible where sporting rights are held in common to some extent. In Sweden, landowners have the option of a short uncontrolled season, or a much longer period in which they have to comply with a shooting plan. The snag about a mandatory shooting plan is that the more rigid it is, the more vital to have a reliable biological basis for the game laws which are imposed. In many ways we seem to muddle along reasonably well without it, if the production of trophies is any guide.

Where the 'random cull' idea falls down is the fatal combination of scope-sighted rifle and males with antlers. The biologists might claim that they got

a true slice off the population by the short-season heavy cull, but if a mixed bunch of deer come into view, no matter what instructions have been issued to the shooter, somehow when the smoke clears away there will be a pair of horns lying flat, and forty does have escaped again into the tall timber. One only has to look at the fallow in this country to see what a heavy preponderance of females remain at the end of the season. The idea of manning a number of high seats in a stretch of woodland one day, so that deer moved by one are likely to drift towards another is gaining popularity. If carefully organised by competent Rifles this method can result in an effective and quick doe cull. Not everywhere lends itself to it, however, and many stalkers like to take things at a more leisurely pace, studying their animals before deciding to shoot.

Having said that, there is no doubt that stalking one area, or one buck, day after day is self-defeating quite apart from any ill effect on the animals concerned. Once a good buck has been seen there is a great temptation to go back and back to the same place in the hopes of another chance. It hasn't survived long enough to grow a good head without taking that one on board! Give him two days and try again – then if he does come out it will be you who has the stress!

Typical Questions on Management

The land agent for the estate where I stalk tells me that I must submit a 'risk assessment' and put warning notices on my high seats because of the Health & Safety Regulations. I do the deer control for nothing, so if I tell him I will be responsible, do I have to go through all this nonsense?

I'm afraid you do. You and the land agent have a responsibility under these regulations which you can't avoid. In addition, your seats must be properly designed and be formally inspected (with a report to the estate in writing) twice a year. This is modern stalking. It is a complicated subject which is summarised for stalkers in my book *Roe Deer: Management and Stalking* published by Swan Hill Press.

The deer on my farm are very used to my Land Rover, but when I get out they soon get the message. In our large downland fields they are often miles from any cover. I know you are not allowed to shoot out of a vehicle, but is it okay to take a shot across the bonnet?

The Deer Act states that you cannot take a shot from a vehicle. So far as I know, this definition has never been tested in the courts, but quite apart from that, if you make a habit of it, your deer will just get wild. Better to get another driver to drop you within shot and drive on, so that the deer do not associate the shot with your vehicle. Also you will be keeping inside the law – which we all need to do.

I stalk in very thick woodland where the chances of seeing a deer at all during the summer are thin or non-existent. Maybe I could persuade the owner (he is always complaining of the damage) to make one or two lawns where I could see and shoot them. What suggestions should I make to him which would tempt the roe out without costing an arm and a leg to make and maintain?

The term 'deer lawn' doesn't really apply to roe, because they don't like open spaces, or much grass for that matter. Think in terms of a long, narrow clearing with a straggle of bushes in it, not enough to prevent you seeing them from a well-placed high seat, but enough to give the roe confidence. The bushes should preferably be of species which are either very attractive to the deer, such as willow or young bramble, or strange to them. Anything odd will always interest them. Any shrub nursery will have some exotic rejects at the end of the planting season you can get cheap. Sometimes ride-sides can be tailored to make quite acceptable control clearings without impinging on the plantations. They are likely to be good for butterflies and other wildlife too.

I have some stalking in Angus. When I start the doe cull, should I try to shoot the weaker of each pair of roe fawns, so that the other gets a better start through the winter?

In your part of Scotland the low-ground roe live pretty well provided the food supply is not used up because the deer population is too high. A lot depends on how many does you have been set to take out. If only a few, you can try to be ultra particular in this way, but remember that you may not shoot a buck kid at this time of year if the mother is still living. Most stalkers have a big quota, and I feel that it is much more important to the general wellbeing of the roe to make sure that the right number is taken rather than pass up opportunities to shoot in the early part of the season which may not come again. The weather may well be difficult later on.

Here in the North we can expect periods of quite heavy snow which lies sometimes for weeks. We love to see the roe about the place and would like to do something to help them through these severe spells of weather.

*We could lay in a small supply of hay to give them when it gets bad –
would this help to keep them going?*

To break down cellulose so that fodder can be digested, ruminants rely on
a community of bugs in the rumen. There are a number of types, each
specialised to one sort of feed. To digest a different food successfully the
predominating sort of bug has to change accordingly. This change can take
up to two weeks, so a deer that has been feeding on woody browse which
runs short in cold weather cannot suddenly cope with a feed of hay and can
literally starve with a full stomach.

It is better to cut down out-of-reach natural food, such as ivy if it grows
with you, fir branches or anything else that the deer have been browsing to
help them over the bad spell. Hay also usually gets wet and spoiled.
Alternatively, give them some calf pellets or other concentrated food,
getting them used to it before the hard weather sets in. Deer round the
policies of the house or other quiet places soon get used to the idea of a
roofed trough in which they find their supplementary ration especially if it
contains molasses.

*I want to make a good start with my doe cull but the gamekeeper on my
stalking ground is very unwilling to let me stalk until after the end of the
pheasant shooting. I think I ought to get quite a few does and am afraid
that with limited time and the risk of bad weather, I won't get enough by
the end, and the owner is always on at me about damage. Is there any way
I can convince the keeper that I won't disturb his birds by stalking?*

Gamekeepers have a lot of worries and often a heavy financial pressure on
them at this time of year, so it is understandable if he seems rather defen-
sive. As well, he may be nervous if he hasn't known you long, that he might
be in the way of a rifle bullet one early morning. Confidence takes time to
build up, so talk it over with him – explain about the owner's worries, and
try to go along with his concerns by agreeing not to stalk for two days before
a shoot, plus of course the day itself, and suggesting outlying places which
are away from the main pheasant coverts which could be stalked without
disturbing anything. An offer to beat occasionally may well be appreciated,
and there is no better way of learning about the odd corners – and the odd
characters – on any shoot. Go to see him regularly, sometimes we stalkers
try to be too unobtrusive.

After Christmas the pressure on most shoots tends to ease, and by that
time he may be agreeable to you doing more for the doe cull. After all, deer
spoil many drives, either by eating the undergrowth which holds birds or
by charging across a flushing area at the critical moment, so he doesn't want
too many either. If this means that you still really can't shoot as many deer
as your owner wants, then it's a good idea to explain the situation to him,

telling him at the same time the steps you have already taken to get along with the shoot.

We are told that there are moves to release wolves in Scotland. In view of the fact that there are too many deer, do you think this is a good idea? Would they reduce numbers and weed out the weaklings?

In countries where wolves exist alongside agriculture, as would be the case wherever they were released on our island, the general experience is that they will take livestock; sheep especially, in preference to deer because they are easier to catch. To make any impression on our deer population wolves would have to be present in very considerable numbers and to put it mildly I don't think that farmers and country dwellers would welcome them. It is easy to think of releasing wolves in some remote region where their impact would be negligible, but they are great travellers and could not be confined to one district or another. According to the noted wolf expert David Mech a full-grown wolf can eat up to twenty pounds of meat at one meal, and can repeat that in a matter of hours. Farming has enough difficulties without that!

My stalking doesn't have much woodland, just one sizeable wood, but quite a few roe spill out along the hedges all summer. Are these likely to be mostly yearlings? Because of the crops it often isn't too easy to see exactly what they are. Should I cull them heavily as non-territorial juveniles?

It is true that yearlings tend to wander along hedgerows when they are thrown out of their parents' territories in spring, and if undisturbed there, can hang about until harvest. It's a good idea to take what you can of the yearling buck cull from within established territories, as these individuals have not shown enough spirit to attract the attentions of the resident buck, and are likely in consequence to be poorer specimens than those ejected and colonising the hedges. Having said that, hedgerow deer are very visible and should be thinned as a contribution to good relations with those concerned more with farming and forestry.

Do not assume that they are all yearlings. Occasionally an old buck losing his territorial drive will decide to take up residence in a quiet hedge or planted-up corner. Some of these have poor, going-back heads, but sometimes one can find a cracker!

I seem to be getting in more and more difficulty with my roe buck cull. I try to follow all the experts' advice and leave my trophy bucks until they are in good summer coat, but my stalking is mostly thick woodland with hazel and bracken underneath and arable fields between. Although the roe are out in the fields in spring, the bigger bucks have disappeared early on, and even the yearlings vanish as soon as the crops are sprayed or grow up a bit.

Then I see practically nothing until the harvest is off. Should I try to get my yearlings in March, and then get on with the mature bucks? I have quite a big cull and it just isn't getting done. Advice please?

The old idea was to start the buck season on 1 May, and indeed that is what I used to do in my professional days. However, things are not the same now, most likely due to climate warming as well as changes in the farming scene. The leaf comes earlier in the woods, and fields are sprayed repeatedly which discourages the deer from feeding there. Under your circumstances one has to make a start earlier, but always within the law. In consequence you may not shoot yearling bucks in March, but there is every reason to get going in April in the southern counties at least. Mature bucks will be occupying their territories long before they are in summer coat, and while something of the pleasure of the buck season is lost in taking bucks which still look scruffy with the remains of their winter coat, your obligations to the landowner to protect his crops may dictate this policy. You cannot depend on getting many bucks in the rut if your ground is as thick with bracken as you describe.

Yearlings can be picked off in the fields while they are still there, and you will have another opportunity to complete your cull after harvest when there are often a number of roe out on the stubbles.

With the doe season soon on us, I am doubtful about shooting does while their kids are still with them. Don't they learn a lot from their mothers, even though they are weaned? Even on that point, we do find some roe does still in milk in November when I go north for the doe cull. What should be the guide lines?

You make two valid points: roe kids do learn from their seniors through their first winter, and indeed some do continue to suckle much later in Scotland than in southern England. So far as suggesting some guides lines for you, this depends on the scale of the roe population and the cull you have to achieve. If deer density of all species is high, then one of the most important functions of the doe cull is to ensure that there is enough food left to see the breeding stock through winter and spring. If through understandable reluctance to make orphans you fail to shoot enough, the young are the first to suffer and the whole community loses quality while damage to crops and forestry increases for lack of natural food. If you only have a few does to get and plenty of time to do it, then you can be more overtly humane in your selection of does to shoot. It is a bad policy to leave culling until February because of the extra food consumed by animals which should have been taken earlier. Also the weather can get bad and completing the cull impossible.

Roe on hill land in the north where heavy snowfall is to be expected, have a lower reproductive rate than on low ground so a smaller percentage need be shot, and maternal help is more important to get kids through the winter. Unless under pressure of large numbers, the stalker under these circumstances can concentrate on taking fawns until the New Year, especially one doe out of a pair of twins, to give the survivor a better chance.

My bit of roe stalking is in Northumberland, mixed woodland and fields. The roe seem to be healthy but the heads they grow are rather poor. Should I weed out the worst, or can I put out salt or feed of some sort to improve the antler growth?

The basic reason for a roe buck putting out poor antlers is lack of rich food, principally protein, during the winter when they are growing them. That is far more important than any efforts one can make in selective shooting. It is unlikely that salt will help – roe are usually reluctant to take to it. Sometimes they do acquire the habit of visiting high-protein supplements, either liquid or solid put out for cattle or sheep and I have seen some spectacular heads which were grown as a result. Putting them out specially for the deer is a chancy idea considering the expense, but you might visit one or two farmers round about to see if deer are visiting theirs, and if so, what type they favour.

Probably a better investment of time and money would be to improve the winter browse available to the deer. If it is your own land, or in collaboration with the owner, you might consider widening any tracks so that scrub grows along the edges, or making holes in the canopy by careful thinning to let the sun in for the same purpose. If you are on low ground you may be lucky enough to have bramble and maybe ivy grows up some of the trees. Both of these are sought-after browse. Otherwise a few goat willow plants, protected in their early years and then pruned low will be appreciated.

Of course you need to make sure the herd is not excessive, and this can most easily be assessed by how hard any growth is eaten off by mid-winter. There is only one way to limit numbers – shoot more does progressively year by year until the browse line becomes less well-defined. You may be surprised how big a cull is needed to make any difference!

I hear a lot about counting the roe on your ground in the spring, but on my little patch there doesn't seem to be much point because what my neighbours do obviously affects the deer more than my efforts. Apart from seeing if there are more or less than last year, are there any other things I should be looking out for at this time?

A lot of stalkers will sympathise with your problem, trying to do your best on a bit of ground surrounded by big blocks of woodland you have no control over. One important thing is not to give up and just shoot regardless. Apart from wider issues, one should remember that if you want to encourage trophy quality bucks, they need good food, especially in winter, whatever peace you can arrange for them (loose dogs are usually a problem), and to ensure that there are not too many does. One bit of wood I stalked was tiny, but ideal habitat, so it attracted a number of big bucks each year as residents, and they even threw out most of the yearlings themselves each season by the end of May. Habitat management can be a vital key. At the same time, when you are patrolling in the spring, look to see how many of your does have twins following. This is a pointer to the success rate for breeding in the previous year, and thus how many does you should aim at culling next autumn and winter. See, too, whether there is a marked browse line, showing the impact that the deer had on the available browse last winter (when they were growing their antlers). If everything was eaten up to a metre high, then your bucks were short of food just at the critical time. Ratchet up the cull.

Some places are receiving areas for everyone else's yearling bucks, which can be a headache. If you are in this situation, you may have to shoot far more yearlings than is justified on paper – but only yearlings!

The books all tell one what proportion of the deer herd one ought to shoot and what percentage of each age class.

I am going to try to make a count of the roe deer on my stalking this spring but in my thick woodland somehow doubt that what I see is anything like what I've got. Have you any advice on how to go about it, and what margins of error are likely?

Sad to say, it's easier to lay down the law about deer management on paper than carry theory into practice in the field! All the books can do is to lay down some guidelines which you have to interpret according to the conditions you encounter on your own ground.

Useful questions: *What numbers have been shot in past seasons?*
Are there more or less now than in the past?
Are the deer in good condition?
Are there too many on the ground?
What is the sex ratio?
Is there much forest or crop damage?
Are the roe competing with other deer species?

As you see, there is a lot to think about without trying to make a physical count.

If you have had the stalking for a few seasons, or there are reliable past records, this gives a base. Condition can be assessed from body weight and obvious thinness. Don't go too much on their looking scruffy – this is normal as the winter hair is shed in spring before the new coat comes through.

Having too many deer is bad for landlord relations as well as for the deer themselves. At this time of year, study the browse line. Are the woods noticeably clearer below one metre than above? Where ivy grows on the trees, there will hardly be a leaf left if the deer are pressed for food.

By all means go out early and late to see what is to be seen and take notes – separating the sexes and noting mature and young bucks separately. It's rare to find equality between sexes, which is ideal, but over 1.5 females to each male indicates that last year's doe cull was insufficient.

Good relations with other land users are vital: listen for complaints of damage – and go and check them. Look out for intensive areas of damage. Scattered damage is usually not so important except for special situations – arboreta, cricket bat willow plants, and of course gardens.

Large deer species present compete with roe and muntjac. Fallow, red and sika deer can reach up higher and can completely deny their food sources to the smaller species.

Actual numbers which any place can support depends on the habitat. I feel that the impact of deer on their environment is a good guide for the practical deer manager to back up his theory, important though that may be.

Damage

The first lesson a deer manager has to learn is that you have to start by managing people. Otherwise you won't get to manage any deer, or at least not for very long. The damage deer do to trees, crops and gardens is a make-or-break element in almost any deer manager's success. Many a stalking career has started out with some outraged owner crying 'Vengeance!' because of some mangled trees. Sometimes the luck holds: a quick bang or two and you are in. Claim to be able to stop it and then fail – and you are out! The trick is to be able to assess whether shooting alone will work in a given location; that is primarily whether the owner is going to insist on a zero-damage situation or will he be satisfied by what reduction in damage you think you can achieve.

Quite apart from variations in individual reactions to the sight of trees eaten or frayed (never forget that foresters love trees as we love deer!), some enterprises can accept a degree of damage but others can't. A commercial plantation of conifers will not suffer any loss of final crop with, say, ten per cent of scattered browsing damage in the early years. More than this may involve beating-up with new plants or extra years of weeding and thus additional costs which have to be carried at compound interest until the crop is felled in forty or sixty years' time. Amenity planting, orchards or a collection of rare species in an arboretum need total protection, and there is every degree of variation in between. Damage may be purely a matter of visual annoyance and distress to the owner or whoever was responsible for the planting. But woe betide the deer manager who says it isn't important!

The temptation when you see the possibility of a new and exciting bit of stalking, is to rush in with offers of help and extravagant promises of damage reduction which may be difficult or impossible to achieve. As soon as your failure to back up these promises becomes all too clear, the good name of deer control and yours in particular will be in eclipse. So take a step back when faced with a damage situation and think a bit. Step One is to make sure whether or not the damage is as bad as you have been told. Most reports are exaggerated. Second: what animal has been responsible? Blaming the deer is not only almost automatic, but may well be convenient to the chap who made the original report, and who should have been dealing with the rabbits himself, who knew the sheep got in last spring because he left a gate open and so on. I have seen so-called 'deer damage' by cows, sheep, goats, rabbits, hares, badgers (especially in maize) squirrels, tractors, the weeding gang, mice, voles, last year's Pop Festival, beetles, weevils, pheasants and believe it or not, porcupines!

Next: when did it happen? It isn't much good shouting about killing deer in May because they browsed some trees last winter, or complaining in the autumn about roe fraying. Also is it likely to happen again? Quite exceptional damage can be a one-off business, like a specially attractive farm crop, or unlikely to last long, for example where hazel coppicing will be out of browsing reach in two or three years.

Then the crunch comes: Do you in your honest opinion think that shooting one or a number of deer is really going to limit the damage to such an extent that the owner will be satisfied? If not, then the sooner you take your courage in both hands and tell him so, the better it will be. I know that there is every risk that he will immediately lift the 'phone and call up those rogues from the Blankshire Deer Eradication Service who promise everything from instant results to a whacking rent just for the chance to get their paying clients in next summer and scoop up all the trophy bucks. They will be out on their ears in due course, and the owner just might come back to you to pick up the bits. At least it is their reputation in the bin, not yours. Word soon circulates round in the area.

What can be done by shooting? Certainly fraying by roe can be reduced by a sharp cull of yearling bucks in April, before they either start fraying themselves, or by their presence encourage their seniors to over-indulge in demonstrations of aggression. Fraying by the bigger deer species tends either to be scattered along ride-sides or in the neighbourhood of rutting stands, although red deer in particular can wreak havoc in frustration if they find themselves shut in a deer-fenced enclosure. Wild fallow bucks have the infuriating habit of challenging park deer in the rut and fighting them through the fence which can demolish the stoutest netting.

Reducing browsing by deer is much more problematic. Overall it is a matter of population density – the more deer, the more they eat! The trouble is that we don't usually control the entire range of a herd of deer, so influx can completely negate any attempts to eliminate deer, even if one should want to get rid of them. The other thing is, as we all know, deer are highly selective in what they like in their diet (like us) and will concentrate on the latest fashionable restaurant, no matter how small. So even if the overall density is reasonable, creating honeypots of delicious browse, like new coppice growth, a rose garden or an ornamental clump of red oak just draws in anyone who gets the news. Another element in the scene is that woodland deer are nervous when they are far away from cover, so they tend to spend more time browsing within a few jumps of safety than well out in the open. As a result the worst damage is concentrated in a relatively narrow band next to cover, say twenty yards or so. If the vulnerable plantation is long and thin, or small enough so that the whole of it is within this distance from thicket, then the damage will be universal. So damage depends not only on the deer density, but the relative attraction of the species planted and the shape and size of the plantation. Sometimes the way trees are maintained can attract or avoid damage. For example weeding *in* the rows exposes them, while clearing *between* the rows, or spot weeding protects them.

With large-scale plantings of the majority of conifers there will be a reasonable chance of at least limiting damage by reducing the density of deer in the vicinity, always remembering that this can only be done in the long term by reducing the breeding herd – that is by shooting females. Have you got the skill and the time to back up a promise to do it? Have you got other stalking commitments? Do you spend all the week in the office, while the syndicate shoots every Saturday through the winter and the owner's wife disapproves of Sunday stalking? It is far better to discuss these things before promising great results. Most stalkers are not operating on their own land, so it comes to a point when the landowner's wishes, priorities and personal foibles may have to cost him money because what he wants to achieve cannot be done by culling deer, no matter how rigorous the stalker's efforts may be. The trees, plants or whatever will have to be protected which is expensive. If that is unacceptable then that stalker must be in the position of having put out a warning first.

Anything that is so valuable that no damage at all can be allowed must be fenced, and that's all there is to it. At a lower level of security there are plenty of other expedients, like tree shelters which can be effective particularly if backed up by the stalker's local knowledge of some special situations. Electric fencing can be used for temporary defence, against fallow especially.

So much can be done through good collaboration between grower and stalker once he is convinced you have his interests at heart. It is a two-way partnership which needs very careful propagation in the early days. Once confidence is built up, the important thing to emphasise is that damage is easier to avoid than to cure.

Your Deer – My Roses!

I suppose nearly all stalkers – or at least those not privileged to work in the high hills – are plagued with gardeners ringing up and claiming that 'their' deer are nightly doing such damage as might daunt a hippopotamus.

Coping with messages like this is an exercise in the public relations business which forms such an important, large and intractable part of deer management in our over-populated island. Calls range from aggressive to sorrowful. Sometimes helpful suggestions are tentatively offered; 'Have you ever thought about . . . you know . . . some sort of . . . pill?'

There is no doubt in my mind that the quickest way of converting a rabid Anti to the right way of thinking is to release a hungry roe among his or her (no doubt organically-grown) runner beans. My old aunt suffered just such a dramatic conversion. 'Come and kill them!' she shouted down the telephone as if it were a speaking-trumpet. And this from a real died-in-the-wool Bambi-lover and founder member of the Cats' Home. The buck was, actually, a real wild one, and he only frayed a bit on a shrub which needed pruning anyway, but that was enough.

Joking apart, the damage deer can do by eating or fraying certain garden plants and shrubs really can be serious, and doing something about it is often pretty difficult from the stalker's point of view The arrival of numerous muntjac on the suburban scene hasn't made life easier either.

Of course, if there are too many deer in the vicinity there will be greater pressure on village gardens, and those on the edge of towns, so control measures on neighbouring land may be helpful, but deer are so quick to recognise a sanctuary, let alone one stuffed with toothsome browse. Shooting a few out of the bathroom window, to teach them that gardens offer little sanctuary, has its problems – safety apart. I remember one particularly insistent complainant who never said another word after I offered to spend a night in her bedroom . . . with a rifle, you understand. I was young in those days.

In any case, shooting the odd deer where it can be done is a palliative. Once the local deer have learnt the delights of garden raiding, they or their successors will come back time and time again.

So what can be done to help these unfortunate victims of garden marauding? Every place varies, and it pays, if you are sufficiently benevolent or concerned, to go and have a look. Sadly, the most vociferous are often the most reluctant to spend even quite small amounts of money.

'Somebody ought to do something . . .' They will tell you how many prize roses they have just planted at what cost, how many pounds of runner beans have been consumed, but as for paying for a bit of chicken wire for a critical gap in the hedge or even a tin of deterrent, no — they are 'your' deer and 'you' must do something! Preferably nearby but not in my back yard.

The three old chestnuts which are re-discovered every year are moth-balls, human hair and lion dung. One sufferer from nightly incursions of red deer, and hearing the hot news about mothballs, is said to have gone straight into Boots and ordered a ton of them. On a slightly smaller scale, the inhab-itant of a remote bothy told me that he had no trouble with deer getting into his garden — all he did was to hang last week's socks on the fence to keep them out. My sympathy was all with the deer.

The champagne firm Laurent-Perrier ran a competition to find ways of saving fawns in mowing grass. The winner was a deterrent said to be a chemical edition of lion dung. The argument was that deer would have some ancestral memory of their traditional enemies and would sheer off. Unfortunately, having won their prize, no effort seems to have been made by the manufacturer to obtain the necessary licence or market the product.

The Forestry Commission have a revealing video of captive roe avidly eating conifers which had been drenched with, so far as I remember, a mixture of lion dung and tiger urine. The fact is that all sorts of new smells are regarded with suspicion by deer until they find them to be harmless and that probably won't take long. It then becomes a battle between the ingenuity of the gardener and the relative hunger of the local deer. If they are hungry enough they will eat almost anything, whatever has been done to make it unattractive. It is also true to say that if one admires the beauty of a blooming rose bed the visual impact is slightly marred by hanging small bags made of your wife's old stockings stuffed with sweepings from the barber's shop.

One sufferer locally had the inspiration of making use of all those free CDs which keep arriving. Hang them up with string and they will glitter in the slightest breeze.

Of the deterrents which are commercially available, most cannot be applied to growing shoots. 'Renardine' and similar products have to be applied to rags hung from the trees, or else applied to absorbent twine festooned about the garden. 'Aaprotect', made by Duphar Midox, was the most long-lasting deterrent tested by the Forestry Commission, but it can only be applied to dormant twigs and great care must be taken to keep it off the roots. The snag is that deer are most attracted to buds when the buds are flushing in spring, when the deterrent effect is lost. Various products are on sale at garden centres. It is worth experimenting.

The Belgians had some encouraging results from spraying conifers in winter with latex-based emulsion paint while mixtures of whiting, fish oil, tar and 'fresh frothy cow dung' are widely recommended in Germany and Austria.

Some gardens lend themselves to fencing, particularly where the deer can only get in on a narrow front, and especially if the access to the road is not involved, or where the drive gate is kept shut. One needs to remember that deer, unlike cattle or horses, prefer to squeeze under or through fences rather than jump clean over. I saw a garden fenced in by nine-foot high netting against deer. The owner couldn't think how they got in every night. Colditz had nothing on it. The only snag was the wire started two feet off the ground! In spite of their long legs, deer can crawl under quite low fencing. They are also very clever at finding unconsidered corners through which to creep. If total fencing is out of the question, have you thought about deer-proofing bits of the garden? Especially in the vegetable garden one can often put a temporary netting cover or fence round a vulnerable crop at the critical time. Clipped, growing hedges can be unobtrusively fenced by erecting one-metre high wire netting against the green. It will soon grow through and the wire will be totally invisible. If the bottom of a hedge is wired against deer pushing through, they are unlikely to jump at a well-trimmed six-feet high hedge. Existing walls can sometimes be incorporated into a no-go area, but remember to shut the gates!

If you have a dog who doesn't mind going out at night, you might consider the Invisible Fence, which in effect trains the dog not to stray beyond a buried aerial. Provided with a kennel for comfort, but with a pop-hole into the garden, he can patrol around from time to time, which is a very good deer-deterrent.

Electric fencing has a place, and in some places works very well – provided that it is turned on every night. The basic requirements are more than 5,000 volts and a visible tape at a height to let the deer see and investigate it with a damp nose. A handy switch by the door allows it to be turned off when the dogs are let out, and during the day.

If all else fails, try the expedient of a resident of Baughurst, near Reading. He put a small, portable radio in his garden, tuned it to the BBC World Service and left it playing quietly all night. The variation of talk and music apparently had an alarming effect on the local deer. Personally, I find it irresistibly soporific. Perhaps, like the 'Flopsy Bunnies' they all lie down for a snooze instead of demolishing his roses. It pays to be innovative with deer!

Typical Questions on Damage

My garden has been devastated by deer – they've had the roses, the runner beans – even went into the conservatory and munched about in there. Is there a list of plants that deer really don't eat – or don't they exist?

My experience is that if deer are hungry enough, they will eat practically anything! A few (sadly rather un-attractive) shrubs are somewhat resistant, shallon and snowberry among them. I suggest getting hold of *Gardens and Deer – A Guide to Damage Limitation* by Charles Coles (Swan Hill Press) ISBN 1 85310 965 7.

My stalking landlord is planting up some set-aside to make game coverts, protecting the trees with shelters. He is very keen, naturally, that they get away quickly. The forestry contractor is putting 1.2 metre shelters on the broadleaves, but only large-diameter tubes like wastepaper baskets on the shrubs. I'm sure the roe will eat them, and we also get a few fallow from time to time, which I'm sure will browse the tops of the tree species when they come out of the shelters. Am I making a fuss, or is this throwing good money after bad?

No, you are right to make a fuss before the trees are planted, or for sure you will get blamed when the trees are eaten later! The 1.2 metre shelters are fine for roe, but it is necessary to protect the vulnerable shoots from passing fallow. If he does not want to use taller tubes now, it will be necessary (if anyone remembers at that stage) to add some sort of mesh extension, which will be expensive. So far as the shrubs are concerned, these are vital to give warmth in a game cover, and they need to get away to a good start. However, once they are well-established in those wide tubes (they are usually 400mm long or so) a limited amount of browsing will make them bush out. I say limited advisedly! It isn't just the deer which will have a go. Hares love quickthorn especially, and this is where a continuing effort is essential on your part to limit the attentions of the deer, and of the keepers so far as the hares are concerned. If arguments develop about what is respon-sible, remember that hares bite with a clean diagonal cut, while deer (having no incisors) make a rough bite, or a bite-and-pull to leave a tag of bark hanging.

The roe deer always come into the garden and eat my roses and a lot of other stuff. I have decided to fence them out completely. How small a mesh is needed?

I have known young roe get through 6in (15cm) square mesh, so for complete exclusion you need 4in (10cm) squares. Remember they are expert at crawling under the wire – and don't forget the gates!

I live in a village which is infested by roe deer. They eat all the garden plants and get everywhere. It is much worse now because the woods round about aren't stalked any more. Who should I complain to?

Roe soon realise that gardens represent both a sanctuary and a larder bursting with deer goodies. The trouble is that you can't really complain to anyone because as soon as a deer enters your garden, it is nobody's responsibility but your own. It is a good idea to contact the owner of the adjacent woodland and ask whether he can step up deer control locally. I'm afraid even if he does, the problem is unlikely to go away and you must devise ways of discouraging the deer from raiding.

I am a patient man, you have to be to grow trees, but I am fed up by all the guff I'm given about 'deer management'. I have had a chap doing it for years and he gives me a beautiful report every year, but my trees are still eaten. Is all this management stuff better forgotten, and should I look for someone who will just kill the buggers?

I have a lot of sympathy with your problems, and there is no easy answer. The fact is that England is fully stocked with deer. If you create a vacuum, there will be the biblical 'seven other devils' all too glad to barge in from next door and make the last case worse than the first.

Control of damage has to be approached on the lines of a risk assessment. You don't say if you have, for example, an arboretum, if you grow Christmas trees, are trying to establish shelter belts, or have large-scale commercial woodlands. The first two are enterprises where any damage at all is probably unacceptable. No amount of dedicated work by a stalker will stop all damage. He can't be there night and day, but they are! Fencing is the only solution.

With shelter belts and also specimen tree planting, tree shelters are usually necessary. Depending on the deer species present, either 1.2 metre high for roe and muntjac; 1.8 for fallow and sika, or 2 metres against red deer. Where you need to establish shrubs, short, wide-diameter tubes will get them started even if the tops are eaten off. The root system will get established and some side-growth started. Attention by your stalker should be concentrated in these areas and will help, especially if he weeds out the females in winter.

In commercial forestry, avoid damage by planting wherever possible in comparatively large blocks (deer spend less time at a distance from cover); avoid planting particularly deer-attractive species in places deer tend to favour, and use shelters for any broadleaved plants. Fraying damage by roe bucks can be limited by hard culling of yearling males early in the season; control browsing by ensuring that the population of any deer species is well within the capacity of the habitat to support it. Hungry deer will literally eat anything!

So your stalker has his place and can help in the situations I mention. I do agree that many stalkers who maybe have a bad conscience try to jolly an owner by producing fancy reports at the year-end which fool nobody. You need to know what he has shot, where he shot it and what he thinks needs to be done next season. A lot of hot air about breathless dawns goes straight in the WPB and does nothing for confidence. Tell him so!

How high can deer jump? I have finally decided to fence my garden in desperation, but don't want to make it more obtrusive than need be. I think the deer that come and eat it are roe, or perhaps fallow?

You should aim at something like ninety-five per cent protection as a compromise. If deer are just wandering in to feed, six feet (1.8 metres) will do the job, but when chased or otherwise frightened, fallow can certainly clear more than this. You must also make sure that they are not provided with a convenient taking-off place (like a tree stump or hump in the ground) just outside.

As important is to understand that deer can both creep under wire, through a drainage ditch for example, and squeeze through remarkably small holes. To deter roe, a mesh size of maximum 4in (10cm) is needed at least in the lower tiers. Otherwise you can clad larger mesh fencing with rabbit netting to do both jobs.

The 'big-house' answer to ugly fencing blocking the landscape is, or was, to make a ha-ha. Unfortunately a very expensive undertaking. The height for one of these need only be 4ft to 4ft 6in (1.2 to 1.3 metres) as the deer not only have to jump that high, but get their hind legs up too. It is the difference in deer terms between horse show jumps and the solid obstacles at Badminton!

I am getting serious damage to a plantation. I am inclined to blame the deer but can one be sure what is doing the damage, and so take control measures against the right animal?

You don't say whether the damage is to the bark or leaves and twigs. Deer can mutilate trees in three ways: with their teeth (bark stripping); with their antlers (fraying); and by eating (browsing). Other species likely to do damage are hares and rabbits, and voles. If domestic animals break into a plantation they usually leave evidence, such as cowpats or wool tufts.

Bark stripping (apart from that done by park deer) mostly affects conifers at the pole stage, though I have seen bad stripping done by fallow on beech.

Long upward scoring will be seen, often with a curl of bark at the top, where the deer has fixed its lower incisors in the bark and jerked its head up. Red and fallow are the likeliest culprits. This type of damage has not been attributed to roe. Sika stags also score the bark with their antlers.

Fraying, done either as territory-marking or in the rut, will be at knee-to-shoulder height depending on the deer species. Trees need to be whippy and small enough to fit between the antlers. Roe scrape under the fraying stock; fallow often tousle overhanging branches in their rutting area and again make a scrape below.

Browsing checks and distorts the young tree. The maximum height helps to identify the beast responsible. Muntjac (because of their habit of rearing up to feed) and roe – up to 1 metre. Fallow and sika 1.6 metres, red up to 1.8 metres. Deer lack incisors in the top jaw, and so browsed twigs will have a cut-and-tear appearance. Rabbits and hares on the other hand, bite with a clean diagonal cut.

Mice and voles should be suspected if there is a heavy grass mat. Plants are nibbled round the collar at ground level, although bank voles climb and remove small areas of bark which are identified by the minute tooth marks.

The main thing is to go and have a careful look before taking action which otherwise may be wrongly directed and ineffective.

The deer are driving me demented! Any tree I plant seems to attract them from miles around, even if similar ones growing naturally (but of course not where I want them) escape damage altogether. Is there some simple answer to this, or is it just Murphy's Law?

No, it isn't Murphy's Law, though it often seems like that. They can't actually read the price tickets! The answer is probably quite simple – taste and smell. Deer are attracted to anything unusual, so when you put in one of your favourite exotics, it smells different and so the deer sample it like a new breakfast cereal.

With native species, the plants you buy come from a nursery where for the best reasons they have been grown from seed in the most beneficial conditions. Probably a mist culture to start with, and then planted out in rich soil to promote rapid growth. We all know the difference in taste between one radish which has been quickly grown and another slowly grown and old. No doubt tree shoots are the same. In addition deer are known to be very selective in their choice of plants and shoots which are more nutritious. You can see the results of this in the big commercial forests where fertiliser has been spread from the air. Browsing damage is less on the strips which were missed, more where the trees are responding by rapid growth.

If you can encourage natural regeneration, rather than planting, you will get less vexation from the deer. Otherwise it's a matter of protecting the young plants.

Health and Safety at Play

The population of Britain, according to the deathless phrase of that Government census paper, can be broken down by age and sex. Stalkers, not immune to these hazards, also expose themselves to quite a few other risks in the pursuit of happiness.

Our spouses would probably put divorce at the top, not without reason. The phrase 'Unsociable Hours' describes roe stalking to a tee. Let alone a line of alarm clocks set to go off at five minute intervals from some point marking a low ebb in human spirits.

At a dinner party once, I was quizzed about the dangers of a deer charging *à la* wounded buffalo. I had to say that the chance of serious injury was small, especially if you wait to the very last minute before stepping aside. At this stage, as every experienced stalker knows, the buck puts down its head, is unable to see forwards, and thus goes blindly on until its antlers stick in a tree. Many trophies are collected this way.

'Oh! Really!'

Joking apart, the sika has a bad name for turning the tables when wounded. Eric Masters, for years the Head Ranger at Wareham, who had more experience of the species than most, always told me to be careful when approaching a sika stag *in extremis*, and not to risk letting a dog go in to thick cover when there is a wounded one to find.

Even when apparently moribund, a deer has enormous reserves of strength if you suddenly appear, or try to make a grab. Antlers make the most obvious handle, but watch out for the state of your palms afterwards! In the melee it may not be the stag which gets knifed. A bullet from short range is kinder and safe, but always look out for your companion or your dog, either of whom may be dancing about in excitement on the opposite side.

Long before you get to close quarters with your quarry there are plenty of pitfalls to watch as a stalker. You may be all-keen and fling back the bedclothes at half past three in the morning (what did I say about divorce?) and drive all bright-eyed to your stalking ground. Come the third or fourth morning with a few miles to do and the heater on, the eyelids start to droop and another good stalker finishes upside-down in the silage crop with his car on top.

Everyone is more careful about the booze these days, but some stalkers insist on getting out the flask before the day is over, and may even be offended if you don't join them. Gunpowder and alcohol do not mix, let alone the getting back afterwards.

I remember stalking on some very steep ground in the Highlands where inevitably you got back to the stalker's cottage soaked and knackered. The stalker was teetotal, luckily, but his wife always had a deep, hot, peaty bath waiting, followed by a fantastic Highland tea. Then you had to drive the forty winding miles back home. l fought sleep on that road as if I'd been all day in an opium den.

High seats are fruitful traps for the unwary, and not just sitting in them. There was a jäger in Austria who managed to drop a chain saw on his head while building a seat. It was still running. They patched him up, but as his employer complained to me, he missed work for a whole season!

One has to remember that a high seat is a 'rustic ladder' in the meaning of the Health and Safety Regulations. The construction has to include wires along and across the ladder parts, and it should be quite difficult for anyone to fall out. Employer and employee have a joint responsibility about both construction and maintenance and regular checking.

After years of experience, I am careful which high seats I ascend. Rungs break, pigeons foul the floors making a surface like the skid pan at a police driving school but fifteen feet up. In a wind the whole caboodle blows over. After one or two such vexing incidents, paying guests tend to accuse you of a lack of professional competence and begin to cut down on the end of-week douceur.

Visitors do not take the care in getting up ladders which you might take yourself if you suspect that the structure is getting dodgy. Some of them are less athletic and heavier. I did see a rather portly Belgian stuck between the rungs of one of my seats when he decided halfway up that he ought to have climbed up the other side. Perhaps fortunately for his dignity I was half a mile away when I observed his predicament through the glasses. Two hours later he had extracted himself apparently without permanent harm, so nothing was said.

Nearly all shooting men are deaf. It worries me to see a young man lying down on the range for a zeroing session without ear muffs, and of course the worst sufferer out stalking is not the chap shooting, but his guide lying alongside who gets the full muzzle blast. It would be interesting to get the views of some professional hill stalkers on this, but I doubt if they would stoop to consider any protection, even if it was to their advantage to turn up in the morning looking like a spaceman.

Woodland stalkers care less about appearances, but anything which cuts down the ability to hear a leaf drop would be fatal. However, taking myself as an object lesson, I can now hear very little on the left side, even without muffs! Obviously, range work and other situations where many shots are fired make a much greater impact than the odd bang, but the hearing experts say that every shot adds its cumulative and irreversible contribution to eventual deafness.

Active muffs with built-in electronics to allow normal hearing up to a certain level in mono or stereo are fine for the firing range, but in mono you can't tell where the noise comes from, which is difficult enough on a game shooting day and no good for stalking. The stereo versions are a bit unwieldy, but there is no doubt that one can hear as well or more acutely than normal, just by turning up the knob. Electronic in-the-ear defenders are excellent, but not only are they extremely expensive, but require routine servicing which is in itself not cheap. Come to the crunch, what price do you put on continuing to be able to hear for the rest of your life?

The most dangerous object which a stalker uses, short of the rifle itself, is his knife. Sheath knives may come out of their cases when you fall down, folding knives without a lock can shut up on your fingers with awful results. Knives without a definite stop between handle and blade can slip in a cold or wet hand.

If one is to believe some of the more extreme meat hygiene enthusiasts, we may have to kit ourselves up for stalking with a plastic handled knife straight out of the steriliser, in a plastic holster which goes with your chain mail apron and gloves. This, of course, in addition to the white plastic hat, overall and boots needed to perform the gralloch. That is another story.

Woodland stalking is an activity of the half-light. By the time one has found the beast, an early-dusk shot may easily mean a black-dark gralloch. How many of us take a torch in the rucksack? Very few, probably. We just rely on touch to perform the rites. Can you imagine a more dangerous thing than feeling round inside a carcass with one hand to guide the knife in the other?

Even if you have a torch, it has to be put down somewhere in the hope that the beam goes more or less in the right direction. In my experience it usually doesn't. One of my visitors shot a very big buck late in the evening, cut himself gralloching it, dragged it to his car, turned the car round to get help and ran clean over the buck. Not a good evening.

Recently there have been technical advances in torch design and you can get them with halogen bulbs which give a tremendous light from the smallest battery. One fitting on a head band is ideal.

One can get too 'gadgety', but sensible precautions against the possibility of serious injury out stalking is just good sense. After all, that leaves you free to get broken down by age and sex.

Hashes and Haunches

One of the justifications which we need before killing an animal, particularly one as large and beautiful as a roe, is that we are going to eat it. The better use we make of the meat and the less is wasted, the more the argument holds. In fact, I think we have a moral obligation in this direction.

Acceptance of any wild game by the kitchen may well depend on your own unsavoury exertions in the back regions so that the animal or bird looks slightly less dead and a great deal more eatable by the time it appears. Most of us see ourselves to some extent as the primeval provider. The smoke of the cave still lingers about us, and we do expect to have a degree of praise at bringing in the bacon. This justifies disturbing the household in the small hours; a notable absence when the washing-up has to be done (I've just got to go and boil out that head . . .) not to speak of the stalking fees, a new 4×4 to make sure we can get there, and perhaps more weapons in the gun cupboard than are strictly justified. Everything offered to the kitchen has not only to be good, it must look good too — as attractively packaged as the latest supermarket offering by the time anyone else sees it.

We even have our statutory duty to make sure that any food item has to be hygienically prepared, though an Environmental Health expert did baulk a bit when I asked him where I should hide my white rubber boots and apron while I actually shot the beast!

Anyone with a taste for game and unwilling to do the cooking himself should take care to provide the kitchen with carefully prepared joints that are neither bloody, hairy nor smelly, and more or less in the appropriate state for the dish the cook has in mind. Above all things, unexpected meetings with freshly killed roe bucks first thing in the morning should be avoided. Even mother love has its limits. Maybe the other sort too!

The first roe I ever shot went to the butcher to be cut up, and a proper hash he made of it. I still remember the tiny, dry, blackened cutlets which resulted from his unwilling efforts. Roe venison is not fatty like lamb, so you need to cook it in a way which will retain the natural juices, either by casseroling, or if roasting or grilling, cooking it in fairly large pieces. Although the obsequies should be carried out in decent seclusion, there should be consultation about the joints, boned stew meat and so on, which will eventually be needed.

Creeping for a surreptitious cup of tea into the kitchen of a house in the Highlands where I was staying I found the girl who was cooking for us

166

quietly weeping into her apron. The reason turned out to be that evening's *Venaison en croute Wellington*. Not only wasn't there a recipe in her culinary bible, that was bad enough, but the main ingredient was still hanging in the game larder – in the form of a fourteen-stone stag. We managed it between us, though our efforts were slightly set at nought by our host having a problem with getting a stag, and being two hours late for dinner! This interesting day eventually led to my giving demonstrations at a famous cookery school on 'Preparing Game for the Kitchen'. They were a bit of an ordeal until I told the girls that this was all part of their dream of cooking for a remote Scottish shooting lodge 'full of gorgeous young men!' There was a loud cry from the back of the class 'Yes! That's me!'

A flurry of feathers and gore meant nothing to their finer feelings after that.

Luckily roe are much more manageable than red deer, and once skinned a roe carcass is very easy to cut up. One only needs a few basic preparations to make sure that the meat doesn't get dirty and that nothing useable is wasted.

Hanging game always provokes some questions. One hears lots of stories about venison so high it was halfway to being rotten. Like all meat, a period of hanging allows various chemical changes to take place which do improve both taste and tenderness. This has nothing to do with decay or the strong flavours which our ancestors became used to because of the lack of refrigeration in the past.

All depends on what storage you can arrange. Apart from the hygiene procedures after shooting which we are, or should be, familiar with nowadays, a deer carcass needs primarily to be kept away from flies, vermin such as rats and mice and domestic cats and dogs. Any larder must have free ventilation; nothing makes game go off quicker than wrapping a still-warm carcass in plastic even for a short while. During the summer, temperature is paramount and if you have no cool or chilled storage something has to be done pretty quickly. Even one hot summer night will age a deer quite enough to make cutting and freezing essential the next morning. A poorly-placed shot or a messy gralloch hastens the problem even more. If you stalk regularly and have to store the deer you shoot, then it pays to install a small chiller unit in your larder.

As autumn passes into winter the problem diminishes, though fly-proofing and ventilation are both still essential. Once you have achieved cool conditions by one means or another, then a reasonable hanging time will make for better venison. Personally, I prefer to leave a well-shot beast for the best part of a week before skinning and cutting, more if the weather is really cold. When it is ready, it should gently remind your nose of its presence in the larder – no more than that. Remember not to skin until you are ready to cut up the carcass – the skin keeps the meat from drying and turning unattractively dark.

Tradition provides you with a piece of wood known as a gambrel with which the carcass is suspended. Having only one point of suspension the carcass twizzles round whenever you try to do anything with it. As soon as you cut and remove one haunch, the rest immediately falls on the floor. Throw the gambrel away and use one meat hook in each hamstring separately supported, so that the whole thing stays put throughout the operation. Lay out a bit of clean plastic on the bench or table to receive the joints as they are cut off.

The rest is system. Ease the shoulders off by cutting the thin muscle layers which alone hold them in place. Lay them on the polythene for boning later. Then take a saw and cut the ribs down just clear of the thick meat on either side of the backbone. Lay them aside with the thin belly skin attached. You are left with a long thin strip of meat starting at the haunches and ending at the neck ('I used to be thin like that!' as one burly keeper murmured at one of my courses). Now count forward from the rearmost rib and cut the neck off in front of the tenth. It is pointless trying to bone the neck. The bones are knobbly and most of the meat lies between the knobs. Better far to turn it into Mock Oxtail by cutting it into sections like a pineapple This is easiest done when the neck has been thoroughly chilled but not frozen. Then the meat can be carefully stewed off the bone and there's nothing left worth giving to the dogs. The saddle can be cut off, or disjointed with a bit of practice, just in front of the haunches. Take care of it because it is the best part. If you fancy your butchery you can cut off the thin layer of pearly coloured sinew which covers the meat before presenting the joint to the kitchen. All that is left to do is to divide the haunches with a saw. Because each is hung on its own meat hook, neither of them falls to the floor.

Inevitably a lot of this meat is going to go into the freezer, and venison keeps very well. Have a selection of polythene bags of various sizes and a roll of freezer-proof labels for marking. You always think you are going to recognise what is in the bag but by the time it is covered with frost and a year since you last saw it, mistakes can happen. When the Boss is coming to dinner it is embarrassing to find that you have carefully defrosted a bag of dogmeat and not the best fillet!

Saddles need special treatment because of the rib bones which will puncture any bag. This joint needs to be wrapped up in a good wad of clean plastic on the underside before it goes into the bag.

Unless you are remarkably well-equipped you will not be able to get all the air out of the bag as commercial packers do, but by squeezing and sucking, do the best you can. Sealing is important. The wire and paper ties which come in long strips work quite well, or if you are doing a lot of freezing a small heat sealer does a good job. For small bags I invested in a plastic tape dispenser which commercial traders use. A twist of the neck, push the bag through a slot and it is tied up with a jaunty piece of red sticky plastic. All very quick and effective, but they don't really work on the bigger sizes of bag or if your hands are wet.

What you put in the freezer needs to be all good stuff, or you are wasting space. It should also be ready for the kitchen and in useable quantities. Cutting up a frozen chunk of meat is difficult – if you don't actually cut your fingers off you may get them frost-bitten.

All that is left at the end of this, and it should not take more than ten minutes if you are slick, are the ribs that we put aside earlier. Fallow or red deer ribs are worth boning. The Chinese would, I am sure, make delicious spare ribs of them. The Hungarians make them into what they call Porkolt and we call goulash. Failing this, the most practical solution is to brew them up in the stew-pot.

Do not, incidentally, forget the offal. Liver and kidneys are excellent if frozen quickly or steeped overnight in cold water if you find them strong. Hearts make the most glorious rich mince and it's a sin to give them to the dogs. They can have lights (lungs) which might be thought suitable for a haggis. Even Scotsmen draw the line at a venison haggis.

You see now that a deer carcass should be like the Chicago pork-packer's pig. 'Nothing wasted but the Squeal!' Luckily, in the case of roe, they, and we, are spared even that.

An Important Question on Venison

Round here a lot of roe and muntjac get knocked over on the roads. They look all right, but are they okay to eat?

It's a temptation, but you need to be aware of the hazards and also to visualise the way in which the animal has died. Quality meat is produced from unstressed animals. This deer was caught crossing the road, and probably panicked before being hit, so the adrenaline will have been pumping into its muscles, changing the pH and thus the palatability of the venison. It is possible that the impact just broke its neck, but more likely there will be extensive bruising before death intervened, plus broken bones etc. Third, it will probably have been dragged some yards along the tarmac, with all the pollutants present being ground into the carcass. No – I don't eat road kills! Nor do I make a tasty stew 'for the beaters' which was recently proposed in one magazine to my ultimate horror.

If you think of feeding your dogs, well maybe, but be aware that some sympathetic motorist may have seen the beast wounded and has asked a vet to give it a lethal injection. This is more likely to happen to the larger deer species, admittedly, but such cases are on record. In one, a fallow buck was recovered by a stalker in the early morning from a roadside which had, in fact, been put down in this way though he had no way of knowing. It was taken back to the game larder and dressed out. The stalker's dog ate a bit of the liver and was dead in minutes. So don't eat carrion!

Stalking Diaries: the Benin Factor

You've finally shot one! It's a moment every stalker wants to treasure, to store up in his memory-bank, a pinnacle of excitement, whether it is a first-ever buck, the successful end to a long stalk or maybe an especially good or interesting head. Afterwards one wants to share the magic moment with stalker-friends or just recall the fine detail of that outing which no matter how thrilling at the time, tends to fade and lose its first gloss.

Luckily with roe and muntjac one can usually find some bit of wall (preferably indoors) where a modest collection of nicely-cut and boiled-out heads can be exhibited without too much friction with the rest of the household. The shield, cut and polished or varnished to taste, can be labelled with basic details, with more on the back. Just the sight and feel of those shapely antlers is an enduring satisfaction, but non-stalkers may not react quite in the same way to your prized collection. One young visitor to our house was heard to remark 'Mummy – their house is full of knobbly bones!'

Photographs, if carefully posed and taken in good light are acceptable and can be kept in an album, but endless snaps of very obviously dead beasts can only have a clinical interest to the very committed. Too often flash has reflected unnaturally in the eyeballs, or gore is seen oozing or trickling from the corpse. A little care in composing the picture helps to show up the antlers against a neutral background and stop the buck looking altogether too dead. Personally, I disapprove of photos showing the proud hunter posing on or behind a gory heap. We laugh at the Victorian big-game hunter with his boot on the neck of a dead giraffe, and what was tasteless then is inexcusable now. Proudly showing page after page of dead-animal photos is also risky. The glazed look soon develops among your audience even if they happened to have been there, and some casual onlookers might not be in sympathy with Bambi-bashing.

Lurking on my shelves are nine fat, leather-clad volumes labelled 'Stalking Diary'. They look good, and represent an awful lot of time spent skulking about the woods over the last half-century. What a mine of information they are, and just like a mine, getting anything useful out of them is time-consuming, hazardous (because you start reading all the rude things I've said about people, which isn't the point) and quite likely futile, because the really interesting things either weren't put down, or are hidden in such a mound of impermeable verbiage that the sharpest mind can't get at them.

A lot of very keen stalkers keep diaries, or at least start to keep them, then the pressure of events takes over and yesterday's outing somehow doesn't get written up till tomorrow – or next weekend – and the fine detail, hot with recent excitement, which should go down in a diary gets forgotten. It then slides into a dreary catalogue of dead bucks – so many for that number of shots, a few highlights, and the whole point is gone.

If we stalk for pleasure alone, then the labour of diary keeping can help to fix people, places and events and allows that pleasure to be prolonged by mulling over the pages in the long winter evenings, preferably with a log fire and a tall glass not too far off. It's a personal choice. A detailed account of each stalking foray, if written up when the events are fresh in the mind, may also help to fix patterns of deer behaviour under weather conditions which are likely to recur in other seasons. Times of movement in relation to dawn and dusk, wind or weather are well worth recording for reference when the chance to stalk comes round again.

If you are lucky enough to have talent with pencil or camera, then a stalking diary may become a delight, and not only to its creator. The stalking diaries of Balfour Browne come to mind. Photography is, however, a two-edged sword. You can take snaps of scenes and people with a pocket camera well enough, but serious deer photography doesn't mix with actual shooting. 'You pays your money . . .' but the choices are difficult and any compromise is usually a pretty fair disaster. Deer go off that you ought to have shot, because they heard the camera, and pictures taken as incidental to serious stalking tend to show very small and fuzzy deer which need imagination and a magnifying glass to see in the final result. Friends get restive if shown too many. I have got drawers of puzzle pictures like that when it seemed a splendid chance at the time and I couldn't wait for the film to be developed.

The other side of the coin is serious deer management. Of course you want to learn as much as possible about the deer you manage and a diary may be appropriate, but facts in diaries are like the old sailing ship days:

> Beware, beware the Bight of Benin,
> For few come out though many go in!

Primarily you have to show your landlord or employer how you are managing the deer; how many you think there are; what you planned to shoot and whether the targets set are being achieved. In particular your stalking guests, potential or actual, will have a special interest in the standard of trophies which have been taken in the past. They will need to be convinced that the deer are managed and not overexploited.

As a professional adviser, I have visited estates of all sizes to look at deer management and try to make suggestions about any improvements. One is like an accountant arriving to audit the books. What you need is a clear statement of action in the past, the present situation and future plans. The owner is very unlikely to pay for enough time for his adviser to find out these vital facts, why should he? There is the resident chap to explain everything between 10.30 and a pub lunch.

'How did you get on last year?' Out comes the well-thumbed diary, meticulously kept day by day. 'Twenty-two.' 'All roe? How many does?' 'One, two, five in December. No, that one was a sika, but Fred got two or three . . . I think..' You know the thing.

It is all so simple, just put things down in columns that can be added up.

A loose sheet on a clip board in the game larder is headed **Cull Record**. This sheet can (and will) get flyblown and speckled with gore. It doesn't matter. It can all be transferred to a duplicate in the house at leisure.

In addition you will need a **Trophy Record**, especially if you are involved in letting stalking. Visitors will want to take their trophies away with them so unless you take measurements and photographs you will have no evidence to convince future clients of the excellence of your management. Loose-leaf again.

Then you need a summary, to remind yourself and to show others of the targets set at the start of the season and the cull actually achieved – The **Summary of Season**.

Each of the last five headings are divided into: mature male; young male; female; young and Total.

I used to market sets of them, but all you need to do these days is to set it up on the computer, or rule up one page and trust to a photocopier.

From these simple records you will be able to answer all the essential questions listed above, and some more in addition: average weights, trophy weights, average ages, most successful stalking weeks and some others. Simple, isn't it?

CULL RECORD

No.	Date	Place	Shot by	Species	Sex	Age	Weight	Disposal	Value

BUCK RECORD

No.	Date	Place	Shot by	Points	Av. Length	Skull weight	Age	Remarks & Photos

SUMMARY OF SEASON 20 . . .

Beat	April count	Planned cull	Actual cull	Found dead	Total

5 ALARMS AND EXCURSIONS

Wild Goat Chase

What's this? Big Game? But even a humble roe stalker can dream . . .

For years I had a terrific urge to get some sort of trophy, not with antlers but with horns; wide, out-sweeping at the tips and (of course) magnificent. I fancied an Astor Markhor from the Himalayas, or perhaps a Marco Polo ram from the high Pamirs. Great adventures seemed a bit out of reach at the time, so I settled for a Scottish wild goat, and had some modest fun getting it. As with most of the nice things which have happened to me, it was through the kindness of a friend.

On 1 October 1957, I met Kenneth Whitehead at Creetown in Galloway, where we called on F W Champion, one of the pioneers of animal photography. His book *With a Camera in Tiger Land* shows, even now, what one can do with primitive equipment and real woodcraft.

I was electrified at the sight of a monster stuffed goat in his hall, but although it had been shot in Galloway, it was possibly a descendant of a real Markhor which was liberated there many years ago. Inevitably, another monster had been sighted the previous year, but had not been seen since. Hopes began to run high.

News of goats was fairly promising, and we set off up a rough track which soon gave on to the open hill very much like any Highland deer forest, but on a slightly reduced scale. We left the car where the track became impossible, and set off in the pleasant morning sun, with a fierce wind from the east.

Halfway up to the ridge a spy disclosed both red deer and goats. One could have taken the goats for sheep, as some of them were white. As we advanced, we also found two foxes. A slightly off-hand stalk of the deer commenced, the stag having been proclaimed young. In the middle of crawling up a rock, I looked behind me – and there was a wild billy with a

175

fair head (it looked enormous) regarding our antics. He had some nannies with him, and it was obvious that the rut was starting. Kenneth said he was about five, and there should be better ones on the other side of the hill.

We regarded the stag and tried to pass him without success. Reaching the ridge, we met the full force of the wind which was quite fantastic – it blew under my eyelids, took the breath out of my mouth and pulled fiercely at the slung camera. Even with the telescope on a rock and my head jammed against another, it was nearly impossible to spy. Besides the vibration of the glass, the wind pressure forced copious tears from our eyes. We did, however, manage to locate two decent stags far below near some peaty flats.

We retired behind the ridge again, and looked for stags on the more sheltered side, finding none, but we did spy some more goats but all with shortish horns. My guide then set off down the slope at a half run. The slope became steeper by degrees and then fell off in rock slabs to a heather-covered piece of grouse moor. Peering over the edge, I became aware that there were a number of goats below, among the rocks. They were all colours from white to brownish-black, even blue. The majority of older billies, but not all of them, were rock grey with fine shaggy coats.

Creeping over the rocks to a new vantage point, we found a beast lying in the bracken with the longed-for out-curving horns. It was, however, a young animal. What he would look like in a few years' time! One billy at the far side seemed to have the best head of any to be seen, so we ascended the cliff again, negotiated a gully and went down the other side, landing up on a nose of rock where we could have a good spy. From here we saw a new and better billy, so I took (illicitly, in those days) the borrowed .275 and clipped on the scope sight. We decided that it would be best to take the shot from where we were, and waited for the victim to offer a decent chance. Of course, he decided to lie down under a rock where only his horns could be seen. I was reminded of other agonised minutes spent poised over some intended quarry, quite unable to shoot.

Luckily, this time, there was no agitated stalker or jäger making impatient scaring noises, so we lay there in the pleasant sunshine, myself with rifle poised in one hand and a large scotch bun in the other, or in my mouth. At intervals the goat would move and the bun spewed forth but always he kept behind the rock, although two young goats with him had spotted us plastered on our rock and were making sneezing noises at us about a hundred yards away.

Some way above him we spied a malformed billy with one horn normal and one curled like a sheep. I asked Kenneth if he would like it for his collection, to which he agreed, but generously added that it must not be at the expense of my trophy. After a little discussion it was agreed that I would take the malform and trust to luck with the good billy afterwards. However, at this point we realised that there was a much better billy out on the flats some way to the north west. I looked at this one in the glass, and certainly he was very black and big, with more out-pointing horns, so we decided to have a go at him. Of course, at that moment the billy below us moved out into the open for the first time. Who says game is not psychic? Off we went at great speed, first up the cliff, then across a series of inclined rock faces. I have never fancied my speed on the hill (or even on the flat for that matter) and trying to follow a dedicated athlete would have been humbling were it not for my commando soles which gripped the rock more securely than my companion's traditional nailed shoes. Otherwise I would have been 'distanced' long before we got anywhere near.

We paused (myself thankfully) for a spy far above the beast, when there seemed to be some doubt about the quality of the billy below us. Kenneth offered to go back to the other, but he was delaying his own chance at a stag, and we were in easy shot of him.

He was lying down facing me, but rather than take a hurried shot if he got up, I decided to take a neck-to-chest shot. A wriggle in the heather to get set, and this was achieved with immediate success. Various other goats in the vicinity were more or less unmoved by the shot, but quickly made off when we appeared.

The old billy was quite dead when we got to him, looking surprisingly thin under his great shaggy grey coat. His horns were not exceptional at twenty-four inches (61cm), but showed nice shape.

Then followed an unpleasant session with him. I was assured that the gralloch was needed at Glasgow University for research, and a king-sized polybag had been provided for the purpose. The odour of that goat was no ordinary smell – it came at you upwind and choked the breath in your throat. It hung about your clothes and followed you inexorably across the moor. We also weighed the wretched beast in pieces (it came to just short of a hundred pounds [45kg]) and then thankfully buried the remains under a collection of stones. Kenneth then set off to have a further look at his stags, leaving me to carry head and gralloch to the distant car, with permission to come back and look for the malform.

It was a good forty minutes' walk to the car, with the wretched bag full of insides slipping through my fingers and a malodorous head slung on the outside of the rucksack. At last it was done, and after a cup of tea I was off again, armed for the fray. Duty called me to the malform, the inevitable stink included, and I hoped for some photographs as well.

I did get the malform – and a few pictures, but it was many years before the memory of that appalling stench faded sufficiently to make me want another wild goat chase!

Adventures and Misadventures in the Alps

Add mountain scenery to the presence of a sporting and elusive quarry and you have the stuff of dreams, or at least mine. Chamois to me in my teens were as remote as the Yeti. Then, quite unexpectedly, a chance remark at an early St Hubert Club meeting made a short stalking holiday in Austria possible.

Leaving the train at a wayside station, I was singled out by a burly forester wearing a smart grey and green uniform. Soon we were speeding through the dusk. Exciting silhouettes of upward reaching slopes could be seen by peering out of the window. After an hour or so we swung into an un-tarred side route, where the woods came right down in a series of lovely glades to the stream running swiftly alongside the track. Every minute I expected to see a roe poised in the headlights. It was that sort of country.

At length we drew up at a large wooden house, and there was my host in a more ornate green outfit waiting on the steps to make a welcome.

'Mr Prior! Today we shoot the Mouflon! And when we shoot the Mouflon – we drink the vodka!'

And we did. Good stuff, too, looted off the recently departed Russian occupying forces.

In the morning the beauty of the place unfolded. Below the house a stretch of turf swept down to a small lake which in turn reflected the rising wooded hills beyond. Away in the distance were real mountains looking inhospitable but lovely with their first autumn cap of snow. I hoped privately (having read various hair-raising stories about hunting in the Alps) that it would be sufficient to admire them from a distance, rather than pursue the nimble chamois over their giddy heights. At any rate for a day or two. Could anyone have slept well that night, with the skulls of seven gigantic stags and several chamois trophies to guard one's rest, added to the prospect of rising at five the next morning to pursue their descendants? I know I didn't.

In the early dawn I was escorted to a rustic seat overlooking a steep gully, and left with a long lecture which may have meant volumes to a student of German. Perhaps it was as well that nothing did arrive during the next two hours, as any advent would have entailed much heart-searching as to whether I was supposed to shoot or not.

Seemingly in no time the jäger returned. Having spied my slope and found it vacant (much to my private relief) we walked over to another valley where the sun was already beginning to warm the slopes. Presently, he sat down, obviously interested. After some help, I could just make out that two patches of apparently typical dry grass had heads with prominent stripes on each side like a badger which could be seen when they moved.

'Gams!' He said – chamois! It was just like that. No inaccessible crags, no perilous ledges to negotiate, just three fuzzy animals feeding on a slope only slightly more steep and slightly higher than some places at home. We did not pursue that party, as they were all young ones. We gazed at them until, even with my inferior glasses, the stubby little hooks of horns could be made out.

The next morning, a depressing mist hid all but the west slopes, but that did nothing to detract from the general rosy colour of the prospects. I felt lucky. Past the now familiar clearing we continued upwards, walking under the spruces. The slope was steep, wet and grassy. I was grateful for the nailed boots which had been such a nuisance travelling, and for a heavy spiked stick. Soon another open space could be seen on the opposite side. Although it was still pretty black, and misty above us, we sat down among the wet herbage. I looked hopefully into the murk. The jäger was wearing a heavy green cloak. His alpenstock stuck out behind like a sword. When he wished me to advance he twirled the stick, which gave a ludicrously Machiavellian appearance to his figure, topped as it was by a hat of strange proportions.

At length a band of red deer we had spied disappeared into the tall timber, and I let the glasses hang on their string to await the next move. Franz, however, was still busily glassing the top end of the clearing, and following his gaze there was definitely something rather like a black tree stump which seemed to have moved from one minute to the next. Obeying a twirl of the cloak I crept after my mentor. When I came up to him he was sitting down again, and the black animal could clearly be seen as an obvious chamois. I steadied my binoculars against my stick, hoping that he would not notice how much they were shaking. We rose again and stalked between the gloomy tree trunks until nearly opposite the unsuspecting quarry. Here was one of the seats with a rail and screen in front, just at the tactical position. Turning over the board in order to have something dry to sit on, which I thought at that juncture to be a most unnecessary proceeding, we slipped behind the screen and again looked at the chamois. I attempted with the three or four essential words of German learned-up for the occasion, to find out the sex of the creature – both carry roughly similar horns – and if it was a good one. I crooked my fingers, and made measuring gestures, finally in desperation patting the rifle with an enquiring look on my face. Franz nodded and said 'Gut – something or other.' and I guessed that this was the great moment. It still looked a long way off, but there was no excuse to miss with the rifle well bedded on the bar so thoughtfully provided. A last despairing glance at Franz produced no response. Even now I don't know whether I was supposed to shoot or not, but he had plenty of time to stop me.

When the bang came, all was well and the beast subsided into the long grass with hardly a kick. No movement. We continued to sit, while my impulse was to arrive at the scene at the earliest possible moment. After a long pause I picked up the cartridge case to try to signal a move. We continued to sit. I suppose it is part of the routine. When I was all but ready to burst, we did get up and first went down into the bottom – speaking for myself mainly on my backside – and then up the other slope. It was beastly going, very steep and covered with half-rotten branches all very slippery. When I caught up, the jäger had a small fir twig in his hand and was looking for the bullet hole. He couldn't find it at first and I was thinking the beast had died of fright. It was a reasonable old doe. Looking very black and woolly, and smelling rather like a fox, only stronger.

I was offered the twig, and replied 'Waidmannsdank!' to the traditional 'Waidmannsheil!', suitably coached beforehand, luckily. We shook hands. It was all very solemn. The dead beast was also given a twig, so that it might not go hungry into immortality. This was my day – nothing could spoil it.

Going High

In 1960 Ian Biggs invited me to go with him to Austria for a chamois. We met in Mayrhofen after a tiring train journey to Jenbach, and an amusing one on the narrow-gauge, wild-west style Zillertal-bahn up the valley in bright sunshine, with the mountains towering up and closing in on either side and the populace waving as we clattered past. Ian introduced me to Georgi Trauttmannsdorf, the son of our host, and we drove up the gorge to the village of Ginzling then unspoiled and totally surrounded by mountains which gave one a crick in the neck trying to peer up the slopes.

The next day was disappointingly wet, so we stayed in the house but a start was planned for the following morning. We started later than planned, at half past six because it was still pouring with rain. Ian and I set out with the Oberjäger Mariacher, leaving the Count to follow with Bliem acting as porter, who was said to be 'The last Fighting Poacher in the Zillertal'. We dipped into Ginzling to cross the attractive roofed bridge and took the Floite path which slowly rises as it follows the river, first through groves of Norway spruce, then into alder scrub giving us views of the opposite slope and, when the clouds parted, offering tempting glimpses of the heights above. The lower slopes are mostly cliffs with a short slope below. Above these rise the corries, or *Karrs*, almost invisible from the valley floor.

It pleased me to find roe here. There were three out on the slope and another in the bushes. Later we were to see more above the Steinbockhaus, a totally isolated pub which I later came to appreciate. Apparently, roe first appeared in the valley in 1950, and when we were there the population numbered about forty. The reason I was given even then was climate change which besides favouring the roe had resulted in the glacier at the valley's head retreating a hundred yards in twenty years. Far above us the tree line was advancing: new seedlings carpeted the ground well above some truly ancient Austrian pines which marked the old limit.

After an hour's steady climbing, we came to the Floite Hut, a delightful wooden dwelling some hundred feet above the river facing a splendid waterfall and, in fine weather, a beautiful prospect of the glacier and the head of the valley. This was the house of the Unterjäger Farder, who made us welcome. The interior of the house was quite plain but pleasant, although the gravity 'comfort station' on the first floor, with a full flow of alpine air from beneath the seat, left something to be desired but nothing to the imagination.

We began to see odd gams on the slopes, all pronounced to be female or young. All the adults have horns, so telling the sex is a matter for experts! I was surprised to see so many at low altitude, and feared for the weather.

We passed the last trees and the valley became even rougher and more barren as the height increased. Sitting down watching some beasts, Mariacher suddenly looked behind him and, after a hurried word with the Count, said that if I wanted to shoot a *Gamsbock*, now was the chance! And that I was lucky to find as good a buck so low. We were now about 1,600 metres, or 5,200 feet up.

I trailed after Mariacher, first up the path and then round and over some immense blocks of stone which had, at one time, been thrown like dice across the slope. With risk to ankles and legs I managed to keep up and arrived at a flat stone as Mariacher was patting his rucksack into a convenient rifle rest. Comfortable it was, but could I see that buck? After a long explanation, of which I understood one word in fifty, we were no further forward, so I gave him the rifle and got him to align the sights on the beast. Then I peered through them (I couldn't afford a scope in those days) and still couldn't see it, though I realised that he must be lying down and that he was a long way away, two hundred yards or more.

After a bit, Mariacher got impatient and started to make noises, even shouting to get him up. No result – except to make me feel even more nervous and incompetent. Then he signalled to the Count, down below, to make noises, which I believe he did, but the buck was quite accustomed to tourists doing almost anything down there. Then we moved up twenty yards to a less comfortable stone and the demonstrations began again. At a particularly violent shout the buck suddenly sprang into view. There was a stout bush just in line with his shoulder. Then he vanished into a pocket of dead ground and did not reappear. By now I was completely demoralised. Ten minutes later he came out at a dead run above the shelf, and hesitated in some bushes. I missed him clean.

At the shot he darted into a chimney, down into sight again below some cliffs where I, again, missed. With great bounds he sped up the gully towards a patch of old snow, hesitating every fifty yards. Each time he did so. Mariacher said 'Shoot!' The, now distant, beast stopped under a huge boulder, and I can still see the white splash of my bullet on the stone face over his shoulder.

Deflated, we made our way down to apologise to the Count who said, consolingly, that everyone misses gams high because of the upwards angle. 'One must shoot at their underneaths.'

Chastened, we went slowly down the valley. At the Steinbockhaus we were met by Ian emerging from the kitchen, who had been celebrating on the local *Obstschnaps* for a gams he had shot earlier. He left Bliem there who was seen to be embracing the cook. Celebrations continued in the main room, all among the trippers who must have thought that we were a very rough and wild party.

Next morning, Bliem soon had a fire going by shaving a dry pine log into curling feathers which caught instantly. Outside there was new snow on the tops. Ian elected to come with me up the valley, so we again set off with four in our party. There was a packhorse standing outside the Steinbockhaus as we passed, the only way possible to bring up supplies from the village below. We were soon at the scene of yesterday's Waterloo, seeing, not surprisingly, little sign of gams. However, some marmots were to be seen and heard, whistling in the rocks. Further up, a young buck appeared and then some females, but as we got nearer and nearer to the glacier it began to look as if I had fluffed my only chance.

Suddenly, the two jägers sat down. It turned out that they had spied a buck across the valley. We then started to look for it. Every stalker knows the thing: 'The middle snow, under a black rock, by some small stones . . .' That could have described the whole enormous landscape, but at last we found it, feeding above a snow-filled gully. While we were looking at him, he sat down.

Leaving Ian and Farder to watch the fun, we set off. First towards the glacier across loose scree, then as we neared the torrent we had to jump from boulder to boulder. The water itself looked bad but there were enough rocks in it to make an easy passage, though with my usual skill I got a bootful of meltwater on the way. After this there was a cliff of smooth rock, luckily with broad cracks in it filled with earth and grass. Half way up, in a broader part, Mariacher started fishing in his rucksack and pulled out a short and dog-eared piece of string. This he tied round my middle (thus invalidating my insurance policy – 'mountaineering with ropes') holding the other end in his hand. After I had made fun of dog leads, we went on again. It was not really bad going, though the void below produced a certain hollowness in the stomach.

Above us was an expanse of steep grass and rocks, to the left the spreading expanse of the glacier, with the spectacular U-shaped Floitental valley stretching away north-west. One could just make out the Steinbockhaus, a distant brown dot far below.

The grass was tricky to climb, boots digging into the red clover blooms and trusting to our stout steel-shod bergstocks to save a slide. After a short distance we found the way blocked by a gully partly filled with old snow. Water was flowing underneath, and it ended in a rock chute into space. Stumbling, I pitched upside down into this gutter, but saved myself somehow from shooting over the lip. Mariacher went across boldly, treading steps in the snow. Underneath one could feel solid ice.

In a surprisingly short time we peered round a rock and there was the gams, chestnut in his summer coat, standing up and looking suspicious. A large stone was the obvious objective, and in no time the rucksack was placed. Panting with the altitude, I tried to aim across it. There was obviously no time to lose, so steadying myself I aimed low and pulled the trigger. To my disgust the beast gave little sign of being hit, but for a shiver, and took a couple of paces forward. One more and he would be out of sight. Another shot and he collapsed immediately, falling from sight. Apparently, one can think quickly in an emergency, because the onlookers said later that the second shot came bellowing out hard on the heels of the first as if from a double barrel.

It was difficult to reach the spot as we had another gully to traverse and then more grass – level in a way, that is to say flat but tilted at about sixty degrees! At first we could not find him, but with help from signals from

183

below Mariacher gave a grunt of satisfaction and there against a rock was my *Gamsbock*. Slightly marred as a trophy by having broken one horn long ago, but infinitely valuable to me after such an unforgettable stalk.

We were now on a small sloping patch of grass, nothing but air between us and the valley floor a thousand feet down. Of course it looked worse than it really was. We set off over the edge, Mariacher with my buck on his 'dog lead', sometimes it was ahead of him, sometimes behind but usually hanging from him like a picture from its hook. I was allowed the rifle and lodens, and thus burdened we zigzagged down the cliff, usually on narrow ledges of grass with short rocky drops between. This is what makes the place look so inhospitable from below, but comparatively fertile looking down at it. Many flowers were in bloom up there, including an attractive Turk's head lily, which Mariacher called '*Gold-apfel*'.

At length we reached the stream and a smiling Ian to wish me '*Waidmannsheil!*' and add enormously to the pleasure of the day.

The Wrong Animal!

On a visit to a great man in the Austrian Alps whose knowledge of roe was enormous and from whom I learned a great deal, I was invited to try for a *Gamsbock*. Delighted, I set off with the jäger and a beautiful borrowed rifle which had no fewer than three safety catches, all of which had to be released in turn. In spite of the attendant fumbling and the jäger's deep displeasure and obvious mental comparisons with proper visitors, we came down the mountain with a respectable buck which passed the critical post-mortem for suitability and correct shooting. The next day it was to be a doe – a *gamsgeisse*. The clouds were low on the mountains. It started raining early and never  stopped. However we pressed on and up into the murk, the Unterjäger leading. About lunchtime we stopped, enveloped in wet mist, to empty the water out of our boots. At that moment the clouds decided to lift slightly disclosing a hollow below us in which a dozen gams were huddled. With one sock off, I was manoeuvred into a firing position and received whispered instructions in German which I didn't understand. In the end we agreed it was the *grey* one – *not* the grey one lying on the stone, but the *old grey one lying by the stone!* I made a little map with my finger in a bit of mud. Reassured, I fired and the beast fell over. Congratulations, followed by a cautious descent. As the jäger got nearer, I saw his face go white – it was a buck! Disaster!

Gloomily we stowed the evidence in his rucksack and began the return home, each step slower and more reluctant, so that I really thought he would not finally make it up the wooden steps to the house. With the dreadful news, the *Oberjäger* was summoned with other functionaries and everyone but me, the perpetrator, retired into the kitchen for a post-mortem and Court Martial. I was not allowed in and sat planning the next train/flight/bus home. It seemed hours passed before my host emerged to pronounce sentence. He said:

'You were sent out for a *gamsgeisse* – and you have come back with a buck! This is very serious. So we have considered the matter with the Head Jäger and his staff, and have questioned the Unterjäger about what happened.'

At this, of course, I said that it was certainly not his fault, which comment was brushed aside. He went on 'We have looked at the buck, (of course it should have been a doe you were to shoot!) and I agree with the Head Jäger that it is a very old buck, he is not in very good condition and that his horns *did* to some extent resemble those of a *geisse*. So after careful consideration we think that it is quite an understandable mistake, it doesn't matter a bit, and have a schnapps!'

These things shorten your life. I hope not to go through something like that again, even for a chamois!

Moose Hunt

As correct shooting dress, a plastic poncho in Dayglo orange and a paramilitary hat turned inside-out to show the equally startling lining is a pretty strange idea to us in this country. Yet in 1983 I did find myself in the middle of some rather primeval forest, togged up like a traffic policeman and on tiptoes, not for the odd villain, but an unbelievably prehistoric-looking beast. The place was southern Finland, and the animal we were hunting was that ungainly creature the European elk, which out of deference to its larger American cousin seems nowadays to be called a moose even in Scandinavia. It is the

185

world's largest deer, standing nearly six feet at the shoulder. A good bull may weigh about half a ton.

Finland from the air looks like a dark patterned carpet over which someone has been playing a hose. There are said to be about 55,000 lakes in the country, not including the little ones, and as you descend, the dark land between them turns into a flatly undulating sandy country of pines, spruce and birch forests interlaced with small cultivated fields. Each farm with its own matchbox farmstead painted in earthy colours of rust-red and ochre. The towns in contrast are modern, reflecting Finland's war-torn past and repeated fires which destroyed the older wooden buildings.

The farms on average are small, less than 50 hectares, but most farmers also own tracts of forest land, in which the timber is an important resource. Fifty years ago, there were practically no deer. Farmers used to summer their cows in the woods, destroying the undergrowth, while crops and hay were grown on the fields. These days the woods are left to the deer and they have profited mightily. Though not as dramatic as in Sweden, the increase in moose particularly in the previous fifteen years had meant that the annual harvest soared year by year up to a peak of 10,000 and was stabilised at the time of my visit round 6,000 to 7,000 per year just to contain the population at a level where forest damage is acceptable.

This was only achieved by a well-organised programme of training. Every Finnish deer hunter, and there are about 30,000 of them, or nearly one tenth of the male population has to pass a written examination based on a one hundred-page manual. In addition there is a shooting test on standing and moving moose targets every three years. The ten foreign visitors in this party were not exempt from the practical test. Passing it, with the official examiner and nine fellow sufferers in close and anxious attendance, proved a nerve-wracking business. Luckily for some of us, another attempt was allowed immediately, with further time allocated in our programme the next day 'for those who failed the shooting test on Thursday'. No question of slipping through for the sake of International relations! You pass it, or come hunting as a spectator only.

While moose were undoubtedly the greatest sensation, we also had the chance of seeing white-tailed deer which were imported from Minnesota some fifty years previously and have become well established in southern Finland. The farmers, on the whole, wish they had not been brought in, for unlike the moose they feed mainly on farm crops. Strangely, red deer are absent from Finland and I found no-one who had seen a roe, though they are supposed to exist.

The ten of us had come to Finland from Canada, USA, Germany and the United Kingdom, not only to shoot moose but to visit the Sako factory which turns out 18,000 sporting rifles a year. About one-third are exported to North America where they find a discriminating and ready market.

My toes were getting cold towards the end of the first drive in spite of an unseasonably bright sun as I scanned from side to side through the trees. As well as the quarry, one always looks for unfamiliar birds in a strange land. Standing motionless I notch up three grey hens, a flock of crossbills, two hooded crows – all too familiar – and a juvenile spotted woodpecker systematically dissecting a pine cone wedged into a crack in the dead birch tree against which I was leaning. Eventually the cone dropped beside me and made my over-stretched nerves jump.

Beaters could be heard in the distance when, with scarcely a sound in warning, a vast cow moose materialised through the trees. The first one notices is the twinkle of movement of four white-splashed legs, then a bulbous-nose and two shortish ears which with small piggy eyes gives her a barmy expression. She stands about five feet at the shoulder. Turning away she takes a mixture of boulders, spruce branches and stumps in her stride as if she was trotting down to the start at Ascot.

We aren't shooting cows in this particular drive, part of the careful instructions given us that morning to supplement a small rule book. Luckily it was all translated for us – Finnish is strictly for the Finns. Off she goes, fading into the blackness of the forest.

Rifle back to the birch tree, heart back to normal rate. A short time later one of the curly-tailed elkhounds appears and silently pads past, mute on the track.

Later in the day there is a flurry of shots from the other end of the line. My host came out mopping his brow. 'That was very dangerous! There were bullets all round my hat. It was rather like the Winter War!'

Before the next manoeuvre there was a short interview on the subject of safe shooting Finnish style, and a pointed reminder that one is expected to shoot only at moose which present themselves in front of your own stand!

After this, two calves and a cow were accounted for safely, and a young bull which even at four years old was already a formidable sight. His antlers, like many of the local race went into spikes rather than making a palm. Everyone gathers round taking pictures and talking excitedly. The beaters start a small fire of birch logs.

For such a heavy-boned animal as the moose, a powerful rifle is called for with bullets designed for controlled expansion and deep penetration. The favourite calibres in Finland are .308 Winchester and .30-06 though many of the older hunters use converted military rifles, most of which take the 7.62x53 rimmed case; similar but slightly shorter than our old .303. Sako rifles and ammunition predominate using their Hammerhead bullet which was specially designed for moose. To avoid separation the bullet jacket is actually soldered to the lead core.

It was interesting to hear that the Finns have specified their minimum without reference to calibre. For moose one has to use soft-nosed bullets of more than 10 grammes (150 grains) with a muzzle energy of 3,000 joules (2,220ft/lb). The corresponding figures for white-tailed deer are 8 grammes (125 grains) and 2,500 joules (1,850ft/lb). Hand-loaded cartridges are not allowed for moose.

Moose and white-tail have a high breeding rate, most females having twins, so a heavy cull is needed. On our shoot at Loppi, fifty miles or so from Helsinki, they have an estimated herd of thirty plus moose and fifty white-tails on 5,000 hectares of mixed forest and farmland. That year they were allowed twelve moose (five calves and seven adults) and fifteen white-tail licences. These can represent one adult or three calves per licence. Getting such a monstrous beast home involves considerable team-work. The party of rifles and beaters (those not engaged in taking photographs) heaving manfully on long ropes like the tug-of-war at a village fete. When skinned the bull weighed more than 500lb, (226kg) or something like 800lbs (363kg) on the hoof. There is something to be said for a 50lb (23kg) roe buck when the time comes to make for home! Because they are so big, a moose drive can be heart-stopping in its excitement. To see one of these great beasts pacing through a plantation of six-foot high Christmas trees is unforgettable in its awesome power.

Maybe again, because they are so big and so primeval, one has a certain reluctance to shoot, but in the absence of many natural predators they are far too successful for their own good, let alone the effect that an over-population of these beasts would have on the important timber industry in Finland.

Chinese Roe on Migration

My travels in Russia in the late 1980s were written up in *The Roe Deer – Conservation of a Native Species* (Swan Hill 1995) What follows are brief extracts from my diary of a camping trip we made to study the Chinese roe, a sub-species which is almost unknown in the West.

The broken land east of Lake Baikal separates the Siberian roe *Capreolus pygargus* from the eastern race, *C. p. tienschanicus* (or maybe *C. p. bedfordi*). The Altai mountains serve the same purpose further west. Roe in the Amur Region of Far-eastern Russia must once have seemed inexhaustible when on migration, as no doubt did the buffalo and the passenger pigeon to the American colonists. In the nineteenth century one hundred thousand were killed a year in the Amur Region alone. To cross the frozen Amur River to China they even invaded the streets of Blagoveshchensk, the jumping-off point of our expedition. One year, in November and December, soldiers killed 10,000 just round the town. By the early years of the twentieth century they had been vastly reduced in numbers and in distribution. There is still migration towards the River Amur from high ground in autumn, returning in Spring, and this was the object of the team to which I was lucky enough to be attached.

We camped on the River Nora, roughly 700 miles north of Vladivostok, in the Siberian taiga. The river, about 250 metres across, is fast, shallow and bitterly cold. As part of the research, we were to attempt to catch some of the migrating deer and attach radios so that their progress could be tracked from the air.

At 8.25 pm on our first evening a young doe came out on the shingle spit upstream. She stood for some time then turned back from the river and wandered about on the bank before literally running out to the edge and without hesitation wading into the water. In a few paces one could only see her head and the line of her back as she swum remarkably strongly for the other bank. It took her about two-and-a-half minutes, which is the measure of how long we have for the catching operation. The sight made an extraordinary impression. Her deliberate purpose so clearly demonstrated in the face of an ice-cold, strong stream; the over-mastering impulse to move on. And this in an animal which I thought I understood after a life-time spent watching them, but which under conditions at home is as rigidly tied to a small territory as a pigeon to its loft. In the succeeding days more followed as the migration gathered momentum.

189

I find the quiet, determined movement of the roe very affecting in some way; seeing the uncertainty of the fawns and knowing how deeply the deer at home are attached to their home ground. It is a new light on the courage and adaptability of this beautiful animal. They have already travelled 50 or 100 kilometres, perhaps more, starting off long before there is any snow to drive them down. No doubt they have their long-established ways the females must have learned as fawns and which in turn they are showing the next generation. But what triggers it? What unsettles a whole community of deer so soon after the end of the rut to the extent that this drift to the south begins?

The first attempt to catch a roe was abortive due to engine failure, making the crew rather downcast. However, when a doe and fawn were spotted swimming quite near, they bolted down for the boat again like the Keystone Cops. This time the engine did start and the chase was on. As Official Photographer, I dashed upstream to the likeliest spot with the 'serious' camera which has a 35–105mm lens and a doubler as the most useful compromise I could get, given our luggage restrictions. I was not allowed in the boat 'Because it would be embarrassing to drown a foreigner!'

Very soon they caught up with her, Harpooner ('Crooker') poised in the prow, but she circled, swimming strongly and turning faster than the boat could without tipping everyone out. With the boat to give scale, the size of these deer in contrast to the European race was obvious for the first time. The Crooker made a grab, then another. She came to the side of the boat but came unstuck and the whole circus set off again. More ineffectual grabs nearer and nearer to the bank in spite of hostile demonstrations. Facing these, she made the shore and galloped up the bank. A gallant performance! A depressed post-mortem followed. I decided to keep clear. More circus at 6.30 pm when the catching team set out after a doe and fawns. The performance was not very convincing. After several encounters in midstream the doe evaded her opponents and the Keystone Cops departed in high dudgeon back to camp. Alexei followed down the bank to reason with them.

Third time lucky! There had just been time for the reasoning process when a doe and twins came out on the bank just opposite me and went straight in. I started taking photos first in the reflection of the trees and then, as the distant Keystone Cops got the motor going, in a brighter patch of reflected sky. By this time they were only about 50 metres away. The doe was collared in every sense of the word, going off with the first radio transmitter safely attached.

Several times a family would walk out until the water was up to their bellies, only to turn back. Pretty obviously the fawns are frightened and unwilling. The doe has to judge if they are desperate enough to follow her. I was near one party as they swam in, and both fawns were squeaking loudly the whole time. The doe could also have been replying, but it was difficult to say. It is only at close range you realise how big they are compared to ours. At a distance they are all roe – just the same behaviour and look about them. As they get closer one realises that something about the head robs them of that indefinable charm which is such a feature of the European roe. They have a definite Roman nose, making them thicker, deeper to the jaw line and making the eyes look smaller in comparison. The ears, which are very large, are set on lower and farther back which alters the look of the head, however slightly. In fact anyone who did not spend his time among roe would have difficulty seeing any difference apart from size.

With a better chance in good light to look at the deer as they hesitate on the bank opposite, two aspects of their coloration are obvious. They have a tendency to an ochreous centre to the target, and their white neck patches are more varied than in the European form. One yearling doe had a complete 'blaze' down her throat, her buck companion just a badly-defined pale area below his jaw.

As possibly one would expect in September, most of the deer were still in summer coat but darkening as the winter hair grows through. The majority have a pale rump patch, or target, though in a substantial number the centre of the target was a bright ochre. This tendency gave the sub-species, then known as the Chinese roe, its early Latin name of *Capreolus c. ochracea*. A mature doe was the first to show a typical dark grey winter coat with a very white target. The buck with her was sandy, with no visible target at all.

The majority of adult bucks have long, rather thin six-point antlers. The span is average to wide. I have not seen a narrow-headed buck at all, though some have been rather 'untidy' or lack one or more points. As far as one can judge with animals in water, yearlings mostly carry 4 to 6in (10 to 15cm) spikes with occasional ones still in velvet. No doubt some yearlings with multi-point heads have been taken to be young adults. We have seen some bucks with very long antlers, the actual length difficult to judge without knowing the length of the ear. A number have definitely been over 30cm (12in) and a few several centimetres longer than this. Pearling on the whole is not pronounced, but the odd individual has had strong, thick beams. Unlike the Siberian roe, this sub-species does not produce heads of more than six points to judge by the four to five hundred bucks we have seen.

Alexei organised an all-night watch to see if the number crossing after dark is comparable. I took my spell early in the night, which was an unforgettable experience. Absolute silence except for the occasional clatter of stones on the far bank as a party of deer milled about making up their minds whether to cross. I hoped a wolf just might appear or at least advertise its presence with a hair-raising howl. Alas! No luck. I would like to see a wolf but the chances are slim especially as the river is still running high with the gravel banks covered. Later, the Poles gave me the definition of a Siberian loo: *two sticks. One to lean against and the other to beat off the wolves.* I wish I needed the second!

In the dawn there was a good deal of barking opposite, which rose at one moment to a crescendo, then to a brief scream. One up to the wolves which harass the rear of the migration. Sadly they did not reveal themselves. The sun rose eventually above the dawn mist, and the Great Trek continued.

As the migration continued through those golden autumn days we watched an endless succession of roe slipping quietly across: does with their fawns, an old buck and his fag, sometimes a male or a female alone. Their heads catch the lowering sun, and behind them the straight line of their wake which can still be seen when the swimmers are already on the bank. There are some very big bucks crossing at this late stage in the migration. It has a dream-like quality, as if one had all the roe in Sussex swimming the Thames between Henley and Pangbourne on their way to Wales for the winter.

Suddenly the migration was over. One evening the movement cut off and we gazed over a tranquil expanse of river which for so many days had been the scene of such intense activity. In all we had counted a total of one thousand three hundred and fifty-two roe crossing the river. For each doe (including yearlings) seen to cross we saw 1.29 fawns, while for does which crossed with young the figure was 1.69.

I was reminded of what I was told in the plane from Moscow by three cheerful Red Army men: 'Looking for roe deer? You'll be lucky if you see one this side of Christmas!'

Indeed, I had been very lucky.

Two Hundred Dogs

Not everyone will be pleased that we now appear to have at least two flourishing colonies of wild boar in southern England, but to be sure there will be a number of woodland stalkers who are rubbing their hands at the arrival of this most sporting, if somewhat destructive, quarry. Anyone who has had the chance to shoot boar abroad will have considerable respect for this courageous, formidable beast. Although boar have been absent from this country since the early seventeenth century they seem to have acquired a terrible reputation for ferocity. It was rumoured that when an unfortunate sow escaped and farrowed somewhere in the north, such was the panic that they shut the schools and life came to a stop until the whole brood had been accounted for by armed gangs! Shame.

I have to confess that I thought them only less dangerous than tigers until my first introduction to the species when I was taken round a big boar shoot in Belgium. Of course I was all agog to catch a glimpse of such a strange beast in the binoculars but my host said, 'Just jump out of the Jeep and rattle the bucket!' There was a stir in the bushes and boar of all sizes rushed out at me! These, of course, were animals reared more or less as we do pheasants and were just about as wild – until the autumn! Like pheasants they very soon get the idea at the beginning of the season and after that can be elusive even in the confines of an enclosed shoot. They are thoughtful and brave, weighing the chances of a break through the line of Rifles here or there. On a shoot in the Ardennes my neighbour had not had the chance of a shot all morning and could be seen to be bored. From my oblique view I saw a boar hesitate in the scrub opposite him, on the point of making a run for it, but at that moment a hare came out and my friend had two vain barrels at it with a 9.3mm × 74 express. Of course there was no sign of piggy after that! One has to stay deathly quiet or see nothing, and a couple of hours can be blisteringly cold in those snowy woods. The only solace was the arrival after the first drive of a vast nest of decanters offering three different sorts of schnapps! At lunch there was a big bonfire at which one toasted one's backside and sandwiches. If you were grand enough you toasted your backside but your chauffeur did the sandwiches. It was good fun until the heat of the bonfire started to melt the snow above, and cold lumps deluged down one's neck from the branches.

At another place the chance of a boar was combined with driven pheasants – one of the more dangerous sporting moments in my life. We were issued with Brenneke solids for boar and normal shot for birds, putting slug in one barrel and shot in the other. Boar, I was told, either come out early in the drive or very late so the slug went in the right barrel to begin with, but when the pheasants started to show was changed to the left. Or that was the plan! Maybe one heard something and changed round again, in case of a sudden appearance. At one moment there was a cry of 'Becasse!' (woodcock!) and everybody had two barrels at it regardless of load or safe angle. Wow! It was on that shoot that one of the Guns killed a piglet with No. 5 shot and was promptly fined a case of champagne – which he duly delivered.

Anyone becoming involved with boar control in the depths of Sussex or wherever would be well to remember that they are very tenacious of life and may go a long way with a wound which would put a deer on the ground. You don't need an elephant rifle, but would be well advised to use something more powerful than a .243, for example, and with a fairly heavy bullet. If you take a shot at a boar and it isn't to be seen, don't give up hope but watch out! If displeased they are mighty quick with those twin gralloching knives they carry in their snouts. A good dog may be needed, but kept on a lead; a large boar when wounded and cross is a very different creature from his normal retiring nature. The bigger the dog the worse it is because he will try to hang on and risk serious injury. A small dog is more likely to yap, dance around and stay out of trouble.

Many of the awful and worrying things that have happened to me over the years were connected with boars. There was one very clear instruction which I read in some book which the author felt was so important he put it in italics: *'Never let a wounded boar get back among the beaters!'* Very early on in my boar-shooting career a yearling came trundling across my front; very obviously took my bullet somewhere, turned and *went back among the beaters.* I was horrified. Worse – there soon came the noise of a distant rugger scrum in the trees and loud shouting in Flemish to which was added strident and agitated piggy noises. Was the pig killing the beaters, or were the beaters killing the pig? I was in an agony until an oilskin-clad figure emerged dragging it, by that time very dead. The relief!

One of the reasons that many Continental sights have very heavy reticles in scopes with very large object lenses for maximum light transmission is that they are used for shooting boar at night. It's an exciting but frigid pursuit; listening with all one's might for the scrunch of leaves – straining one's eyes to identify vague forms under the inevitable spruce trees and trying to remember the often precise rules about what one can and cannot shoot. Boar when they are feeding tend to move about, and between seeing a definite male in the binoculars and putting up the rifle, the whole picture will probably have changed. Two or three obvious sows are now directly in the line of the one obvious boar or the whole lot have vanished. Frankly I have always been more worried about not doing the wrong thing than getting a boar at all.

One of my most vivid memories of sitting up for boar was in Portugal one warm night in early autumn. The two of us were placed on a hilly ridge from where we were given a fantastic display of summer lightning in the distance. Later a boar did come out, attracted to a wallow liberally seeded with old sump oil in which the boar love to roll. At my shot the boar rolled down into a thicket of thorns. The gamekeeper who was with me removed his shirt and forced his way in, emerging some time later carrying the beast, which must have weighed fifty or sixty kilos (110–130lb). Between sump oil gore and mud, I could only admire his strength and tenacity.

Where boar inhabit very dense thickets some form of driving has to be employed. When the thicket is studded with enormous boulders and is inclined at about sixty degrees, as is often the case in Spain, then dogs are the only practical way of tackling the situation. This need has evolved into the *monteria*, in which a large area is surrounded by Rifles manning likely crossing points while two hundred or more dogs are released to stir things up. The result can be explosive! Of course it is not as bad as it sounds: the dogs are hunted in packs of about fifty, each with a beater/huntsman whose loud cries keep his pack more or less together and alert the Rifles to the progress of the drive. Where I have been lucky enough to be a guest on one of these very fashionable and expensive shoots there is only one drive, but the beaters move over the ground twice. While there is more chance of seeing something when they come near or you hear a dog in pursuit, the old and cautious males may move out at any time, and can shift their bulk through tinder-dry scrub with scarcely a sound.

The dogs are a mixed lot, mostly long-legged and usually thin, but must be fit to run for three or four hours through that rugged terrain. One might assume that their owners economise a bit on the day before a shoot, because any fallen game they find tends to have a rough time before the drive is over and the bits can be picked up. One cannot, of course, for safety leave one's post while shooting continues. One day my neighbour shot a red deer calf which was set on by what looked like a hundred dogs. A couple of hooves were all that could be retrieved at the end of the day! It wouldn't do for Dorset, but if those lovely pigs start to breed as they are capable, say six or eight at a time, we soon may be inundated with red-hot phone calls, 'Your boar are eating my potatoes! Come and do something!'

I am reminded of something that old Frank Wallace quoted in his deathless book *Hunting Winds*: 'The slothful man saith "There is a lion without, I shall be slain in the streets!" I wish he would say it now.'

Wild Boar and Mixed Drinks

I am sorry to say that a good many of my memories of boar are centred round some quite splendid parties; the latest expedition not least when we sat down eighty-five to lunch after a *monteria* (lunch was at 7.30 pm, being Spain) at which we were regaled successively with every bit of pig anatomy, pieces of air-dried raw *jamon serrano* ham from pigs living semi-wild in the oak forests, barbecued spare ribs and so on, all washed down with the splendid local wine. There were more sophisticated pre-battue banquets in Belgium with waiters in white gloves, and at the other end of the scale, a decidedly tipsy evening in Poland where the abundance of vodka made up for a certain simplicity in the food supply.

The last came leaping to mind when I was leafing over a diary which I kept of my travels in the collapsing communist world of the late 1980s. Thanks to a vastly helpful host I was wafted from expert to expert round Poland, mainly talking about field roe which were the main object, but as well a host of other topics to do with the management of game. When, at a field station near Poznan, I told them of my admiration for boar, no effort was spared to show me a Polish specimen, and even have a shot at it. We drove out into the woods and sat for the evening on the high seat normally reserved for VIPs. There was a pricket red deer out on the clearing when we arrived, then nothing for some while. The seat overlooked a long clearing with pine and oak struggling against competition from deer and very coarse high grass in the open bits. Toward dusk a hind came out, but just at that moment there was a bang from not far off and she decamped. The Professor was much put out at the lack of game. As the light began to go, he suddenly pointed out four yearling boars in the long grass, thrust his rifle into my hand and whispered 'You can shoot one – shoot all of them!'

Although I had a steady position from the seat, the boars were three parts concealed in the high grass and were shifting around. Momentarily one would show up well, but with another behind it. Then another would offer

196

a shot and instantly vanish. I was struggling to sort them out through a 6-power scope with a very narrow field of view and with a horrible rubber tube on the eyepiece to which one had to clamp one's eye. Luckily I had been schooled in the set trigger mechanism of the 12-bore and 7mm × 65R drilling. In the end one looked right and I banged off, seeing absolutely nothing afterwards.

Then the commentary: 'One has stopped! Now he is going on – that's very bad!' This was accompanied by sad head-shakings. I took the used cartridge case out and forlornly descended the ladder, trying to maintain a stoical British attitude. At such moments there is plenty to say, but nothing to be said.

We struggled across some deep forestry ploughing concealed by the high grass and the gathering gloom. No wonder they had been difficult to see. We found the place where they had been – and there was some blood. Not much, but looking to me like good bright lung blood. We cast about, leaving markers of loo paper and then decided that it was too dark and we would need a dog. Departed in profound depression. All I could say was 'It looked all right when I fired' but knowing in my heart that all I could see was that the reticle had been 'in the black'.

Back at the Field Station we recruited some help, including 'Box' a young German pointer said to be 'Not much good because he was too petted.'

We went back to the place and showed Box the blood, in which he didn't seem very interested. However, he and his owner set off with a torch, and in a different direction from our first search. In ten minutes there was a gruff bark and encouraging Polish shouts – they had it! What a relief. In fact it had been well shot in the lungs and had run less than 100 yards. A large yearling weighing 42kg (92lb). Good boy, Box! Home in jubilation, spruce twigs in hat, to supper and vodka.

Even after six weeks' practice in Russia I still can't take to vodka – slugging it down 'for the effect', but in celebration one has to go through the motions and avoiding too many repeat toasts. At a certain stage (hunting songs) I felt that the party would feel less inhibited without a cold-blooded foreigner present and went to bed.

Friday 13 October – not an auspicious date! Rendezvous at 5.15am, but there was a distinct hiatus before anyone else appeared. My designated assistant was one of last night's revellers. We went to the same high seat, in which he went immediately and heavily to sleep for two-and-a-half hours – still completely blotto from the previous night's potations. He kept falling over on to me, needing a firm return push to set him upright again. By degrees I became slightly peeved, and a firmer push had the satisfactory effect of more or less collapsing him in one corner of the seat where he continued to snore regardless. I did have a moment's unease in case he woke up and a fight should develop. A small high seat fifteen feet above the ground is no place for fisticuffs.

Not surprisingly after the shooting and dogging last evening, nothing came out.

The second evening was spent in another 'guest' high seat – a tall structure overlooking another long pine plantation with high grass. The Professor says it is a lucky seat for guests, and indeed a roe doe ran off as we went up the ladder. There was a large ploughed-up area in front where some boar had obviously been busy. We settled down to a regular sweeping of the clearing, which was maybe 70 metres wide and 500 long, with high trees on three sides and 15-year-old larch facing us. In this I spotted a movement which turned out to be a fair-sized boar, hull down in the long grass. I was again told 'Shoot!' but the seat was awkward and I had to get to my feet, change position and start again without ever getting a really comfortable aim. All this time the boar was working into the corner, and never gave a good view. However, I did see a good shoulder and fired, hearing a loud knock.

Not good at all. The boar went quickly across the corner of the clearing and when last seen was going strongly up a ride. Oh Dear. Much deflated we went down to look for signs where it had been, or thereabouts. Nothing. The Prof thinks I missed it. I wish I had. Then we went to the only certain spot, where it had turned up the ride, and there we found a sparse trace of blood with a couple of white spots which looked suspiciously bony to me.

There was nothing to do but go home, get Box and hope. Mine was NIL. Remembering the driven boars of Belgium I thought it would go at least a kilometre and then think about what to do. Back at the Research Station we had a bad wait – Box and his master were out in the forest, and anyway the longer we left it the better. We agreed that next morning would have been best but for the risk of rain. The Prof was consoling, but obviously not hopeful. We had tea and vodka 'for the boar' who no doubt needed it even more than I did.

The stalking party at last turned up. Luckily I was unable to understand the inevitable comments about foreigners who always needed a dog at Bloody Midnight. . . However, two helpful students, plus Box and owner and ourselves all turned out, found the loo paper markers and off Box went on a lead into the dark. It was pointless to follow, so the Prof and I stayed waiting, straining our ears for any signs. The lights vanished into the forest, and for a long quarter of an hour nothing happened. Then Box came back! Worse.

There was a good deal of light flashing at one spot; Box went back and shortly afterwards we heard a bark from him. Flashing lights in a different place, then shouts – untranslated – then the party coming back. Well, I never did expect to get it – so back to England with a bad taste. Why does one go on shooting when there is such a risk of total disaster? The party were coming back with a good deal of crunching of branches, finally emerging 50 yards away – with the boar!

Box, you marvellous dog! It had gone 200 yards with a liver shot before dropping dead. A barren sow of 64kg (140 lbs), very silvery in coat and typically long-nosed in contrast to the Belgian boar.

So we went home a much more cheerful party than the outgoing one. There's no doubt of it – wild boar are special!

6 LOOKING BACK

The Origins of South-Country Roe

Petworth – A New Fragment of Roe History

The origins of the roe in the south of England have always been a source of intense interest. Piecing together the story of the reappearance of roe where they had almost certainly died out is rather like a jigsaw puzzle – one bit lying in an old book, another lurking deep in a pile of dusty handwritten letters. Often one finds that a likely lead turns out to be one more dead end. Recently a new piece turned up unexpectedly and to put it in its context it may be worth summarising what we know.

Roe deer became rare in the south country during the eighteenth century. Whether a few survived in some of the great woods which then existed is a pipe dream. I have a letter written in the 1920s by Maurice Portal who knew North Dorset and its wild life at the beginning of the twentieth century. His opinion was that there had always been a few roe there 'and the shepherds on the high downs always said their fathers spoke of them. One old man of eighty had a wonderful story of one his father had found wounded, which he killed and ate.' All lovely romantic stuff, but if one assumes that these tales relate back to the early nineteenth century, they might have been talking about animals which had already travelled from their release point at Milton Abbas, especially if the date of importation was 1780, as suggested by Richard Fitter in his book *The Ark in Our Midst* and not 1800 as is generally accepted. I do not know of any similar folk legends from Sussex, though they may still exist.

The resurgence of this species, in Dorset at least, was due to an enthusiasm for hunting on the part of one or two landowners which led to roe being released in central Dorset. The actual date and especially the origin of these deer and others which were supposed to have been liberated about the same time in Petworth Park in Sussex has never been clear. Research has been frustrating in the extreme. The great estates of the period should have been repositories of local history, but a combination of occasional

200

house fires and a tendency on the part of their owners to clear out and burn old ledgers from time to time has led to many dead ends. For example, the Drax family of Charborough Park, who were involved in roe hunting in the early 1800s and could have been a fruitful source of contemporary documents. Their archives were transferred at some stage to another family house which subsequently burned down. So it goes . . . Disappointment again.

The earliest date proposed for the Dorset reintroduction was 1780 involving Lords Dorchester and Portarlington, but accounts in *The Sporting Magazine* about 1817 led to the generally accepted notion that the Dorset roe were liberated by Lord Dorchester in 1800 'Some of which he procured from the Menagerie of Mr Brooke in London, at a considerable expense, and some were presented to him by The Earl of Egremont' (the owner of Petworth Park). If this was true, then roe must have existed in some numbers at Petworth prior to this date.

Other accounts in succeeding years made other suggestions, perhaps the wildest being that some came 'from Ireland – another couple were brought from North America'. Of course they existed in neither country. Another story coming from the grandson of a neighbouring landowner, Mansell-Pleydell stated that they came from Scotland, 'he had often heard his Grandfather say so' but this was not written until the 1880s. A further suggestion, backed up by contemporary accounts in the Dorset archives was that they 'came from France'. Perhaps these were the expensive animals from Mr Brooke's Menagerie. Who knows? The reverse was also suggested, that roe were sent to Petworth from Dorset to found that herd. Kenneth Whitehead, that indefatigable researcher, reviewing the available evidence in 1964, concluded that the Petworth roe were imported by the Earl of Egremont about 1805, although it is just possible, as suggested by Edgar Barclay about the same time, that a relict population had survived in Sussex until that time, and that some were enclosed when the thirteen-mile long park wall, first built 600 years ago, was completed by French prisoners during the Napoleonic War.

If the colony of roe was established at Petworth before 1805, then some foundation stock could have been supplied from there to Dorset, as *The Sporting Magazine* stated, but if so, it is curious that typical heads from Sussex and Dorset are noticeably different, the Sussex heads tending to be narrow in span with heavy, dense pearling, while Dorset bucks tend to have wider but less well-pearled antlers. With the development of sophisticated DNA analysis, one might have hoped that problems such as these could be finally solved. It was reasonable to assume that genetically isolated communities in Dorset and Sussex might show vital differences, or more particularly between the roe of Scotland and France. Unfortunately this technique has not apparently advanced enough so far to prove anything.

Humble Pie

Some years ago I wrote to the County Archivist of West Sussex to find whether there was any mention of roe in the Petworth archives which had been transferred to them. A regretful letter followed saying that they had not had time yet to study the archive in detail, but would let me know if they found anything. That was in 1993. Imagine my surprise and delight when I received a letter ten years later from the Assistant Archivist:

> I am pleased to tell you that to date I have catalogued a number of bills for the supply of animals, including 7 from Joshua Brookes. I find that in June 1789, Brookes supplied two roe bucks to the Earl of Egremont. This is the only reference I have found to roe deer, though the Earl was buying various other breeds of deer at this period. There is one bill of 1802 for 'ten live does' bought from George Othen, a venison dealer, but there is not indication of their breed.

One can possibly disregard the ten live does, which could be assumed to be fallow. However, much can be deduced from this one fascinating invoice, of which they sent me a photocopy.

The first conclusion is that if he got two bucks, but no does, from Mr Brookes, (or Brooke?) there must already have been roe in the park in 1789 and these were needed to improve or supplement the stock. When the invoice arrived, I was surprised to see that while an 'Amber-headed Paroquet' cost £1. 11s. 6d, the two roe bucks were priced at the formidable sum of £42, plus carriage of £3. 13s. 6d. A very expensive purchase indeed at a period when that sum might have built a reasonable house. Did they come from France via Mr Brooke, like the ones for Dorset? I wonder. It would have been easier in 1789, before the French Revolution, rather than in 1800 when the world was at war, though even then there was a lively trade across the Channel in brandy, silks – and maybe roe bucks!

The next stage was to find out about Brooke's Menagerie, but there again I ran into a blank wall. Not even the London archives or the Natural History Museum had any record of this animal collector who was so obviously well-known and successful at the time. A resourceful merchant too, judging by his ability to supply twelve reindeer from Lapland for the Duke of Norfolk's estate near Penrith in the year 1799. Maybe all trace of him was obliterated in the Blitz. Did the Dorset roe come originally from Petworth, descendants of the imported (or native plus imported) stock within the park? Or was all this a fine cloak for some fairly illegal imports from over the Channel, along with a few barrels of brandy and some silk? Who is to know?

Various articles in *The Sporting Magazine* (*The Field* of its day) admittedly written some years later, do give some details of how the deer were settled 'in Lady Caroline Damer's woods, within the wall [presumably of Milton

202

Abbey?] to which their descendants invariably made when they were hunted'. The Dorset roe became established and started to expand. Within fifteen years they were sufficiently numerous round Milton Abbey to hunt. The first buck was killed in 1815 by Mr Pleydell, of Whatcombe House.

Packs of roe hounds were kept by the Pleydell, Drax, Radclyffe and Yeatman families. Mr Harding's Mountain Harriers were another such, but despite their picturesque name appeared to be willing to hunt almost anything they encountered! Special uniforms were designed and worn by Huntsmen and Whips – buff with a black collar in the case of the Drax hounds, and a field of sixty horsemen indicates the general enthusiasm for the sport early in the nineteenth century. The vogue gave way to the more fashionable sport of foxhunting and had practically died out by the 1860s. The roe, however, survived and soon spread throughout Dorset. We hear of them again from the pens of some early enthusiasts for stalking with the rifle, notably Martin Stephens and Henry Tegner, who wrote of their stalking exploits round Milton Abbas in the 1930s and 1940s.

Roe Stalking in the 1930s

The roe stalker of today has, to a great extent, inherited a legacy left by a small number of sportsmen for whom the species represented a worthy quarry, and who believed that they deserved a better fate than snaring or shotgun drives.

Stalkers who are keen enough on roe to study the literature will know that roe stalking as a sport was promoted against the weight of tradition from the late nineteenth century onwards by a very small number of enthusiasts. The names of John Guille Millais, Frank Wallace and Henry Tegner leap to mind because of their memorable books. Nobody could communicate the sheer excitement of a roe stalk and the beauty of the Scottish woods and hills better than Frank Wallace. He was a man who had travelled the world for big game but still did not disdain the humble roe – far from it.

Henry Tegner caught Frank Wallace's enthusiasm, and went on to write extensively. His book *The Buck of Lordenshaw* was my bible when it came out in 1953 and still keeps its magic for me as an evocation of the unalloyed pleasure which his generation took in chasing the roe for the fun of it in the days before we became involved in the necessary business and disciplines of careful management.

Edgar Barclay was friends with all these and other roe stalkers of the period, but who through his innate modesty was less well-known. He was a keen shot, fisherman and roe stalker, writing fluently not only about roe, but on the management of small game and general mammalian natural history. Running a regular column in the shooting press for years, he never failed to put in a word for the better treatment of roe in the days when they were still 'Those uninteresting little beasts' to be shotgunned or snared as a perk for the keepers.

I got to know Edgar early in my roe stalking career in the 1950s, soon finding – mostly through his regular letter-writing – that I was in touch with a man who, if limited by finance and the demands of his job with the Ministry of Works, was as great an enthusiast as any of the other household names of the roe world. Five years older than Tegner, he was born in 1896, one year before the publication of J G Millais' *British Deer and their Horns*, and served in the army in the First World War and then as a civilian in the RAF from 1939 to 1945. Always a keen rifleman I still have his NRA Rifleman's Certificate awarded when he was at the Haberdashers' School in 1911. His diary of the time recalls shooting over the family property in Sussex and fishing for trout not only in the Rother but also for carp, tench and roach in private ponds. That was followed by mainly fishing expeditions to Scotland and shooting as occasion offered.

His interest in big game and his passion for accumulating facts about them started soon after the First World War and resulted in the publication, in 1932, of *Big Game Shooting Records* – a companion volume to Gladstone's *Shooting Bags and Shooting Records*. This book, now hard to find, contained some extraordinary accounts of shooting on the grand scale – 'Feats which can never be equalled again' in the words of a contemporary reviewer. In the section on roe he quotes the bag of 16,864 killed by The Elector John George II of Saxony between 1656 and 1680, suggesting that he probably killed more roe than any other man. As an example of the enormous shoots which took place in Imperial Russia he gives the bag killed between 31 August and 12 September 1900: bison 32, elk 36, red stags 53, fallow 26, roe bucks 325, wild boar 138, winged game 11, Total 685. This was at Bialowicza near the present Polish border, a famous place to this day for its remnant of the primeval forests. Barclay accumulated this mass of data on a long-vanished way of life by writing directly to the people concerned and kept up a lively letter-friendship with several of them for years.

Scotland features in the roe records, with details of bags between forty and sixty in a day's driving to shotguns. The Bad Old Days indeed. Although not included in the text, a letter pasted into his copy of the book also gives the personal bag of a contemporary roe stalker, Robert Hargreaves, who took 330 roe to his own rifle between 1887 and 1932. Not perhaps a big total for these days, but a good indication of his dedication. They would probably all have been mature bucks. Henry Tegner recounts of this stalker that he had a caravan specially designed for stalking. It was 'luxuriously equipped with cupboards for his rifles and racks for his fishing rods'. Besides using it in Dorset, one year he took it to Scotland and spent three weeks in early summer passing from the estate of one friend to another as the fancy took him, stalking roe bucks. Was it horse-drawn one wonders? How romantic – and inconvenient – if it was.

Barclay was always a meticulous correspondent and recorder of facts, and no mean photographer. He spent some years at the Natural History Museum where he wrote a number of papers on the cervids and became an internationally-known authority, though circumstances always limited his ability to travel. Roe were a particular interest for many years. Under 'Petworth 1934–1936' he wrote: 'At Petworth in the spring roe deer may be seen feeding on the move at all times of the day, and I have seen them out in the fields far from cover. On April 6th 1934 I counted twenty-two in three hours, three of them out in the fields . . .' A former huntsman at Petworth kept a tame roe, 'Minnie' which he had as a fawn and successfully reared. 'Minnie' became so tame that she would feed from the hand and would run with the foxhounds. Her constant association with the pack taught the hounds to ignore the scent of roe.

Milton Abbas in Dorset saw him stalking roe from 1934 onwards, and an undated photograph shows a youthful Henry Tegner posing outside the keeper's lodge. This keeper was Arthur White, whom Tegner praised for his exceptional knowledge of roe. On occasion Edgar Barclay stayed with Major C R E Radclyffe (author of *Round the Smoking Room Fire*) at Hyde near Wareham, and at other times and during brief war leaves at the Hambro Arms in Milton Abbas, sometimes accompanied by Henry Tegner, Martin Stephens (author of *Fair Game*) and others. They seemed to have the freedom of all the woods round Milton Abbas which used to be enormous, though sadly many were bulldozed in the name of food production after the Second World War including the 2,000 acres of Houghton Wood of which practically nothing remains. To judge by Barclay's photographs and my own schoolboy memories of the area at that time, the stalking – then totally un-exploited – must have been fabulous; rough valley bottoms with a straggle of scrub leading up to solid woodland cut in small patches by rotation under the old scheme of 'coppice with standards'. The heads they shot, some of which are illustrated in Tegner's classic book *The Roe Deer* were typical six-pointers which reflects the sporting philosophy of the time to shoot good mature bucks but leave young beasts, and the does too, as potential mothers of more bucks. One cannot criticise them, bearing in mind that the total number taken can never have had any effect on population structure or density while the ones they left would have to run the gauntlet of indis-criminate winter shotgun drives.

Essentially a very modest man, Edgar Barclay had the gift of being able to make friends with everyone, high or low. In his obituary in 1973, Henry Tegner wrote 'He was a very gentle man, always willing and eager to help anyone in trouble and with affection for the young and those who wanted to learn more about the field sports of this country and his beloved deer'. To this I subscribe, as he became with other equally kind members of that select coterie my mentor, regular correspondent and friend. What a debt I owe to him and them!

A Plague of Monsters

Quite a few stalkers have queried what exactly is a 'Baillie Monster,' or what is meant by that inelegant word 'Bailliesque' which has been used to describe certain forms of malforma-tion in roe trophies.

Way back in 1974 Major Peter Baillie, then the chairman of the British Deer Society, shot a monstrous roe buck which might have been the world record. It was disallowed, quite rightly, because most of the extraordinary weight of the skull – 1,140 grammes – was due to thickening of the pedicles and skull bones, the additional bone having the appear-ance of poured and hardened cement.

Shortly afterwards another similar skull was found in the same district west of the New Forest by Ranger Vic Pardy and yet a third turned up in 1980. It began to look as if something serious might be affecting the deer there, and nobody could produce more than vague theories about the cause. One problem was that there was no fresh tissue or blood samples for a pathologist to work on. Two had been found as long-dead skeletons, and the first was eaten before anything could be saved for examination. Not even the kidneys remained for veterinary research in the Baillie freezer – 'They were excellent for breakfast!'

The distinguished pathologist Dr Archie McDiarmid's original theory was that it might possibly be due to a tumour in the vicinity of the pituitary. He said that the first 'monster' might be unique but that if a second turned up, there could be more. Since then we have almost a plague of them!

In the following years I began to see odd specimens with the same problem, but to a lesser degree. The area concerned also began to widen: in 1985 a buck was taken east of Salisbury with swollen pedicles, and in 1988 I was brought a skull from Berkshire (retrieved from a nettle bed, having been discarded by the stalker) which had a skull weight of 896 grammes and a provisional score of 214.88 C I C points. Another very large specimen was shot by a Belgian stalker in East Wiltshire about the same time, but it only later became clear that his much-heralded gold medal owed much of its score to swollen skull and pedicles.

Still no fresh material until the following year when, on 8 May, professional stalker Roger Cray, in an understandable state of excitement, unloaded a freshly-shot buck on my lawn which in many ways rivalled the very first. The antlers were slightly more normal than Major Baillie's, but short, multi-pointed and incredibly thick. Not only the pedicles, but the whole face could be seen to be swollen. It had been shot by Jeremy Pilkington the previous day. Here was the longed-for fresh material, thanks to Roger's foresight and Jeremy Pilkington's public spirited offer to delay the obsequies. Some frantic phone calls finally led me to Mr Cooper and Mr Williams, of the Royal College of Surgeons, who were willing to carry out tests. The result? Nothing! It must be said that they were not given access to 'the cranium', which even Mr Pilkington was unwilling to sacrifice. Rumours were even then circulating about how much 'a passing German' had offered for it in fresh Deutschmarks!

The stalking world is a small one, and who should turn up in August with the next exhibit but Vic Pardy, the needle-sighted Ranger who had discovered the second skull. That morning he had shot himself a monster. Not only that but when we met on the Game Conservancy's lawn for a photo session, he had two more; a buck from Thetford and even a doe skull! Later I was shown a buck shot by Mr Lewis in east Wiltshire with the typical thickened pedicles, but with normal antlers on top. Vic Pardy also returned with a buck's skull which had been found dead (as so many of the others) with two enormous lumps of antler. All display, in varying degrees, the same additional layering of the pedicles and skull (even the doe has pedicles) to the extent of reducing the diameter of the eye sockets.

Vic was even prepared to have the fresh skull taken apart, but in the meantime mishaps and foreign postings meant that the Royal College pathology team could not continue their researches. Sadly, even the details of their examination of Mr Pilkington's buck have disappeared in a most frustrating way between London and Kenya. However, the stalking bush-telegraph put me in touch with a Surrey vet, Alastair McVicar, who volunteered to carry out a post-mortem. Unsavoury bags of remains were hurried across country and we lived in anticipation of a real answer to the mystery at last. The result? Negative! No tumour near the pituitary, nothing abnormal at all.

Every one so far has come from a limited area of Southern England. What can one guess from all this? We are left to speculate between heredity, the effects of agrochemicals or the greenhouse effect. Whatever the actual cause, for sure there will be more monsters turning up in due course.

MEASUREMENTS OF MONSTER ROE

YEAR	OWNER	COUNTY	SKULL WT	C I C	
1974	Maj. Baillie	Hants	1140	241.01	Shot
1974	V Pardy	Hants	1120	–	Fd Dead
1980	Sir G Meyrick	Hants	975	144.0	Fd Dead
1985	A Bergengren	Wilts	460	133.3	Shot
1987	S Whitfield	Berks	896	214.88	Shot
1991	J Pilkington	Wilts	1080	236.25	Shot
1991	V Pardy	Hants	–	–	Shot
1991	G Lewis	Wilts	680	161.48	Shot
1991	V Pardy	Dorset	772	–	Fd dead
1992	D Andress	Hants	742	208.55	Shot
1994	M-P White	Hants	862	215.33	Shot
1999	P Vastapane	Hants	780	174.15	Shot
?	J Bundy	Wilts	955	228.78	Shot

Winter Browsing

No! Not roses this time, but the long winter evenings. By the time you have sharpened all your knives to what they should be, got round to searching the deep freeze for heads which ought to have been boiled out long since; thawed out those hearts and processed them into delicious mince all in neat cook-acceptable packets; dusted the cobwebs off the trophies on the stairs and loaded a batch of super-accurate rounds, what is there left but watch videos about stalking until late at night? Bookworm-stalkers have the answer: turn to the shelves, or pore over the latest catalogue from David Grayling or Paul Morgan and rattle the piggy bank.

Books to me are friends – patiently waiting for the moment when you say 'Ah! I know, I'll mug up on how to tell young does from old before tomorrow's outing. Then I really ought to study building designs for next year's high seats.' In a more reflective hour you can just sink back and join Henry Tegner on the Northumberland moors; prowl the New Forest with Arthur Cadman or follow Lady Breadalbane (plus female photographer with box camera) on the High Tops of Blackmount. There they are, all ready to share their triumphs and disasters once again. Or maybe they aren't there yet, and wouldn't it be nice if they were! Collecting sporting books is a hobby in itself aside from the advice and information which many of them have to offer. If you don't go for first editions in pristine condition it needn't cost an arm and a leg. Only the other day I found Tegner's *Buck of the Saughs* at the local village fete, and a lot of the real classics have been reprinted at a tithe of the price tag on the originals. If the publishers have been over-optimistic on reprint numbers, there may be some real bargains on offer only a year or two after publication. Some amazing prizes lurk in the darker corners of non-specialist secondhand bookshops to whom overtly sporting books may be almost an embarrassment.

Most books which get published these days are in the 'How to Do It' category. Depending on your particular interest, any enquiring stalker needs a basic collection, even if it's only to check if the local guru is talking out of the top of his deerstalker. A few gunmakers' catalogues are also handy, either to scan the latest wheezes if you are a gadgety sort of chap, or to update on the choice of ammunition available and their ballistics on which the technicalities of your zeroing depend. Either you buy publications like *Shooter's Bible*, which contain all sorts of things, some which are of very little direct interest, or alternatively write for the different manufacturers' lists from both sides of the Atlantic and get more information for nothing.

One of my sadnesses about books is that the ones which were too expensive for my purse early on but at prices which look terribly cheap now, are still too expensive to have just for the pleasure of possession. I always had a yen for Millais' massive tome *British Mammals*, but quite apart from the difficulty of physically lifting one of the volumes and lacking a lectern for reading it on, the equally massive price has been a total deterrent. However, a butchered remnant containing just the deer section appeared out of the blue in David Grayling's list, nicely bound. Goodness knows what happened to the rest of it.

The other sadness is the limitations of shelf space. From time to time there has to be an agonising clearance sale. Inevitably after only a month or three I stretch out my hand for one of the Dear Departed, only to realise that it went in the last turn-out.

Everyone knows that lending books is the quickest way to disaster. You lend, and friends borrow, with every expectation of giving or getting the thing back 'in a day or two'. Some people are very meticulous, but all too often it is R I P Book, and that is that. A card inserted in the gap with the borrower's name may help, but it gets dusted or blown away and one can rarely think who it was who promised faithfully . . . Some genius invented Bookcheques, which are now my mainstay. You fill in the counterfoil with the borrower's name, telephone number and if necessary bank reference, while the 'cheque' with your name and address on it goes in the borrowed volume as a threatening bookmark, a constant reminder to the borrower who may have honestly forgotten who it was he borrowed it from.

Looking at my bookcase, it is remarkably short on ballistic technicalities, although I do have things like Burrard's *Notes on Sporting Rifles*; Taylor's *Big Game and Big Game Rifles* (not that I have ever shot an elephant, or want to) and Sharpe's *The Rifle in America* which are all somewhat historical. O'Connor's *The Hunting Rifle* is a fine source of transatlantic expertise. Reloading as a hobby or an economy has passed me by, mainly because when I was using a lot of rounds, a grateful government paid for most of them and emphatically banned reloads. I was always more interested in bullet performance, leaving the chemistry of going bang to cleverer chaps. Of course there is a lot of useful stuff about choosing rifles and ammunition in general stalking works, especially the Americans. I enjoy George Sell's books *The American Deer Hunter* and *Advanced Hunting on Deer and Elk Trails* and for practical native advice Kenneth Whitehead's *Practical Deer Stalking* has a good deal to offer. Sell's idea of having an 'understudy rifle' similar in action and build to your full bore weapon for low-cost practice and experiment is a wonderful tip.

My shelves tend to be fuller on the side of natural history and behaviour.

Rory Putman's *The Natural History of Deer* is pre-eminent for giving a scientist's viewpoint on all our deer species without a trace of unnecessary jargon. If you want to know why deer do something, not just what they do, that is the book. His second book *The Deer Manager's Companion* is essential reference. For red deer in particular one should have Fraser Darling's classic *A Herd of Red Deer* also *Red Deer in the Highlands* by Clutton-Brock and Albon and there is nothing better than Donald and Norma Chapman's *Fallow Deer* for that mis-managed species. Sika and Chinese water deer are under-represented in the literature, relying on two modest BDS publications and three important but hard-to-find papers, one by Arnold Cooke on the water deer of Woodwalton Fen, and two long-forgotten but useful papers on the sika of the Poole Basin by Michael Horwood. Probably the best source of up-to-date information is Kenneth Whitehead's *Deer of Great Britain and Ireland* and his monumental *Encyclopedia of Deer*. The latter has appeared recently in CD-ROM, which makes the mass of information in it so much more readily accessible. (It is marketed by Country Books Direct, Palmers House, 7 Cove Street, Ludlow SY8 1DB.)

Muntjac are beginning to attract the attention which up to now they have lacked, just as the challenging sport of stalking them has been terribly under-rated. There lies the greatest opportunity for any young stalker with more energy than money. It is still cheap, and the techniques for getting on terms with them are still a mystery to most stalkers. Charles Smith-Jones' *Muntjac – Managing an Alien Species* is very welcome.

The literature of roe starts with J G Millais' *British Deer and their Horns*, now available on CD and in reprint. This was followed by a book which was long before its time: Snaffle's *The Roe Deer* published first in 1904 contained a plea for their better treatment which was not achieved for half a century or more. The author, not to be confused with 'Snaffles' the sporting artist, was a somewhat enigmatic character who was known among his contemporaries as the Marquess of Ivrea (a town in Italy). Peter Davenport researched deeply into his identity, proving eventually that his name was Guy Hardwin Gallenga, army officer, travelling sportsman and roe enthusiast. One can pick up good reprints of *The Roe Deer* at bargain prices. Frank Wallace, in *Hunting and Stalking the Deer* (1930) and Henry Tegner with his book *The Roe Deer* from the 1950s (reprinted by Tideline Books) both carried the flag through the years when they were largely regarded as vermin in this country. In our own time Frank Holmes' *Following the Deer* contained much of deep interest to the roe man. I am writing of books that I can read and re-read with continuing pleasure, so my own do not qualify. If I pick one of those up, I see so much that isn't right, or could have been better put, and that is no pleasure. Let others make up their own minds! Recently Dominic

Griffith's book *Deer Management: Quality in Southern England* contains some important and first-hand information from an experienced professional.

For really sitting back and revelling in the pure delights of stalking, I think one must return to the days when they went out shooting with no hesitation about enjoying it! No self-justification about 'conserving the species' or substituting 'culling' for 'killing' in the pages of the classic authors. Their pure gusto is refreshing, though completely out of date: 'We were not likely to see a better – so I took the shot.' Of any of them, I like most to turn to my old friend and mentor Frank Wallace who had been everywhere and done everything but recounted his doings with the enthusiasm of a schoolboy and an extraordinary degree of modesty. Whether he writes of high jinks in the Highlands, mostly with himself as the scapegoat, stalking big game almost anywhere or still-hunting roe across two continents, his deprecating sense of humour, charm and skill as a storyteller are unmatched. Perhaps *Hunting Winds* is the best place to start. *The Buck of Lordenshaw* by Henry Tegner was one of the first books on roe I ever discovered, and I practically memorised it. For anyone who loves the Highlands and open-hill stalking Duff Hart-Davis' fascinating delve into the early days of the sport *Monarchs of the Glen* is a must.

Stalkers like to keep up to the minute and so one should not overlook our latest quarry species, one which may be both important and exciting in the near future. Martin Goulding is the only wild boar specialist in England, so his book *Wild Boar in Britain* is an eye-opener and may be the start of great things.

The Making of a Stalker

What is it about roe deer that grabs one? Not so long ago they were dismissed as 'Those uninteresting little beasts'. Like a lot of other roe deer fanatics, I beg leave to differ! Roe deer have been my obsession – a love affair – for fifty-five years. I love them for their unique charm, for their total unpredictability, for the way they live at our expense whether in the vast northern conifer forests or your own back garden. To me they are the Brownie of children's books; elusive, fascinating, and yet with a definite spice of menace. There's nothing cuddly about a roe buck in his territory, especially if you happen to be another roe buck!

To begin with, to a shooting-mad teenager they were Big Game in capital letters. Imagine my excitement when a neighbour who let me shoot rabbits (mostly with a .22, and good training it was!) told me 'If you get a roe we'll share the venison!' The thought of it sent me prowling the woods straight off, and I suppose I have never stopped. Nobody said 'You will have to get up early to see one, or stay out late' because nobody stalked them in those days round my Devon home.

Roe were in fact thin on the ground in Devon in the 1940s, but that is no excuse for my taking four years, no less, to get my first. Youngsters were more regulated years ago and it was not until my parents happened to be away for a couple of days that discipline was relaxed enough for me to plan a dawn-to-dusk onslaught on the one buck I knew about. I knew the path he took, judging by the tracks, so ambush was the thing. I lay on the lip of a badger sett, ideally placed for a steady shot as he advanced unsuspecting along the path below. Hours later there was a breath of movement – and there was the buck watching me from behind, no doubt with some amusement. I made a wild shot off the left shoulder (I had graduated to a .22 Hornet by that time) and the buck vanished. No sign of him. Not a vestige. I looked everywhere in complete despair. The very first chance in four years of effort – and I had muffed it!

Looking for any indication of where the bullet might have gone, I went to where he had been standing on another exit of the badger sett. Three feet down the hole there was a hoof. If he had kicked once more, he would have been completely out of sight. He went back ungralloched and messily draped round my shoulders. To say my cup of pure joy was filled is an understatement.

Once hooked, the roe bug had me. Through enthusiastic letter-writing I met by degrees all the woodland stalkers of the day, both established figures such as Frank Wallace and Henry Tegner, and the wave of returning ex-service men, among them Andrew de Nahlik, who had seen what roe stalking could offer during their time in Germany, Austria and Poland. Through these one tended to appreciate some of the minute attention which sportsmen in other countries lavish on the roe.

There was a great contrast between the native and Continental approaches to roe stalking as a sport. The handful of pre-war roe stalkers did it because they loved to be out early in the summer woods, and they were proud to bring back as large a buck as happened to present itself. There was no point in leaving a good one when it would be butchered in winter drives anyway. This was the evil they campaigned so hard to bring to an end.

The Continental approach had an instant appeal because the whole philosophy was to value and manage the deer, admittedly with the main object of producing the best possible trophies. What we did not understand at the time was that conditions abroad, especially the heavy shooting pressure in Central Europe, created a different situation from our own, nor that the rules so rigidly held and taught might in the end turn out to be at odds with biological fact.

In the end we turned to research in other countries where the deer were no less admired, but where trophies were less important in sporting tradition. The work at Kalø in Denmark began the process of breaking down the notion of roe as a textbook animal whose behaviour was so well-understood that the rules for managing them could be handed down from one generation to another without change or argument.

I was fortunate to get a full-time job with the Forestry Commission to study deer and primarily to stop them eating trees. I never succeeded in this, but enjoyed my sixteen years in the open air, though getting married on nine pounds a week, getting up two hours before light and coming back late in the evening did put a strain on daily life which many stalkers' wives will appreciate all too well. The more I looked at roe, the more conundrums they offered. We thought of them as strictly territorial with 'a pair' in each territory. Yet there were stories of roe living all the time in the fields – how did the bucks mark their territories in a cabbage field, or was the territory a certain distance round the doe? Certainly they did not behave like a pair of breeding birds, in fact they seemed to me to be much more like humans with a definite matriarchy, females dominating males and resenting their spouses' definite tendency to philander. I knew bucks with two wives – even two territories – and those were no better than they ought to have been in our terms. We were told that 'Button Bucks' and 'Rubbish Bucks' should be shot

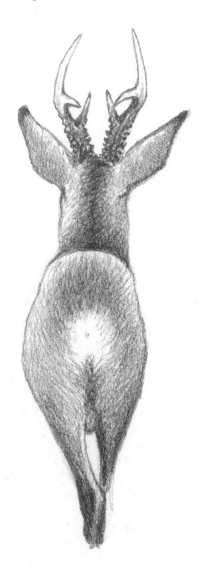

because they would never grow good antlers, yet marked bucks at Kalø (and soon after, similarly marked animals at Chedington) grew very different antlers from year to year.

One effort which we made early on was to give roe a money value, thinking that if they were valueless they would only be regarded as forest pests and be treated accordingly. We started to let stalking. Of course some established stalkers were very critical who saw the end of enjoying their sport for nothing or who resented the knowledge that our best trophies were going out of the country. Nobody could doubt now that roe are better treated because of the value they represent, and many dedicated roe stalkers are employed to manage their deer and supervise the summer visitors. That is all to the good.

In recent years the roe has been subject to much more study than before, and what a wonderful bunch of people the researchers are! Always welcoming, free with their findings, and going to enormous trouble when language difficulties got in the way. I started to travel, trying to talk to as many experts as possible, and if after a meeting one problem seemed to have been resolved, there were half a dozen more thrown up to bemuse me. Over the years I have visited fellow roe enthusiasts in nearly every country where these animals exist, from Portugal to Siberia and watched roe with them – some territorial, some living as so-called field roe, one full-scale migration. Seeing this enormous variation in behaviour to take advantage of changing conditions, the notion of roe as a text-book territorial species is completely blown away.

One of the prime hazards they cope with is the presence of man; mostly harmless to them, sometimes highly dangerous! If there is one thing I have learned in my life of watching roe it is this: We may look at roe for a few hours a day or week and think we know something about them. They study us 24 hours a day, every day, and they know a very great deal more about us, as humans and as individuals, than we can ever understand. No wonder I love them!

Last Word – Numbles

If you really want to try Humble Pie – the culinary version – Janet Burdge found the following gem, which is reprinted with kind permission from her book *Venison Cookery* published by The British Deer Society.

𝕹𝖀𝕸𝕭𝕷𝕰𝕾

𝕿o mak numbles tak hert middrif and kidney and hew them smalle and prise out the blod and seethe them in water and in ale and colour it with brown bred or blod and fors it with canella and galingale and when it boileth kole it a little with ale and serb it . . .

Reading this I am reminded of Beatrix Potter, who wrote of Jeremy Fisher enjoying 'Roasted grasshopper with lady-bird sauce; which frogs consider a beautiful treat; but I think it must have been nasty!'

If eating humble pie in our terms is often nasty, I have a feeling that real Humble Pie (or Numbles) may have been just as bad – or even worse.